# The Economics of

# Collective

# Action

# The Economics of
# Collective
# Action

———◆———

## John R. Commons

*Edited with Introduction and Supplementary Essay by*
KENNETH H. PARSONS

*With a Biographical Sketch by*
SELIG PERLMAN

THE UNIVERSITY OF WISCONSIN PRESS
Madison, Milwaukee, and London, 1970

Published by
The University of Wisconsin Press
Box 1379, Madison, Wisconsin 53701
The University of Wisconsin Press, Ltd.
27–29 Whitman Street, London, W. 1

First UWP printing, 1970

Printed in the United States of America
SBN 299–05360–1 ; LC 69–17328

# Contents

[ v ]

vi ]     Contents

# Foreword to the 1970 Edition

The re-issuance of the *Economics of Collective Action* by the University of Wisconsin Press provides an opportunity for a few comments on possible keys to the theoretical writings of John R. Commons. In this book, first published posthumously in 1950, Commons attempted a simplified statement of issues which he had argued more fully in *Legal Foundations of Capitalism* (1924) and *Institutional Economics* (1934). These three books, as well as Commons' autobiography, *Myself* (1934), all published originally by Macmillan, are now in print under the auspices of the University of Wisconsin Press.

The availability of these volumes will facilitate serious study of Commons' writings. Few of his contemporaries survive; even his youngest students are well along in their careers. His accomplishments stand as historical evidence of a fruitful career, but the ideas which directed his remarkable achievements in humanizing and stabilizing the American economy are not well understood. These ideas deserve the most careful consideration—for Commons was both a systematic and a creative thinker.

As with all innovators, to understand Commons' point of view requires that he be met on his own ground. What was he trying to do? He was trying, as we understand him, and particularly in his later years, to achieve an approach to, or a formulation of, economics which honored the dual needs of analyzing our twentieth-century American economic system as a human organization and incorporating the insights of the great masters in the history of economic thought. Commons worked primarily as an investigator, attempting to find clues as to how economic conflicts, such as those between labor and management, could be resolved creatively and how the powers of the state and other forms of collective action could be used constructively.

[ vii ]

As he sought a perspective upon the deeper issues of public policy and industrial government, his approach became more and more comprehensive. In all this, his thinking was anchored in philosophical conceptions which came to be known as instrumentalism, or more popularly as American pragmatism.

To him groups, not individuals, were the basic units of economy and society. The freedom, dignity, and security of expectations for individuals are achieved, he maintained, through group action, "in control, liberation, and expansion of individual action." Reacting against theories of economics which treated individuals as mere atoms, he set out to devise an approach to economics which recognized that all human beings had wills of their own. Thus, no person was completely powerless. From the very beginning of his career, therefore, he accepted power as a pervasive elemental fact of life. His analysis of power culminates in Chapter III, *Legal Foundations of Capitalism,* "Physical, Economic, and Moral Power."

Accepting power as an elemental brute fact of life, and holding the view that willing participation is the leading principle of social organization in a society honoring freedom, Commons then had to reconcile power and freedom. The question was, How can power be made to serve public purposes? His conclusion was that this can be done only by ingenious public procedures which balance power with power. This is the root of his views on reasonable value. The great public purposes are realized, if at all, only through rules which place reasonable limits to the exercise of power.

This emphasis on procedures required that the postulates of economic analysis should be comprehensive enough to embrace and articulate an interpretation of the economy not only as a mechanism overcoming natural scarcity but also as a system of working rules. Thus, the opening chapter of *Legal Foundations* is entitled "Mechanism, Scarcity, Working Rules."

It is this attempt to systematically analyze working rules which channel action—especially joint or collective action—as a part of economics that makes Commons' analysis so complex and so baffling to economists who take as their field of primary attention the universe of commodities which can be analyzed in terms of mechanical interactions.

As Commons observed in the opening chapter of *Institutional Economics,* his viewpoint grew out of a lifetime of participation in experiments in collective action in America. "I do not see how any one going through these fifty years of participation in experiments could fail to arrive at two conclusions: conflict of interests and collective action" (p. 3). "The problem now is not to create a different kind of economics— 'institutional' economics—divorced from preceding schools, but how to give to collective action, in all its varieties, its due place throughout economic theory" (p. 5).

Thus the greatest value of Commons' systematic writings is likely to be that he was a true disciple of the great tradition of political economy—especially of Locke, Smith, and Malthus —which he sought to bring up to date in order to provide an intellectual basis for economic policies in an age of power, in an era in which the Western economic systems, with their historic roots in liberalism, confront and are challenged by avowedly Marxian-based systems of national economy. As early as 1909, in his remarkable analysis of industrial organization, "American Shoemakers, 1648–1895: A Sketch of Industrial Evolution" (*Quarterly Journal of Economics,* 24 [1909]), he seems to sense that Marx is the economist to be reckoned with in the twentieth century.

Even if it were granted that Commons' attempt to widen the horizons of economics was both advisable and successful, it does not follow that all economic analysis should attempt such generality (nor does it follow that Commons' attempt, if valid in his own time, would be equally valid in subsequent decades). But it does follow that Commons cannot be understood as a dissenter from or a protester against the more traditional approaches to economics. Few economists have studied the development and history of economic thought with the thoroughgoing respect and appreciation that Commons did.

What he saw there may have been something different from what others saw; this was at least partly because he was asking different questions.

Commons attempted to study economic performance from the perspective of seeing an economic system whole. In this, his work is closely akin to the work of those of his contemporaries called institutional economists, most of whom were attempting to analyze the economy as a system (Allan G. Gruchy, "John R. Commons' Concept of Twentieth-Century Economics," *Journal of Political Economy*, 48, no. 6 [1940]). He differed from some of these institutionalists, notably Veblen and some of his disciples, in that Commons held to the view that choice is central to economic behavior; in fact he struggled for fifty years to formulate a theory of volitional economics—out of the recognition that all persons have wills of their own.

Thus, there is in Commons nothing of the renunciation of "sufficient reason" that Veblen asserted in his famous essay on "The Limitations of Marginal Utility" (*Journal of Political Economy*, 17, no. 9 [1909]), in which he accepted the principle of "efficient-cause" as the key to scientific economics. The difference between "sufficient reason" and "efficient cause," notes Veblen, "may seem trivial. It is serious only in its consequences. The two methods of inference—from sufficient reason and from efficient cause—are out of touch with one another and there is no transition from one to the other: no method of converting the procedure or the results of the one into those of the other."

The mention of Veblen is not for purposes of invidious comparison. Both Veblen and Commons were genuine pioneers in social thought. But the writing of each can be understood and evaluated only by going to the foundations of his thought. It is worth noting, however, that Commons' writings have suffered neglect as a result of the superficial lumping together of all institutionalists as protesting dissenters.

The problem actually is how the insights of these unortho-

Foreword                                    [ xi

dox thinkers in economics can be integrated with the main
body of economic theories. My suggestion here is that Commons' formulation may be of unique value in such an integration because Commons honored the creative role of choice
and decision. In this respect Commons was a traditionalist.
His differences with the tradition, of his own day and later,
come in his attempt (a) to formulate a theoretical statement
sufficiently comprehensive to include in the analysis the "social
framework" of the economy which a mechanistic analysis
treats as a datum, and (b) to work within a conception of
philosophic method which recognizes that mind is a creative
interaction in the ordering and reconstruction of human affairs.
As economists come to grips with the great problems of human
organization and philosophical analysis, they will surely find
Commons' writings to be a treasury of insights.

The four decades following the American Civil War were
tumultuous—with Reconstruction, panics, and depressions;
the completion of the intercontinental railway system; the
industrialization of the North; a flood of immigrants pouring
in, to free land and especially to the rising industrial cities,
where many lived in poverty-ridden slums, without effective
citizenship; the anti-monopoly "Granger" movement among
farmers, which culminated in the regulation of railroad rates;
and the eventual achievement of stable labor unions in the
1890's. Born in 1862, Commons shared intimately in these
experiences particularly as an investigator, studying many of
the controversial issues.

By the early 1900's, Commons had acquired a vision of the

Although Commons spent most of his professional career
as a university professor, he was always a participant investigator. In this capacity, he responded to the successive chal-
lenges of an American economy and society undergoing an
urbanizing industrialization. This consideration, together with
his association with the La Follette reform movements, goes
far to account for the particular emphases in the economic
problems he tackled.

possibilities of the reconstruction, stabilization, and humaniza-
tion of the American economic system. Thereafter Commons
was a progressive, demonstrating a remarkable capacity for
social invention, or institutional innovation. This aspect of
Commons' life has attracted much comment, especially in the
recognition that his insights and ideas, as well as his experiments in Wisconsin, laid much of the groundwork for the
American system of Social Security. In fact his remarkable
successes in grappling with the great problems of his times
drew both him and his students into the administration of the
numerous agencies which grew out of the suggestions of his
fertile mind.

His originality and especially his deep insights were appreciated and admired by both his contemporaries and his students. The result, however, has been, and remains, that
Commons is known and respected principally for his influence
upon public policy and administration. Thus, the more durable
aspect of Commons' work, his tough analytical and philosophical thought, remains little understood. Perhaps it was inevitable in the nature of Commons' intellectual enterprise that he
should have no disciples to carry his work forward—for what
he was attempting was so comprehensive and difficult that his
students could not really grasp what it was all about.

One of the keys to the understanding of Commons, it may
be suggested, is that he was one of a small band of indigenous
intellectuals who matured about the turn of the century. In
many respects, this was a confident, hopeful era. It is also
noteworthy that the twenty-five years or so before World War I
were times when at least a few young scholars could find
great teachers to study under in universities that were genuine
centers of learning, and could thus think out their own points
of view. The greatest of these teachers both knew systematic
European thought and understood the restless, volatile America, in which the plain people, as self-respecting citizens, were
clamoring for reform. The American dream was being frustrated by panics, the practices of monopolistic railroads, un-

conscionably hazardous working conditions in industry, and an unspeakable squalor in urban slums. Yet beneath such bitter fruit there was also a vigorous self-confidence born of successes in subduing a continent and building an industrial system which commanded the respect of the world, providing economic opportunity for millions of hitherto poor immigrants.

Out of these experiences came a philosophical movement popularly known as pragmatism, or more technically as instrumentalism. Commons was a creative member of this group. This is not to suggest that one can find somewhere in Commons' voluminous writing a concise integrated statement of an analytical philosophy. For Commons was an economist, investigating the most complex of social problems.

What was truly great about Commons was no doubt his "naked insights," to use Neil Chamberlain's phrase (Joseph Dorfman et al., *Institutional Economics: Veblen, Commons and Mitchell Reconsidered* [Berkeley: University of California Press, 1963], p. 93). Commons had something of a poetic sensitivity to the great issues of his time. Perhaps no one could have worked the implications of so copious a flow of insights into a really comprehensive systematic statement without losing the capacity for fresh insights.

Commons drew his deepest philosophical inspiration from the writings of Charles S. Peirce. His life and work ran parallel to that of John Dewey, but there was no direct communication between them. Even so, one can learn much about the implications of Commons' basic ideas by a study of Dewey's writings: *Human Nature and Conduct; The Public and Its Problems; The Quest for Certainty;* and especially *Logic, The Theory of Inquiry.*

Commons had the deepest respect for human experience and the lessons which can be learned therefrom. He was a masterful historian, but he studied history for its deeper meanings, as he demonstrated in the remarkable historical chapters in *Legal Foundations of Capitalism*—in which he distilled out of the experience of feudalism and the guilds the basic and objective meanings of property, sovereignty, negotiability, liberty, and opportunity. His respect for experience is evident also in his emphasis upon reasonableness rather than pure reason. There is, in Commons, an abiding faith in man's capacity to reconstruct the world in which he lives; that is, he recognized that mind and thought are not merely reportorial but are creative interactions in events.

From these philosophical premises he moved not so much to the classroom discussion of implications, consistency, and system building after the manner of academic philosophers, but rather to research into the crucial issues of industrialization and industrial government, policy and administration— attempting to humanize and stabilize the economic system.

Although Commons rarely used the term, his thinking is problem-oriented; his expression for problem-solution was attention to the limiting factor or to the strategic factor. In this he reflected a conception of causation as putative; cause is attributed to that factor, among countless interdependences and interactions, which yields control, enabling man to give direction to events. His system is thus a system of problem-solving, a method and set of ideas which have instrumental status. This he perceived as being essential if man is to be recognized as having a will of his own, capable of rising to new heights of attainment through the achievement of a dignified status. Commons' analysis comes to a focus upon the procedures by which debilitating conflicts can be reconciled sufficiently to permit the enjoyment of the mutual advantages of order—epitomized in the phrases "willing participation" and "security of expectations."

The main drift of formal economic analysis during the past three or four decades has been in other directions. The system of state and economy is treated as a given framework. The study of collective action, the nature of property rights, and the structure of power is not included in contemporary formal economics. Where Commons struggled with the problems of public value and social value, contemporary economics accepts value systems as given—to be treated as systems of preferences, or matters of degrees of indifference; where Commons struggled to understand how individual conduct and even personality was shaped by collective action in its many forms, contemporary economic analysis posits given individuals and even treats society as a sum of individuals.

This, quite obviously, does not mean either that Commons' view is superior, or right in some sense, or the opposite. That is not the point. What is important is that Commons, working in different premises, was a man who knew what he was doing, in a controlled philosophical sense.

Furthermore, Commons worked as an economist trying to widen the horizons and broaden the concepts of economics. As Kenneth E. Boulding observed in his comment in "Institutional Economics: A New Look at Institutionalism": "In Commons I would argue that we see the most successful attempt to enlarge the borders of the economic abstraction, not so much, however, by drawing in contributions from other social sciences as by the generalization of concepts originally derived from economics. Thus his idea of the transaction is a generalization from the concept of exchange: his idea of the 'going concern' is a generalization of the concept of the firm; his concept of 'working rules' is a generalization from the notion of economic behavior. None of these concepts derives much from other social sciences; and while Commons always seems to stop short of building his conceptual framework into an orderly scheme, he foreshadows much that is happening today in the theory of organization and behavior" (*Papers and Proceedings of the Sixty-ninth Meeting of the American Economic Association, American Economic Review,* 47, no. 2 [1957]).

In this comment I have attempted to point to a few issues or ideas which might serve as clues to the interpretations of Commons' voluminous writings. This is a search for avenues which may open new vistas into Commons' thinking, thus facilitating the growth of a community of systematic criticism of Commons' writings. Although such an evaluation can come only from an academic or similarly intellectual environment, we may be sure that the larger issues confronting mankind will set the stage for serious examination of Commons' writings. If the world is moving into an era of vast institutional reconstruction, with the necessity of creating new operative systems of political economy in the now underdeveloped areas, with conflicts of revolutionary proportions over access to economic opportunities, then the academic community may turn to Commons' writings for the insights and the suggestions of principles regarding the way in which the Anglo-American economy evolved from feudalism, the guild system, and mass poverty. Also, in the United States, in what is now called the emerging post-industrial society, the academic community is likely to find Commons' study of industrial society to be most illuminating.

Commons hoped, obviously, that he had achieved something of a general system—culminating in this last book. At the very least, Commons was attempting to create a more inclusive statement of economics than that which prevailed, and prevails, among academic economists. In the terms of Thomas Kuhn (*The Structure of Scientific Revolutions,* Chapter V), Commons was trying to think his way out of, and free himself of, the limitations of dominant paradigms in economics derived from Ricardo. Research within established scientific paradigms, says Kuhn, is basically puzzle-solving, not problem-solving. If Commons' thinking can contribute something to the creation of a more creative paradigm for some future generation of economists, his work will not have been in vain.

KENNETH H. PARSONS

University of Wisconsin
University of Ife, Ile-Ife, Nigeria
*June, 1969*

# Editor's Preface

With the publication of *Institutional Economics* and his auto-biography, *Myself*, in 1934, Professor Commons might have considered his work finished. He had retired from teaching and was then 72 years old, frail, and in poor health. Those of us who saw "John R." in those days wondered whether he would have the strength to see the two books through the press. But soon after they were published he gingerly set out on a new chapter in his life. He sold his home, purchased a trailer, and with his niece set out for Florida. The healthful climate and warm friendships among the "trailer-folk" soon revived John R. and restored his health. Here he worked for a decade, encouraged by his students, in a persistent attempt to explain in simple terms the essentials of a complex system of thought.

Had he lived to see this book through the press, I am sure that he would have acknowledged his indebtedness to the scores of persons who helped him in its preparation. As one who worked with him in his last years and as editor of the present manuscript, I can make those acknowledgments only imperfectly.

He felt deeply indebted to Mrs. Theresa S. McMahon, who prodded and encouraged him to write this volume, when he had almost concluded that he "was finished for good," to use his own phrase.

Professor Selig Perlman, student and colleague, worked with him from Madison, checking manuscript, supervising the typing and safekeeping of the steady stream of writing year after year.

Mrs. Leona Spillman worked with him several months in Madison about 1936 and 1937. She later presented a dissertation for her doctorate in which the points of view of Commons and Veblen were compared.

After Professor Commons was again left alone, in 1941, by the death of his niece Bertha Best, Chester Meske became his companion and assistant. Meske was then a graduate student in economics at the University of Wisconsin; he worked with John R. until July, 1942. The two of them worked through the whole manuscript, shortening it considerably and clarifying the statement in many ways.

During the winter of 1941–42, H. H. Erdmann, Office of Federal Milk Market Administrator, Chicago, visited Professor Commons in Florida. The section of Chapter X on "Similarities and Differences" grew from their conversations. As a student, Erdmann appreciated the significance of this part of Commons' methodology as few other students did. Finding the concept extremely valuable in his administrative work, Erdmann encouraged his teacher to make this part of his thinking more explicit. This section gives a taste of the way Commons sought in his investigations for significant similarities among the multiplicity of differences.

Philip Glick, of the Solicitor's Office of the Department of Agriculture, came to Florida in 1941 through the kind offices of Secretary Henry Wallace and M. L. Wilson to help Commons on his investigation of the invalidation of the original A.A.A. act by the U. S. Supreme Court. The analysis was originally published in the *Journal of Farm Economics* in May, 1942, as "Legislative and Administrative Reasoning in Economics" and is here republished as a part of Chapter XIV, "Agricultural Administration."

To some of his "trailer friends," students and friends of Professor Commons owe a special debt of gratitude. In 1942, Mr. and Mrs. A. B. Carpenter took him into their home. As he neared 80 Professor Commons could no longer stand the Florida winters in the meagre comforts of a trailer. The warmth of the Carpenters' fireside and of Mrs. Carpenter's devoted care filled Professor Commons' last years with comfort and affection. He left the Carpenter home in the spring of 1945 to go to North Carolina with his son and join his one surviving sister to spend his last days with his own family.

In November, 1943, Professor Commons wrote me inquiring whether I could take the time to work with him for "a month or two." His strength was failing and he expressed fear that unless I could help him, he would not be able to finish the book. I had been giving attention to Commons' theories for some time. Beginning in 1929, I had attended his class on Public Value during my graduate work at the University of Wisconsin. I was deeply impressed by his viewpoint and genuinely puzzled by the profound difficulties which even sympathetic readers had in understanding what Commons was driving at. After some ten years of reading and reflection I published, in 1942, an essay in which I attempted to expound the fundamentals of Commons' viewpoint and to show some of the relationships to the larger issues in social thought.[1] Professor Commons appreciated this essay very much and asked the privilege of using it as the introduction to the present volume. We later agreed that I should write an introduction dealing more directly with the contents and significance of this volume. However, the essay on Professor Commons' viewpoint is included in an appendix to this volume.

I was able to go to Florida in June of 1944, upon a travel grant from the Research Committee of the Graduate School of the University of Wisconsin. I spent five weeks with "John R." working through the whole manuscript with him.

During this seminar together we followed the practice of discussing the manuscript for about two hours each day. I would then make the editorial changes or modifications of statement which we had agreed upon. The next day Professor Commons would work over the text of the revised manuscript. The chapter on "Valuations" was the last one written, having been composed in the spring of 1944. This required somewhat more of our joint attention than other parts of the book. His recent study of the theories of the physical scientists is reflected in this chapter. Here, also, he virtually abandons the conception of causation in valuation, centering his thought rather on the instrumentality of the practical judgment. My role in the revision of this chapter, however, was only editorial; at the most I prepared a few transitional paragraphs making explicit some implications of Professor Commons' shorthand statement. Here, as throughout the book, my purpose and practice were to substitute my hand for an enfeebled one

[1] "John R. Commons' Point of View," *Journal of Land and Public Utility Economics*, August, 1942.

so that a vigorous and creative mind could find satisfying expression.

After my return to Madison, I checked the references, including court cases cited, made a few minor changes in the wording of the manuscript, and had it retyped. The manuscript was returned to Professor Commons in the spring of 1945; he again went over it carefully and returned it to me with a few suggestions for modification late in April, 1945. He was satisfied with it and pleased that it now required so little revision. His work was done.

He spent a few delightful days in North Carolina, visiting with President Frank Graham and Professor Howard Odum of the University of North Carolina at Chapel Hill, and with Professor C. Bruce Hoover of near-by Duke University. As he revelled in the university atmosphere, he was young again for a few days; and then the little canter at the end of the race was over and he died rather suddenly in May, 1945, at Raleigh, North Carolina, with his son and sister at his side.

I have gone over the manuscript again lately, attempting to clarify the statement by slight modifications here and there. In this I have been helped greatly by the criticisms of graduate students in the Department of Agricultural Economics who have read the whole manuscript, especially John Bowditch and Erven Long. With the latter especially I have discussed many critical points in the statement. Professor Edwin E. Witte, a colleague and long-time student of Professor Commons, read the manuscript and made several valuable suggestions. I have tried to take all these suggestions into account in clarifying the statement. In a few places the manuscript lacks completeness; a few indefinite references must be left, since only Professor Commons could clear them up.

As I have prepared the manuscript for publication I have had to make several decisions on questions of policy. In these matters I have sought the advice especially of four of my colleagues who were both my graduate teachers and students of Professor Commons: Professors Perlman, Glaeser, Witte, and McNall. The latter was the first of my teachers to point out to me the uniqueness and originality of Professor Commons' approach. I am deeply grateful to these men for their counsel, encouragement, and assistance in this effort. *

This volume is more than the last chapter in a long writing career; it is a monument to a persistent, inquiring mind which never faltered in its devotion to humanity.

Professor Commons and I had not agreed upon a title to the book at the time of his death. He favored some title that would emphasize the investigational nature of his approach to economics; I preferred some title that would point to the significance of his work for the analysis of collective action and administration, both public and private. But we were never able to work out and agree upon a phrasing which both thought adequate. Since Professor Commons' death we have explored again the possibilities of appropriate titles and have decided to call the volume "The Economics of Collective Action." This title acknowledges his great resolve to work out a theory of economics relevant to the dominant problems of the twentieth century, which he considered a new age of collective action by corporations, labor unions, and political parties.

When I left Florida in July, 1944, Professor Commons entrusted the manuscript to me, asking that I edit the same and see it through the press. This trust I have endeavored to keep in the belief that future students of economics might be able through this volume to participate to some degree in seminar with John R., whose penetrating observations opened up the vast field of the economics of collective action to the thousands of students attending his classes.

K. H. P.

[* The bibliography of Professor Commons' writing included in the original printing of this volume has been omitted from the present edition. An extensive bibliography of Commons' work is available in Richard Allyn Gonce, "The Development of John R. Commons' System of Thought," Ph.D. dissertation, University of Wisconsin, 1966.]

# The Economics of

# Collective

# Action

# John Rogers Commons*

## 1862–1945

John Rogers Commons was born in Hollandsburg, Darke County, Ohio, on October 13, 1862, and died at Raleigh, North Carolina, on May 11, 1945, at the age of 82.

He studied at Oberlin College and The Johns Hopkins University, and taught at Wesleyan University, Oberlin College, the University of Indiana, Syracuse University, and the University of Wisconsin.

An enumeration of the fields in economics in which he did original work reads like the table of contents of a comprehensive textbook: Value and Distribution, History of Economic Thought, Public Utilities, Immigration, Housing, Labor Legislation, Social Insurance, Trade Unionism and Industrial Government, Labor History, Monopoly Price, Index Numbers, Business Cycles and Stabilization, and Tariff. To these one will have to add the following from Political Science: Civil Service and Administration, Municipal Government, and Proportional Representation.

Commons was the creator of American labor history, although in this he had been preceded by his teacher and original inspirer, Richard T. Ely. Ely brought him to the University of Wisconsin in 1904 to prepare the *Documentary History of American Industrial Society* as well as to teach. The history was published during 1909–1911 in eleven volumes. Commons retired after thirty years of teaching at Wisconsin. However, during the decade between his retirement and death he steadily continued his researches and publication as well as his close connection with his students in administrative posts and in academic life.

*Reprinted by permission from the *American Economic Review*, Vol. XXXV, No. 4, Sept. 1945, pp. 782–86, with additions for the present volume.

[ 1 ]

He was officially connected with the following public bodies: President McKinley's Industrial Commission, the Wisconsin Industrial Commission (1911–1913), and the United States Commision on Industrial Relations (1913–1916). In 1923 with Professors Ripley and Fetter he represented four western states before the Federal Trade Commission on the Pittsburgh Plus case, involving price discrimination as practiced by the United States Steel Corporation. He organized and directed the Bureau of Economy and Efficiency of the city of Milwaukee during the first Socialist administration, 1910–1912.

His connections with unofficial bodies were equally varied. Early in the century he promoted agreements between employers and unions for the National Civic Federation. In 1906 and 1907 he also investigated for the same organization municipal and private operation of public utilities. In the same years he investigated with others labor conditions in the steel industry in Pittsburgh for the Russell Sage Foundation. The American Association for Labor Legislation began operations in 1909 in a corner of his university office at Madison. Between 1924 and 1926 he was chairman of the voluntary plan of unemployment insurance in the clothing industry in Chicago. He was president of the American Economic Association (1917), associate director of the National Bureau of Economic Research (1920–28), president of the National Monetary Association (1922–23), and president of the National Consumer's League (1923–35).

Among his appearances before Congressional committees doubtless the one in 1913 in support of the elder LaFollette's bill for the physical valuation of the railways by the Interstate Commerce Commission was the most comprehensive in scope. His intimate cooperation with LaFollette had begun in 1905 when the latter, as Governor of Wisconsin, requested him to draft a civil service law. In 1907 he drafted a public utility law for the state of Wisconsin.

Perhaps Commons' greatest contribution as a scholar dealt with the life cycle of economic institutions. He defined an economic institution as "collective action in control of individual action." Commons had no liking for either the winged phrase or for what one might call the winged theory: he knew from experience that human motives have a way of appearing in innumerable combinations. He therefore doubted such master juxtapositions as bourgeoisie and proletariat, technician and business man, and felt that they appeared convincing only from a seat in the British Museum or from an academic armchair. To him the social terrain was far too broken to conform to any sweeping description, but demanded the labor of tireless and meticulous topographers who had the experimenter's imagination and were unafraid to "wade in." He began with the institutions of labor, to which he had received an early introduction as a member of the Typographical Union.

Commons accorded a supreme attentiveness to the institutions contrived by workingmen without the aid of mentors from those of high social station and education—institutions such as trade unions, cooperative buying clubs, cooperative workshops, and the like. He rejoiced in tracing the steps of the unlettered statesmen— the phrase is the Webbs'—whereby these movements laid stable foundations underneath these organizations by the method of trial and error. And as a student of such movements he knew how incompatible such creativeness from below was with external domination by employers, messianic intellectuals, or government.

To Commons the working men were not abstract building blocks out of which a favored deity called "History" was to shape the architecture of the new society, but concrete beings with legitimate ambitions for a higher standard of living and for more diginity in their lives. Both objectives, he agreed with labor, were primarily realizable through the attainment of citizenship status on the job and in the place of employment, paralleling the worker's status in the democratic state. As self-determining beings, the workers and their movements were to set their *own* objectives, their *own* values, and were entitled to claim from the intellectuals expert aid in the road they should take to attain the goals set by leaders risen in their midst. If labor's goals were mutually contradictory, the intellectual should so inform them. If labor's objectives were not for the benefit of society and ultimately not for its own, he should tell that too. And above all, the intellectual should be an expert social topographer and trained forecaster of group behavior.

Commons applied this same pattern of fruitful interplay between the undogmatic intellectual and struggling movements to past history. He thus came to formulate a gripping theory of the interrelation between group customs and the common law, of the rise of new social classes, and of their struggle for recognition. In his *Legal Foundations of Capitalism* he showed how in the struggle around the "rent bargain" the barons had reduced the King of England from an over-all owner to a recipient of a land tax fixed by collective bargaining between their representatives and his. In a similar way, the merchants of England began through their participation in the piepowder courts at the fairs to impose the customs of their group upon the presiding judge, who was only too glad thus to fill the void of his ignorance. Out of this unimpressive beginning, through a process of osmosis over several centuries between judges increasingly appreciative of the growing importance of the merchants to the Commonwealth of England and a continuous custom-making by that merchant class to suit changing conditions, came the law merchant, and finally the latter's incorporation in the common law. What produced this significant result was the unremitting pushing by the merchant class; the willingness of undogmatic intellectuals, the judges, to absorb pressures from below and thus prevent frustration; and ultimately a judicial sifting of these merchant customs, the rejection of some and the acceptance of those that looked acceptable from the standpoint of the moving pattern of the law. The intellectual mechanism employed was the expansion of the meaning of *property* from the mere "physical" to embrace the "incorporeal" and the "intangible."

Commons delighted in seeing the judges of America during the last years of his life do with the customs of the labor movement—the fair wage, the normal working day, the union shop, and seniority—what their English predecessors had done with the customs of the merchants. Earlier he had been greatly impressed by the statesmanship of Australia's Court of Conciliation and Arbitration, although not by her system of compulsory arbitration of labor disputes. But the shift away from dogmatism by our official "intellectuals" came only after the labor movement had gathered momentum both in industry and government under the salutory climate of the New Deal—altogether in conformity with Commons' conception of how social change takes place.

Thus ran the Commons theory of the class struggle: it is not a struggle by the rising group to liquidate the old class or to raze the social structure which the latter controlled, but laboring instead to add to the old edifice new and spacious wings to serve as the dwelling places of the customs of the rising class. Such a "class struggle" might appear to some as pathetically limited in its objective, but there was nothing pathetic about its driving qualities. And those who pioneered in the struggle of recognition were in the front ranks of the history makers. As an intellectual democrat Commons held in the highest esteem Samuel Gompers, who had to develop his theory of the American labor movement as he went about keeping the American Federation of Labor from disintegrating on his hands.

Commons' intellectual democracy perhaps showed clearest when he was interviewing. His was no "technique of modesty" or a simulated ignorance to appeal to the other's ego and thus evoke information. It was a genuine groping, questions without any definite goal—a mere stabbing in this direction and in that. What kept the conversation from degenerating into a boring experience to the person interviewed was Commons' deep earnestness and his unmistakable assumption that the latter's problems were not just his own private worries but of general concern and deeply instructive to any serious-minded interrogator. And then, sometimes after hours had elapsed, a question or a series of questions would come forth which not only touched the nerve of the whole situation but as if by sleight-of-hand made the earlier groping appear as an orderly quest with little waste motion. The result was a fuller grasp of the problem and a suggested solution possessing both freshness and promise. To the bystander it was an absorbing spectacle of intuition and reason pulling in common harness.

In Commons genuine personal modesty went hand-in-hand with unusual intellectual courage. He never shrank from taking risks with his reputation when among the tentative interpretations of a body of factual material one finally loomed as *the* interpretation. There was neither laziness nor lack of regard for accuracy in this flouting of the much over-praised academic caution. Commons was an indefatigable worker whose working day began at four in the morning, and his co-workers knew he would have the manuscript of a whole volume re-checked from the original sources, himself participating, on account of an error in a single quotation.

Probably Commons' boldest theoretical *coup* was his "American Shoemakers, 1648 to 1895," the Preface to Volumes VII and VIII of the *Documentary History of American Industrial Society*. In this study he has given us a breath-taking picture of changes in economic structure, of the formation of "bargaining classes" and the vicissitudes of their respective "bargaining power." He based it on testimony given in the early labor conspiracy trials by strikers, "scabs," master workmen, and "gentlemen of the trade." Little did these witnesses realize that they were providing material for a future economist who would emulate the reconstruction work of the paleontologist.

But great as Commons was as a social investigator inspired by the ideal of the equivalence of all men, he was no less great as a statesman. In fact, with him scholarship and practical statesmanship were forever inseparable. As a statesman he knew that the democratic objective in industrial relations could not be attained through a bureaucracy, however well intentioned or trained, but depended on self-action by all the groups concerned, the government aiding but not dominating. Nor would he enthrone the underdog group. For much as he identified himself with the so-called "common man," he was far from disdainful of employers' and manufacturers' associations and other organizations among the better-situated groups. Though he fought them before legislative committees when they impeded industrial safety, workmen's compensation, shorter hours for women and the like, he strove to harness the power of these same organizations alongside the trade unions on behalf of an efficient administration of the laws enacted.

And within the groups on the conservative side of the alignment, he sought to enlist and to energize on behalf of those measures the individuals of high purpose and high standards. He thus came to grapple as early as thirty-five years ago with the so-called "road to serfdom," the alleged discovery of our own day, and in the device of the "advisory committee" of the leaders of the groups affected he provided for an effective preventive of the bureaucratization of the governmental process.

As teacher and inspirer of graduate and undergraduate students, Professor Commons ranks with America's greatest. In Commons' presence the student while aware of contact with greatness yet never felt dwarfed, for Commons made him feel that he was genuinely dependent on his contribution whether to check a theoretical point or to invent a workable device. Professor Commons never tired of acclaiming such contributions, as when a member of his seminar suggested the "employer election device" in the workmen's compensation law of 1911, for long the keystone of that law's constitutionality. In fact, his generosity in allotting credit to his students and co-workers was a source of endless embarrassment to the latter. The same generosity and solicitude extended to the students' other concerns and wants.

There are hundreds of Commons' students, including some most prominent in the academic life and in the public services of this country, who largely owe their careers to the untiring and tender encouragement by Professor and Mrs. Commons. At the Commons' weekly "Friday Nights" at their home near Mendota Beach, students, frequently numbering as many as sixty, had the opportunity of meeting some of the most prominent economists and public men of the world and to present before the group their own observation in the "field." To the Commons' "Friday Nights" many a public man looks back today as the informal and friendly "Parliament" that heard his "maiden speech."

SELIG PERLMAN

University of Wisconsin

# INTRODUCTION*

John R. Commons' life epitomized the growth of American industrialism. Born in 1862, he began his career as a printer, and moved in an ever-widening circle of understanding and influence—as printer, union member, teacher, investigator, administrator, and counsellor to public officials. He was supreme as an investigator, with a rare faculty for ferreting out the strategic factors in a situation, and then devising ways of resolving the difficulties. Commons developed a comprehensive and original viewpoint through economic investigations into the "hot spots" of an emerging industrialism. He saw the American labor movement grow from infancy; he understood the day-by-day workings of American capitalistic industry as few university men ever have; he participated as counsellor, investigator, administrator, and social inventor supreme, in the creation of programs and administrative organizations to stabilize a turbulent industrialism and direct its growth toward civilized goals by means of a created "security of expectations" which served both public and private interests. Through it all he attempted to work out a system of ideas which would contribute to the foundations of a genuinely democratic economic government in this twentieth century of collective action and economic power.

The present book is the capstone of that long career. Here he attempts to expound, for the first time, in simple terms, the basic ideas which he developed through sixty years as a participant observer in American economic life. His other theoretical books, *Legal Foundations of Capitalism* (Macmillan), 1924, and *Institu-*

* By the editor, Kenneth H. Parsons.

[ 9 ]

*tional Economics* (Macmillan), 1934, are research treatises. This is an exposition.

But with John R. Commons exposition was also creation. As he pulled the threads of the argument from the tangle of experience and wove the fabric of a systematic statement, he revised and re-shaped his conceptions. Two problems, or perhaps better, two aspects of one problem, absorbed his attention in his last years and give a distinctive tone to this book: (1) the fundamental differences between the physical and social sciences, and (2) the need to see valuation as an aspect of judgment. His thinking on these two points represents definite advances from positions held in earlier writings.

This last book is, therefore, logically the first book in understanding Commons' thought. Here the elements in his viewpoint are presented systematically in relation to the problems or experiences from which he gleaned his hypotheses and insights.

Commons' attack on the problem of industrial accidents in Wisconsin about 1905 revealed his genius as an investigator and social inventor. Industry was torn by intense conflicts between employers and workers over the conditions of employment. Feeling was especially bitter over accidents. Working conditions were hazardous, with legal liability for accidents following the common-law rule of negligence. Where accidents were held by the courts to be due to the employers' negligence, the usual recourse in case of a corporation was to arrest and perhaps imprison the foreman or superintendent. The persons of the stockholders were beyond reach of the law.

Commons had been impressed earlier by the possibilities of safety engineering in the steel industry. Here in Wisconsin he proposed to compensate workers for injuries regardless of fault and make this a cost of the industry; correlatively he proposed to reduce accidents in industry by safety devices on machines and the creation of a "safety spirit" among workers and employers alike. He believed that the actual cost of accident compensation could be more than covered by increased output due to improved safety. He then proposed the elimination of criminal prosecutions for accident liability—substituting accident compensation commensurate with the injury as a penalty or charge upon the company. As he liked to observe, "The fines got at the pocketbook nerve of corporations; criminal penalties didn't touch them since corporations couldn't be put in jail." Finally he helped employers form their own mutual insurance company by which the benefits of safe employment could accrue to the particular employers responsible for the improvement.

This experience in first investigating accidents and then working out adequate administrative procedure for a permanent program made a deep impression on Commons' whole viewpoint. Here he saw the possibilities of actually lifting the whole level of performance in industry by enlisting the willing participation of both workers and employers in a common effort to achieve goals already proven possible by the more enlightened men in the industry. This is one of the roots of his conception of reasonable value. He found that the use of safety experts as factory inspectors, in the place of earlier "policemen" in search of violations, both enlisted the employers' interest in safety and gave the inspectors a new dignified usefulness. This was a demonstration of how ideas could help resolve conflicts and make way for a rewarding mutuality.

This experience also gave him deep insight into the significance of economic power and how it might be directed toward achieving public as well as private purposes. The substitution of economic penalties upon the corporation in the place of the primitive common-law criminal action upon the person of participants gave him clues which he generalized into his views on kinds and degrees of power in securing performance. Finally, the procedures worked out by the Wisconsin Industrial Commission for the actual participation of the various interests in the industry in the drafting of safety codes gave Commons a great vision of the way investigations by experts could be combined with representative interest groups in administrative commissions to work out the new "fourth branch" of government needed in this twentieth century of collective action. Commons discusses this experience in accident prevention in Wisconsin in this volume under the suggestive title of "Cooperation of Public and Private Administration" (Chapter XVI—"Capital-Labor Administration").

Commons' experience in drafting a public utility law for Wisconsin, about 1910, may have influenced his viewpoint more than any other investigation. Here he sought a plan of public action which would both provide economic regulation in the public interest and meet the judicial tests of "reasonableness" within the due process of law. This investigation launched Commons and his students upon an exhaustive study of the economic principles followed by the courts. This study matured into *Legal Foundations of Capitalism,* in 1924, and carried him well into the analysis of "reasonable value."

In his investigations into "reasonable value" Commons concentrated upon the analyses of court decisions, but his purpose was even broader than the study of legal theories of valuation. He was searching for a laboratory in which to study the operation of the human will upon the most difficult problem in social thought—the achievement of joint valuations and agreements for action in situations involving genuine conflicts of interest.

He is speaking out of this experience in his comments on valuation in this volume when he says: "But when economists came finally to the study of the political theories of bankers and lawyers and their implicit theories of valuation they discovered the foundation to be nothing less comprehensive than the whole of the *human will,* individual and organized . . . consequently, in what was really their experimental laboratory, a court of law in examining witnesses and documents, the lawyers had to discover and measure the behavioristic dimensions of the human will as a power of self-control or self-command." (Chapter XI, "The Economists' Theory of Value," pp. 145–169.)

The essence of Commons' approach to reasonable value was to devise ways of drawing upon the vast treasury of human experience for suggestions as to possible courses of action that would actually carry civilization forward step by step especially from conflict to mutuality. In Commons' view, social values can be dealt with objectively only by attention to the working rules by which performance is guided as valuations are acted upon; these working rules can be made more precise as the relevant performance is measurable.

The fundamental unity of Commons' whole intellectual history appears to be found in his efforts to bring the human will within the scope of economic analysis. As he remarked in the summer of 1944, "I began fifty years ago to work out a volitional economics but then I couldn't make anyone understand what I was driving at." It was his firm conviction, as he neared the close of life, that economists have been misled by mechanical analogies and the imitation of the physical sciences into an inadequate doctrine of subjective valuation, by using methods of analysis which assumed that human beings were propelled by external "forces" rather than purposefully by their own wills. Commons sought a relativistic theory of valuation, whereby the purposes in action would be inherently related to the possible or accessible alternatives for action. He strove to achieve this inherent relevance by arriving at value judgments out of the analysis of experience. In this way he would avoid the arbitrariness of his own wishful thinking and habitual assumptions. He therefore investigated the valuations of joint actions in the "laboratories of the human will" wherever he could find them.

In reflecting upon his quest for a volitional economics he observes in this book that: "During the stages of economic science when the economists imitated the physical sciences, the individual was treated in economic theory like atoms, molecules . . . and the like, controlled by external forces and not self-controlled . . . Their [the economists'] science was founded on materialism, and when businessmen, as well as economists, came up against such facts as labor turnover, trade unions, secret ballot, and emancipation of slaves, where laborers had 'wills of their own,' they had to treat them either as dishonest and call in the army or begin to adopt methods of investigation and understanding based on purposes of the human will instead of the economic theory of causation by physical forces." ("The Economists' Theory of Value," pp. 154, 155.) Commons devoted his life to devising and using methods of investigation and understanding which explicitly recognize that human activity is volitional.

Commons' approach centers on the problems of social control, through the analysis of the structure of collective action in an age of economic power. He knew that the economy is not an automatically self-directing mechanism. In his view, the economy moves forward on the decisions, judgments, and actions of persons —on operations of the human will, individually and collectively. The common ground of all democratic (i.e., nonauthoritarian) control is therefore the procedures by which the wills of participants, including those with conflicting interests, are brought together into a created collective will.

Commons blazed a broad trail through many virgin areas—labor history, labor conciliation, accident compensation, industrial government, industrial commissions, unemployment insurance, social security, and public utility regulation, among others. His contributions in these practical fields were monumental.

These contributions were rooted in a viewpoint which was being worked out as Commons moved from problem to problem—from insight to insight. His general theories are elaborations and generalizations of particular insights; he integrates his ideas around positions on the fundamental issues in social thought. This approach, this method of working out a theory of economics, may seem bewildering to persons who are schooled only in the techniques of logical exposition from assumed premises. The true measure of Commons' genius can be seen only when one realizes the boldness and originality with which he worked out a viewpoint from insights which he derived from putting ideas to work in the actual solution of economic problems.

Commons' ideas are grounded in his conception of social relationships. He proceeds from a postulate of the economy as a social organization, rather than as mechanism or organism. As a social organization it is the way participants act; organization is achieved through the stabilization and regularization of activity. Activity is regularized or controlled in a society of citizens (persons with legally recognized wills of their own) by the working rules which define the limits within which individuals may exercise their own wills.

It follows from these conceptions that individuals are not self-sufficient, independent entities; and society is not the summation of the individual members. Individuals are what they are through their participation in the institutions or going concerns of which they are members. Commons was deeply impressed by the way in which membership in labor unions lifted workers from a level of fear and servility to a new dignity and courage commensurate with their rights of economic citizenship. This aspect of Commons' thought is summarized in his conception of an institution as "collective action in control, liberation, and expansion of individual action."

Similarly values are conceived of as fundamentally institutional and relative to social organization. Freedom, for example, is not conceived of as a natural right; rather it is a social achievement. In this view, freedom is created by collective action controlling, liberating, and expanding individual action. Individual freedom is achieved through the proportioning of inducements and sanctions to individuals by collective action. Through collective action a zone of freedom for secure individual action is created—the security of expectations for individuals and going concerns. Commons summarizes the issues neatly by one historical comment in this volume: "Coke's common law rights of Englishmen became Smith's natural rights of man."

These few remarks may suggest why the argument in this book moves to a brilliant climax in the chapters dealing with economic government. In Chapter XVI on "Capital-Labor Administration," Commons analyzes the emerging economic government in the area of most intense social conflicts—the conflicts of labor and capital. The twentieth century is an age of collective action, Commons emphasizes time and again. Three forms of collective action predominate: corporations, trade unions, and political parties. Here are fundamental conflicts, economic and political. It is not simply that persons misinterpret their own self-interests in relation to a harmonious totality of interests. Conflicts and economic power are real.

It seemed strange to Commons that economic power should be so little comprehended. From this limited comprehension comes one of the basic confusions of our times, in Commons' view—the failure to distinguish collective bargaining from totalitarianism. To him trade unions and corporations are simply the modern forms of economic activity. The task of economic government is to create a genuine economic democracy within these forms. As he observes in the chapter on "Capital-Labor Administration": "The preservation of the American economic system against a totalitarian world, and against its own internal disruption, consists mainly in the collective bargaining between organized capital and organized labor, as against government by the traditional political parties. Other economic organizations, whether of farmers, merchants, bankers, or the professions, must conform their policies and methods to this major economic issue of 'capital and labor.' . . . If American democracy is 'saved,' it will be saved by collective economic organization of corporations and labor unions. Instead of the traditional equilibrium between equal individuals of economic theory, the alternatives today are betweeen an economic government based on balance of power between self-governing corporations and unions, and a suppression of both organizations, or their leaders, by military power. . . . Yet the whole system of political economy, as theoretically developed in the nineteenth century by professional economists and approved by the public generally, has been so built upon the ideal of a perfect society of liberty, equality and fraternity among individuals, under the ideal name of 'democracy,' that people have not learned to think and act in terms of the actual 'collective democracy' of economic organizations" (pp. 262–264).

The order of problems to which Commons devoted his major attention promises to take on a renewed importance in the years ahead. During the war, the necessary dominance of the emergency powers of the president and military force pushed the problems of economic government into the background. But with the peace, the great questions of security, power, conflict, and economic government in an advanced industrial-financial economy are again before us.

The viewpoint which embraces a formulation of possible courses of action on these great problems is necessarily comprehensive. As Commons sought the requisite breadth of interpretation and statement, he necessarily dealt sketchily with many problems which other economists have worked out in greater detail. But this viewpoint has in it the elements of a truly general theory of economics, embracing the more particular problems of production, pricing, equilibrium, etc., as well as those of social control.

The comprehensiveness of Commons' approach may be indicated by his early attention to rationing. By 1924 he had worked from the traditional conception of exchange through an exhaustive analysis of the social relations in transactions. He once commented that he spent seven years working out his theory of transactions. In his *Institutional Economics*, 1934, he simplified the statement by distinguishing transactions into three kinds, according to the issue and social relations involved: bargaining, rationing, and managerial transactions. His analysis of rationing transactions, for example, was a pioneer work, in showing the fundamental differences in the social organization implicit in the adoption of price and production rationing in the place of the usual (market) bargaining relations. With the outbreak of the war, and the necessity for curbing the exercise of individual choices and bargaining through a system of rationing, Commons' previous analyses were extremely valuable in the administration of rationing and price control.

Commons is not only original in the subject matter investigated, his ideas are grounded in a different philosophical context than most systematic economic thought. Commons was a truly indigenous thinker; his was one of the most creative minds in the American stream of pragmatism. This aspect of his thought deserves careful and exhaustive investigation. Here we can only note certain issues which are definitive in his system of thought. Ideas for Commons are essentially possible courses of action, not replicas of an assumed reality. The function of thought is accepted as creative and reconstructive, not simply reportorial. Causation is viewed as an imputed effectiveness in the control of the social process; a social affair is "caused by the control of the limiting factor"—hence causation is not simply a mechanical antecedent or coexistent "force," but is an aspect of the form which accrues to subject matter through and by investigation. Truth is not to be tested merely by consistency or argument from assumed premises; the ultimate truth or validity of an idea is to be tested only by the consequences of acting upon it. As Commons once remarked, he spent his life persuading public officials and union leaders to try out his ideas to see whether they were true.

The issues run the whole gamut of social philosophy. Commons took his stand on the grounds of a social pragmatism which he seems to have worked out independently by devising procedures in his own investigations. He did, however, build upon the ideas of Peirce as a foundation; as a young man he was delighted to discover Peirce's essay on "How to Make Our Ideas Clear" and find that Peirce had worked out in terms of physical sciences the central problems with which Commons was then struggling.

Few academic people have had the intellectual courage to tackle the order of problems to which Commons devoted his life. His effectiveness in public affairs stands as a challenge to future students of economics to understand the source of his mastery. He struggled for fifty years to articulate and systematize the insights which came to his fertile mind. He passed on in the hope and calm belief that at last he had been able to explain the essential points of his message.

# PART ONE

Economic Activity

# Introduction

Economics deals with the problems of mankind as they go about trying to make a living or get rich. Thus the economists are interested primarily in the problems which arise from the production of wealth and the distribution of income. Virtually all economists would agree with this generalized statement. The disagreements come over how these problems should be approached.

We begin our investigations into economic problems through collective action. Our experience and observations over sixty years teach us that collective action is inclusive. Other persons may call this social. But collective action is the general and dominating fact of social life. Human beings are born into this process of collective action and become individualized by the rules of collective action. Thus an institution is collective action in control, liberation, and expansion of individual action.

From investigations into economic activities we conclude that the human will is central to economic life. Human activity is behavioristically the human will in action. Consequently the stragetic relation in economic activity is the place where the wills of men meet. This meeting of the wills can be analyzed in terms of the transaction. A transaction is two-sided: it is joint action. In the transaction the terms of performance are agreed upon; or performance is executed according to working rules previously established or agreed upon.

In this way our theories of economics come to center on transactions and working roles, on the problems of organization, and on the way collective action becomes organized into going concerns. But these forms of collective action are not something different from what people do. The organization of activity is simply the more stabilized aspects of activity. The form is a part of the process.

In modern capitalism the most important stabilized economic relations are those of private property. But property relations are not something fixed and permanent. They are undergoing change all the time within the processes of collective action. We have made studies in *Legal Foundations of Capitalism,* and elsewhere, of the changing meanings of property, liberty, and due process of law which the courts have followed in the settlement of disputes in transactions.

Capitalism in its highest form, as found in the United States, is built upon this legal foundation of private property, latterly modified by the emergence of joint-stock corporations, holding companies, banks, labor unions, and political parties seeking control of the sovereign power of the state.

If economic investigations are to implement the search of mankind for liberty, security, justice, equality or other great goals it would seem that economists must analyze these political, economic, and social relations by which the values are made available to, or secure for, the individual.

# Chapter i

## COLLECTIVE ACTION

———◆———

This is an age of collective action. Most Americans must work collectively as participants in organized concerns in order to earn a living. In this collective process, persons engage in collective bargaining—for this is the way individual wills meet and become a part of the collective will. Collective bargaining, in the case of labor relations, means that the representatives of two organizations, the labor union and the capitalists, meet together as equals and agree upon working rules that shall govern all individuals within the two concerns.

For several years and on various occasions I have participated as mediator, conciliator, and as arbitrator when agreed upon by both concerns, to help these conflicting organizations to agree upon the joint working rules that should, for the time being, govern their members. I have been able to introduce the principle of collective bargaining into the administration of labor laws in the state of Wisconsin. At first I failed when I tried to introduce it into the civil service law of the state in 1905. The legislature was then alarmed at the suggestion of collective action by employees of so sacred an organization as "the State." But since that time the employees of the state government, that is, the employees of the politicians, have effected an organization on their own initiative, and have even obtained a considerable amount of recognition by the politicians in modifying the working rules of the civil service of the state. It turns out that "the State" was the collective action of politicians. The three principal kinds of collective economic action in the twentieth century are corporations, labor unions, and political parties.

Collective bargaining was introduced into the Industrial Commission law of Wisconsin in 1911 under the name of "advisory committees." As I was appointed one of the three members of that Commission, it fell to me to organize the advisory committees. They were organized on the principle of collective bargaining. The boiler safety committee, for example, on nominations made by the State Manufacturers' Association and the State Federation of Labor, was composed of representatives of the organized manufacturers, the unions, and the insurance companies. They worked out, in the course of a year, a safety "code" under the general rule, contained in the legislative act, that "safety" should mean the highest degree of safety that the nature of the industry or of the employment would "reasonably" permit. This code, after a public hearing to conform to the constitutional rules of government as formulated by the Supreme Court, was then issued and published by the Commission and became the law of the state as though it had been enacted in detail by the legislature itself.

The same principle of collective bargaining was afterward, in 1933, incorporated more explicitly in the Workmen's Unemployment Compensation Law of Wisconsin, designed to prevent unemployment as much as practicable, as the safety law was designed to prevent accidents. The advisory committee in this case, as in the safety laws, was selected by the same State Manufacturers' Association and the State Federation of Labor, with the secretary of the State Industrial Commission acting as mediator or chairman, but not voting. The rules, unanimously agreed upon by collective bargaining and mediation, were then issued by the Commission as the law of the state, subject to review by the courts, governing all employers and all employees designated by the legislature. Many amendments and improvements of the statutory law were also unanimously agreed upon by this collective bargaining process, and these amendments in the legislative sessions of 1935 and 1937, were unanimously accepted under suspension of the rules, without debate, by the legislature.[1]

Thus, collective bargaining became a law-making procedure of the State. It was afterward that I named it "collective democracy," in order to distinguish it from the individualistic democ-

[1] See chapter on "Capital-Labor Administration," p. 261.

racy of Adam Smith, the founder of political economy in 1776, and from the dictatorships of Europe and Asia. Collective bargaining applies not only to the so-called "conflict of capital and labor," but also applies to other economic conflicts. It rests, for us, on the common law of England and America, carried forward from the decisions of American Supreme Courts on "reasonable" value, reasonable practices, and fair competition, in place of the free-competition theories of the economists.

These are the subject matters set forth for investigation in this book. The assumption is that whatever is "reasonable" is consti-tutional, and that reasonableness is best ascertained in practice when representatives of conflicting organized economic interests, instead of politicians or lawyers, agree voluntarily on the working rules of their collective action in control of individual action. This may not be ideal, and it is not logical, neither is it revolutionary. It is the discovery, through investigation and negotiation, of what is the best practicable thing to do under the actual circumstances of conflicting economic interests, organized, as they are, to impose their collective will on individuals and on each other.

My acquaintance with collective bargaining was begun five decades ago, in the year 1883. In that year I joined local Typo-graphical Union No. 53 at Cleveland, Ohio, in order to get a job on the *Cleveland Herald*, owned by a corporation. Across the street was a nonunion office, the *Cleveland Leader*, where my brother had a job. The hours of labor and rates of pay at piece-work were the same. We worked eleven or twelve hours afternoon and night, and I could earn about fifteen dollars per week if I worked seven nights a week; this was more than I had ever earned before.

The two offices were alike, except in the rules that controlled the foremen and the printers. In the nonunion office the foreman was a dictator. He had his "pets" to whom he gave steady work; and he gave to them the "fat," meaning the kind of work, like advertisements and baseball scores, that paid better wages than other kinds of work. This kind of activity would be named, in the science of economics, "the distribution of wealth."

But in the union office the foreman was restrained in these

matters by rules agreed upon by the labor union and the owners of the newspaper. We had a rule of preference for vacancies, instead of leaving it to the foreman. I started as a "sub" on the "waiting list," and then became a "regular." The rule provided that if a regular wished to lay off, he might ask anyone on the substitute list to take his place until he came back. A regular asked me to substitute for him one night, and he then left for Chicago and did not return. I had the job.

A regular could not be "fired" without a hearing. In this hearing the "father of the chapel," named a "steward" or chairman in other less medieval unions, represented the members and had equal voice with the foreman who represented the proprietors. The "fat," instead of going to "pets," was auctioned off by the father of the chapel. I bid on the baseball scores, which paid double rates. I got the work by paying 10 per cent. Then, at the next bidding, the boys forced me up to 40 per cent. It was fat at 10 per cent, and I could make about 20 dollars a week of seven nights' work. But at 40 per cent all the fat was squeezed out. I paid my bid in kind by clipping off that much galley proof from my "string" and handing it to the father of the chapel, who then distributed it around the office to all the printers. So with the others who bought at auction the other kinds of fat. We were all provided with an equal opportunity in the distribution of wealth. Then when I moved to other towns north and south, the union gave me a "traveling card," which would admit me to any "union shop," where I could take my chance on the waiting list. I was thereby a member of the International Typographical Union of the United States, Canada, and Mexico.

Many years afterward, when I had investigated other labor unions as well as business corporations and farmers' cooperatives, I gave the name "institution" to my little union in Cleveland and to all the others. I now define an "institution" as collective action in control of individual action.[1] The rules, regulations, or bylaws I name the "rules of action," or "working rules of collective action." I can recall that my little union had created certain rights

[1] See my *Institutional Economics*, New York, The Macmillan Co., 1934, pp. 69 ff.

and liberties for the members which were not to be found in the
more dictatorial government of the nonunion shop. That dictatorial shop operated under the historic common law of "master
and servant," whereby the master—that is, the foreman—was
authorized to "fire" a man without notice and without giving a
reason, and the servant also had the equal right to quit without
notice and without giving a reason. The common-law rules under
which people worked had been created in past history by the
courts of England and America and were supposed to be the law
of liberty and equality. But I knew from experience that I had
more liberty in the union shop and, therefore, earned more wages
steadily, and enjoyed more equality when it came to the "fat,"
than my brother enjoyed across the street in his nonunion shop.
I had, indeed, acquired a "right to work," which he did not have
in his shop—not a "legal" right, but an "economic" right.

This right to work was merely an "immunity"—an immunity
against being discharged arbitrarily by the foreman, although I
could be discharged—and others were so discharged—after a hearing, where I could have the father of the chapel to protect me
against the foreman in defending myself on the merits of my case.
This was our "court of law." The "father" had a similar immunity,
if he talked according to the rules of order.

My rights, liberties, and immunities came from the working
rules of my little experiment of collective action in control of
individual action. The "control" was the duties imposed equally
on each member and upon the foreman in his dealings with members. Indeed, my rights and liberties were assured only because I
and the others were subject to corresponding duties. The so-called
working rules were themselves only the duties imposed on individuals by the collective action of all together.

The nonunion establishment had to pay the same or even higher
wages than in my union shop, else their employees would join our
union. Yet, what is the good of high wages if you do not have a job,
or if you can be fired at will by a foreman who need not give any
reason for firing you? People may question why it is that even
high wage earners go out on strike, and employers often think that
by offering workers still higher wages they can induce them to

stay at work or win them back to work. But what the union wants
is a hearing for each individual before he is fired, or when he
alleges that he has been discriminated against. This is the most
that the members mean by "recognition of the union."

Such "recognition" meant simply, in this case, that the father
of the chapel had immunity from discharge if he went over the
head of the foreman and appealed to the general superintendent
or even to the board of directors of the corporation in his effort
to get a hearing on behalf of any individual member of the union
who claimed a "grievance" against the foreman.

Years afterward I joined with others of my teaching profession
to form the American Association of University Professors, headed
by the eminent Professor E. R. A. Seligman of the economics department at Columbia University. The purpose was to establish
"academic freedom." I found that what was meant by academic
freedom was exemption from the law of master and servant, so
that we could have security of tenure and a hearing before dismissal. In one of the investigations made by the committee of the
association, a member of the board of trustees of the university
in question justified the removal of a professor by saying, "If I
have a clerk in my store that I do not like, I fire him. These
teachers are our employees. We drop them if we do not like them."
He stated correctly the law of master and servant. But what the
association of professors wanted was a hearing on the merits of
each case of dismissal as to whether the dismissal would be justified in the interests of liberty to teach and speak. We wanted
immunity from the common law of master and servant, and named
it "academic freedom."

The science of economics has been endeavoring to catch up with
this collective action which was condemned at the beginning of
the science by its founder, Adam Smith, in 1776, and by the courts.
Collective action proceeds, indeed, not from the intellectual logic
of philosophers and economists, but from the arguments, debates,
conferences, compromises, mass meetings, agreements, disagreements, negotiations, propaganda—among ordinary people themselves, like business men, laboring men, farmers, or professional
classes, when forced or persuaded to consider their common in-

terests. The psychology of this give-and-take process of conciliation and agreement may be named negotiational psychology, to distinguish it from the pleasure-pain psychology of the individualistic
economists since the eighteenth century.

The illustrious American philosopher and economist, Thorstein
Veblen, at the beginning of the twentieth century, condemned the
collective action of business men and laboring men even more vigorously and satirically than did Adam Smith in the eighteenth
century. He was equally opposed to corporations and labor unions.
Where Smith condemned them as monopolies, Veblen condemned
them as "getting something for nothing," which is the same thing.
But toward the end of the nineteenth century there began to
emerge a distinction between one-sided collective action and two-
sided collective action, known latterly as "collective bargaining."

My little union of 1883 was two-sided collective action. On one
side were the investors and stockholders of the *Cleveland Herald*
acting collectively as owners. On the other side were the type-
setters acting collectively as a labor union. Each side negotiated
through representatives of its own choosing. Where the economists
contended that a free trade was individual bargaining, there now
appeared a kind of trade that was collective bargaining. Where
formerly it was assumed equality of individuals existed in individual bargaining, we endeavored to achieve equality of bargaining
power between two organizations of individuals. And the bargain
which was agreed upon collectively between the organizations was
not the exchange of commodities but the construction of working
rules. These rules were intended to govern all the individual bargains of "hiring and firing" between foremen and laborers as to
wages, hours of labor, tenure, vacancies, promotions, seniority,
"parity income," and other points where disputes might arise.

There was nothing logical, inevitable, or natural in this bargaining. One could see strategy, weighing of alternatives, and
reasoning about what they were up against if they did not agree.
It was collective negotiation and compromise between the conflicting interests and the conflicting reasoning of capitalists and laborers, a process of reasoning which has historically been known
since the time of ancient Greece as "dialectics," that is, argument

back and forth instead of logic. They might not arrive at logical truth, but they arrive at agreement to work together for the time being.

This process of collective negotiation and compromise has been enlarged to cover the whole nation. In a railway case, in the 1930's, there were 67 railway corporations and 5 railway brotherhoods, representing billions of dollars of investment and thousands of operating employees. The employee representatives reasoned that they must have a 20 per cent advance in wages. The capitalist representatives reasoned that, since their corporations were going bankrupt already on account of competition from trucks on free highways, they could not logically and would not practically grant a single cent advance in wages. The dialectic continued for a month and was a deadlock until the date announced for the strike was near at hand. A mediator, William M. Leiserson, not a judge or arbitrator with compulsory power to decide and enforce his decision, but merely a negotiator appointed by the government and thus representing "the public," began his argument, which was merely a summary history of the labor movement. He was confronted by two-sided collective action. Each side was logical in its own contentions on the preliminary assumptions that the capitalist system should be preserved and that laborers should be paid in proportion to their responsibilities, increased output, and cost of living. At the conclusion of Leiserson's argument, and without further debate, a 6 per cent advance in wages was agreed upon. This was not logical, but it worked.

Many other cases I have investigated since 1883. Some of them were ostensibly collective bargaining but were, in fact, one-sided collective action. A number of years ago, as a member of the Federal Industrial Relations Commission,[1] I investigated, with the other members, the building trades of San Francisco. The building trades were united in a complete federation and controlled the municipal government of that city. They drew up their so-

[1] See *Report of the Commission* to U. S. Senate, 1915. *Collective Bargaining in San Francisco, Senate Documents #24,* 64th Congress, 1st Session, 1915–16, Vol. 6, pp. 5169–5402. *Final Report and Testimony of Commission on Industrial Relations* submitted to Congress, 11 vols.

called agreements with employers, but they did not consult the employers as an organization. The unions took these agreements around to the employers individually, and the employers signed individually "on the dotted line." The local union officials claimed that this was collective bargaining, but it was not. Eventually, the employers could organize better than their own employees. And they finally perfected their organization whereby they compelled the unions to strike, and compelled the individual employers to violate the dictated agreements. The associated employers, through the banks, were able to prevent these individual employers from getting credit, and, through control of merchants and "material men," were able to prevent the employers from getting construction materials. The unions were defeated. The union members went back to work on individual contracts dictated by employers. One-sided collective action was not collective bargaining.

In Russia one-sided collective action became the dictatorship of the "proletariat"; in Italy, Germany, and Japan it became a dictatorship of the property owners. I call two-sided collective action "collective democracy." Smith and Veblen were right in opposing one-sided collective action. It is monopoly and getting something for nothing.

But even two-sided collective action may be monopolistic, and it has also been condemned on the same allegation of getting something for nothing. The building trades unions and the building employers of New York City were organized separately. When a general strike took place in 1903, I participated as a mediator representing the National Civic Federation. Eventually a joint Board of Arbitration was created with an impartial secretary representing both sides. All local disputes were then to be referred to this joint board. The general public which paid for housing was not represented. Hence this arbitration agreement was denounced as "capital and labor hunting together," their prey being the people who needed cheap housing. But this exploitation of the public was possible because of the nature of the housing market; the consumers had no other accessible alternatives.

In the year 1902, I investigated for the National Civic Federation, the stock exchange and the musicians' union in New York

City. The two were organized quite alike. The same individuals, stockbrokers in one case, the musicians in the other, were, indeed, members of two different concerns. For each group one concern was incorporated under the laws of the state—known as a joint stock corporation; the other concern was unincorporated—known as a cartel, or a union. They were incorporated in order to own and operate huge buildings, the stock exchange building on Wall Street, or the musicians' building uptown. As owners of these buildings they could borrow money, employ laborers, sue, and be sued in court. But either as a cartel, or as a labor union, the same individuals turned about and rented these buildings to themselves as an unincorporated association of brokers or musicians, which could not be sued or sue others in court or own the collective property. As such, they were simply a so-called "voluntary" association of buyers and sellers, a cartel or union, the brokers as buyers and sellers of stocks and bonds, the musicians as buyers and sellers of musical labor.

They operated as incorporated associations to buyers and sellers because they did not wish the courts to interfere in their business, but desired to regulate their buying and selling among themselves by their own working rules which created their own rights, duties, and liberties among themselves. In the musicians' union the buyers were the "leaders" of bands or orchestras. Any member could become a leader and buy the labor of his fellow members, subject to the rules, and he might sell his own labor to other leaders. Any stockbroker in the association could buy stocks or bonds from other members and could turn about and sell to other members, provided he kept within the rules. In both organizations there were "discipline" committees that enforced the rules, but these associations did not want the courts to make the rules or enforce them, or let members appeal to the courts in a suit at law where their own rules might be overruled as monopolistic interferences with free competition. They hoped to accomplish this avoidance of the courts by remaining a voluntary association of brothers— like a club, fraternity, or church.

But individual members might make contracts with outsiders, which might bring them as individuals into court. The stockbrokers had their clients all over the country, namely, the investors, speculators, and corporations, that acted through the brokers as their agents in buying and selling. The Congressional legislation of 1935, creating the Securities and Exchange Commission, has since subjected the stock exchange cartel to regulation.

In the Musicians' Union the members who made contracts for the employment of musicians became "leaders." These contracts were made with theatre owners, picnic parties, or with parade managers, to hire the musical workers for a band, orchestra, or symphony. But the leaders continued to be members of their own union, as the stockbrokers continued to be members of their own "union." These unions were, in general, the kind of organization known as "guilds" in the Middle Ages, which included both employers and employees in the same union. At that time these guilds were organized to protect themselves against the feudal nobility.

To simplify matters we give the name "pressure group" to each of these different forms and degrees of collective action. Corporations, unions, and political parties are organized pressure groups; others are unorganized, the latter acting together by the leaderless force of custom. There are also the maneuvered pressure groups, some acting together under the lead of politicians, others under the lead of spokesmen for religious "causes" or movements.

A notable fact about the economic pressure groups is the recent concentration of their headquarters at Washington, D. C., the political capital of the country. The economic pressure groups really become an occupational parliament of the American people, more truly representative than the Congress elected by territorial divisions. They are the informal American counterpart of Mussolini's "corporate state," the Italian occupational state.

In organizing the unemployment insurance plan in the Chicago clothing market in 1924, I found that the Amalgamated union leaders spoke of "the activity." "Get the activity together and see how they will take it." That was a good term. It sorted out precisely the individuals intended. They were by no means only the elected or the salaried officers. They were the "organization workers," that part of the "rank and file" which attended meetings, reported on the sentiment of its members, and with the elected leaders formulated the policies of the union and established the collective agreements with their employers. I had figured that in this and in other unions "the activity" approximated about 10 per cent of the membership. "The activity" is the "party workers" in the political machine, the "business activity" in the employers' organization, the "church workers" in an ecclesiastical organization, always a very small fraction of the total membership. Upon "the activity" depends the daily continuance of the concern as a whole, and the daily contact with the official leaders. Together with the outstanding leaders they are "the politicians" of the concern.

Economics should be a science of activity. The formula of collective action in control of individual action, which is the "institution," gives us a mental tool of investigation, application of which brings together similarities and differences in the varied and innumerable modern economic activities.

Business men, professional people, and laymen have each a name for the many forms of collective action, and the popular name used by the courts when settling economic theories of value and valuation is "a going concern." The concern "goes" as long as the participants earn a living or a profit through collective action; it may die by bankruptcy, be dissolved, or be absorbed by another corporation. Individuals come and go, but the concern goes on, if not in one form, then in another. Hence our "institutions" are, in reality, "going concerns." A going concern is an organization.

The modern business corporation, consisting of stockholders and bondholders, is becoming the dominant form of business in the twentieth century, except under the totalitarian states where its functions are made subservient to the rule of the dictator. The modern joint-stock corporation is a creditor-debtor relationship between credit bondholders and debit stockholders, but with limited liability for debts. This relationship, which has been legalized, is continuing as the going concern more vigorously than other forms of collective action, such as cooperatives or the voluntary commercial societies—which Karl Marx termed "utopian socialism."

Collective action means more than mere "control" of individual

action. It means liberation and expansion of individual action;
thus, collective action is literally the means to liberty. The only
way in which "liberty" can be obtained is by imposing duties on
others who might interfere with the activity of the "liberated"
individual. The American people obtained liberty for the slaves
by imposing duties on the slaveowners.

Collective action, in the form of present-day corporations, labor
unions, and political parties, did not begin generally, for America,
until the decade of the 1850's. These organizations seemed revolutionary to the economists who followed Adam Smith. To them,
only individuals felt pleasure and pain and did the bargaining on
the markets. And the only kind of individual bargaining was the
sale and purchase of physical commodities. These economists did
not even investigate individual action, much less the variety of
transactions between individuals, nor the variety of organized
collective action which was forcing itself into control of individual action. These, as we shall see in the next two chapters,
became the foundations of twentieth century economics.

# Chapter ii

## *INDIVIDUAL ACTION*

———◆———

The early nineteenth century economists patterned their work upon the materialistic sciences of physics and chemistry, instead of on a volitional science of the human will as developed by the courts. According to the materialists, the human individual acted somewhat like an atom, or like a natural law, and only in the one direction of overcoming the resistance of nature's forces in the production of wealth.

To materialists the *real value* of a commodity was its *labor costs* of production, toward which its money value on the markets would gravitate if not interfered with by governments (laissez faire), by corporations, or by labor unions (either monopolies or conspiracies). And *real* money, as distinguished from nominal money, was metallic money which also had its *real value* in its labor cost of production.

Thus, these economists, basing their theories on material forces, adhered to the costs of production in the valuation of commodities and made little or no attempt to lay the foundation of their argument on a science of the human will—the twentieth century foundation. They believed that the will acted capriciously and arbitrarily, both in individuals and in all collective organizations.

The human will is the "will in action." Whether one is earning a living, getting rich, or avoiding a loss, one is always confronted with alternatives in every choice of action taken. It is not merely a choice between one act, or direction, and another; it is a choice between alternative objects, and also a choice as to degrees of power or control exerted in the alternative actually chosen in the performance of any act.

Another science, jurisprudence, the outgrowth of our "common law," followed a motto of the human will—"a willing buyer and a willing seller"—as its criterion in judging the validity of a contract between individuals. This was a definition of willingness discovered or invented by the courts when deciding disputes in the enforcement of private contracts. But the human will, or willingness, was not recognized by the courts as existing in the statute law enacted by legislatures, nor in the administrative orders issued by executives. These departments of government, the courts thought, were arbitrary or capricious, as described in their assertion "government by men" in contrast to "government by law," meaning the courts.

Jurisprudence, the science of the courts, may be said to have developed through two stages in America. In the first stage, the primitive "common law," descended from England, applied to both criminal law and economic contracts; in the second stage, a further analysis of the human will in economic transactions was developed by the courts. This latter stage began about 1890 with cases on the constitutionality of legislation regulating public utilities and restraints of trade.

When, in this latter stage, the courts became involved in reviewing orders issued by administrative commissions regulating economic transactions, or in deciding upon the coerciveness of corporations and unions in control of individual action, the older "common law" was found to be inadequate. The requirements of early jurisprudence were met with proof or disproof of guilt in performing an unlawful act, and were, therefore, satisfied with interpreting the act in an alleged violation as an "act" or an "omission" to act.

The new decisions, turning mainly on the collective action of governments, corporations, and labor unions in control of individuals, required that account be taken of the *degrees* of economic power exerted in the "act," and the choice of *alternatives* open to the individual in his regulated activity. These two considerations were really two dimensions of the will-in-action at the moment of action—a two-dimensional will, instead of one-dimensional.

The first dimension is a choice of *degree of power* in choosing between two alternatives; the second dimension is a choice of one *direction* of acting instead of an alternative direction. This second dimension is properly described as an *avoidance* of the alternative, instead of an "omission." The court is no longer satified whether the individual performed the "act" or not. Now it is also a choice of the degree of power in the act, and a choice of alternative degrees of power confronting the performer of that same "act."

Since we are concerned in economics with both the directions and the degrees of power in controlling individual action, this power, or control, may best be expressed by three terms, as developed by the courts: *performance, forbearance,* and *avoidance.*

A performance is an act. It is positive; the actor does something. In this he may be doing what he has agreed to do; something he must do. Or he may be doing something strictly by his own volition. But his performance may be limited in either of two ways, by avoidance or by forbearance. The first pertains primarily to the direction of his performance, the second to the degree of power exercised.

The performance follows a certain direction. A choice is made from among the available alternatives; thus the actor omits all alternatives at the moment other than the one chosen for the course of action. This is avoidance. Some alternatives must be avoided, according to the working rules of collective action; in this case there is a duty of avoidance upon the performer. Yet within the limits imposed by the duties many alternatives may be allowed, only one of which is chosen. Thus is performance directed.

But within these directions the performance is modified in still another way, according to the degree of power exercised, by forbearance. The human will has the faculty, unique among all the forces of nature, of limiting its own exercise of power. Other natural forces, such as gravity, go to the limit of their power at all times: the human will forbears to do this except in moments of great stress or emergency. Thus the degree of forbearance is correlative to the degree of power exercised.

Forbearance may be exercised either in the actions with (non-human) nature or in transactions with other persons. A farmer may forbear to work his horses to their limit, or to drive his tractor at full speed. An employer may refrain from driving the hardest possible wage bargain with an employee. Or, a buyer may not exercise his full economic power in purchasing materials at the lowest possible price. Forbearance is self-restraint in doing.

Yet it is not wholly voluntary, just because the limits to performance cannot be defined with absolute and invariant precision. While many courses of action are clearly prescribed by the rules of collective action, questions of reasonableness may arise over either the direction of the performance or the degree of power exercised. Since the rule of reason is the final rule of valuation in collective action, there is also a certain indefinable duty of forbearance in collective action. We are under a compulsion to act "reasonably," especially regarding the degree of power exercised in performance.

If we extend the application of performance and forbearance into judicial decisions of the courts, we immediately come to what is known as "reasonable value," a kind of value which had already been coming into the common law. Performance, moderated by forbearance, then, is an "act" with a limited degree of power.

Avoidance, as different from "omission," is a choice between alternatives. It is not a total omission, but a preference of one act, or performance, over the alternative act or performance.

In place of accepting the "free competitive value" of a commodity, or adhering to the cost of production doctrine of nineteenth century economists, we arrive at "reasonable value" through performance, forbearance, and avoidance. The trend in economic history is no longer the old *laissez faire,* or "let alone," in human activity. Now it is becoming evident that the choice lies in the degree of power of an individual confronted with choosing an alternative—a double choice which is the all-inclusive foundation of modern economics.

We now can turn to the different *kinds* of collective action and their different degrees of control over the performances, forbearances, and avoidances of individual action. The different kinds may be grouped according to the kinds of pressure, influence, or sanctions, which any one may use, as moral power, economic power, or physical power. An ecclesiastical organization, since the time of the separation of church and state, has neither physical power over the bodies of individuals nor economic power over their opportunities of earning a living or getting rich. Churches, in this country, for nearly two centuries, have had only the moral power of persuasion. In other countries, such as Spain, we lived to see a civil war fought largely on the issue of trying to deprive the church and the nobility of their economic power as owners of large estates and possessors of the sovereign physical power of taxation.

These distinctions of *kind* of power, as moral, economic, or physical, run immediately into differences in *degree* of power, meaning by degree the intensity of the inducement, or pressure, upon the will of the individual towards a particular performance, forbearance, or avoidance, ranging from mere friendly advice to fear of loss of livelihood, fear of violence or imprisonment, or even death. The degree of resistance by individuals differs, as is well recognized, according to differences in character or personality, and the circumstances of time and place.[1]

All organizations must act through individuals who are entrusted with authority to give direction to the combined force of the collective action. They are the "officials" of the organization. The simplified formula of their relation to individuals is that of an appeal from one individual, a plaintiff, to use the collective force against another individual, a defendant, who is alleged to have acted or is about to act contrary to the working rules of the organization. In the ecclesiastical organization this is a trial for heresy; in an economic organization, such as a stock exchange or a labor union, it is a trial for unfair acts or practices in getting a living or getting rich; in a sovereign organization it is a trial for any act or practice alleged to be unjust or unfair according to whatever ethical rules the sovereign organization imposes on individuals by physical force at the time.

Organized in this way, each kind of collective action is a government, differing in the kind of "sanctions" employed to bring the individual into conformity with the rules, as the moral sanctions of opinion, the economic sanctions of deprivation of property, or the bodily sanctions of physical force.

[1] See "Degrees of Power," p. 170.

Since the bodily sanctions are, for most people, the most extreme of all, the collective activity that attempts to monopolize physical force is known as sovereignty, and the officials who direct its use are sovereigns. In the American system they are collectively the politicians, including the legislature, the executive, and the judiciary.

But sovereignty is inseparable from property. It is the sanctions of sovereignty that make property what it is for the time being in any country, because physical force, or violence, is the last and final appeal when the other sanctions are deemed inadequate to control individuals. Economic science, in England and America, began with the separation of property from sovereignty, on the assumption that private property was a natural, primordial right of individuals, independent of sovereignty which might artificially and unjustly interfere with it. But this was a substitution of justification for fact, as is often the method of argument in economics and politics. Property rights were justified on the ground that the object of property was a product of labor, and belonged, therefore, by right to him who had embodied his labor in it by giving to nature's materials the quality of usefulness. Having this natural right of ownership of his own product, he had the right to exchange it for the products of other laborers. His product thus obtained "exchange value," which was the quantity of other products which he could obtain in exchange. If his product was a pair of shoes, its exchange value would be a bushel of wheat or two bushels of wheat, or any quantity of anything else which he could command in exchange for the shoes at the time.

This was the simplified formula with which economic science started at the hands of the nineteenth century economists, and it is the formula followed by traditional economists down to the present day. "Goods exchange for goods," and if there are grave complexities that get into the process, these are eliminated as irrelevant, because the real thing that everyone is concerned about is the quantity of other goods which one can get in exchange for his own goods.

But if we examine the formula in the light of present-day economics, we find that it does not fit a credit-and-debit economy where performance is measured by a unit of account. This failure to fit is the source of hundreds of misunderstandings in the variety of remedies proposed or experimented upon for overcoming the economic maladjustments of the present time. Also the simple formula of goods exchanging for goods does not fit, because goods are sold for money at prices measured by the amount of money at whatever prices happen to be current or manipulated. And even this money is not metallic or paper money—it is bank credit enforced by sovereignty in enforcing the performance of contracts.[1]

[1] See "Credit Administration," pp. 239–260.

# Chapter iii

## *TRANSACTIONS*

Private property, owned by individuals for executing the will of the owner, was assumed and taken for granted, without investigation, by the nineteenth century economists. The kind of property with which they were familiar was "corporeal" property, the rights of ownership of lands and physical commodities, which were the products of labor. Their buying and selling was merely a "voluntary exchange" of one item of physical property for another item.

But the incoming of joint stock corporations, labor unions, and universal suffrage without property qualifications, changed the legal foundations of economics. Corporations now began to own the bulk of corporeal property as valued on the markets, and individuals owned the stocks and bonds of the corporations. Laborers, backed by the new universal suffrage, obtained legal rights to organize and bargain collectively with corporations and individual owners. Political parties became the organizations through which these legal foundations of economics were maintained or changed.

In this process three types of transactions may be distinguished instead of the one type of voluntary exchange of physical commodities by individuals. These are the *rationing* transactions by the "policy-makers" of the organization—boards of directors of corporations, or similar directors of labor unions and administrative political governments—in laying down working rules; the *managerial* transactions between superiors and inferiors, mainly wage earners and salary earners in the production of wealth; the *bargaining* transactions on the markets which transfer ownerships of corporeal property and the new kinds of incorporeal and intangible property of bonds and stocks of corporations.

All of these varieties of transactions are in operation at the same time, and the problem is not the total elimination of any one kind, but the balance among the three in the processes of economic activity. The latest to come historically into prominence were the bargaining transactions; the most ancient were the managerial transactions. Rationing transactions, which are also of ancient origin, have latterly become of major importance through the activities of corporations, unions, and governments.

The free bargaining transactions among individuals were the legal foundations of the early science of economics. But exactly what it was that the bargainers "exchanged" in these transactions was not made clear at the hands of the economists. There developed a double meaning of the word "commodities": a proprietary meaning, intended by the courts, of the acquisition and alienation of ownership; and a technological meaning, used by the economists, for the production, transportation, and physical delivery of the thing owned. The proprietary meaning was assets, the legal capacity to pay debts and taxes which were known as liabilities. The technological meaning was wealth, the product of labor, and the enjoyment of consumers.

That the two meanings of wealth and assets were widely separated became evident at times, but did not become the main political and economic issue until after the widest of all separations, which began in the year 1929.

The ownership meaning had become the foundation of the credit system and its method of creating credit money in place of metallic money, by the businessmen and the banks. This ownership meaning had been working itself into economics by decisions of the courts in enforcing contracts, and, therefore, had become dominant over the technological meanings of the economists. For example, I deliver to you a horse, you deliver the money. It is an exchange. But I may not own the horse. You may not own the money. Only the owner of the horse can sell it and give legal title. The owner of money is different, however. A thief can give, under certain circumstances, a legal title to the money which he has stolen and with which he pretends to buy a horse. Money becomes a privileged kind of asset. It alone pays taxes and debts.

For this reason everybody tries to get the ownership of money. It cannot be taken even by its rightful owner if the payee accepted it in good faith, even from a thief who had stolen it.

It is not even the owner or a thief who transfers the ownership of property and gives a good title of ownership. It is sovereignty, the law of the land, as worked out by court decisions through the centuries in the form of the "common law." Business economics has more or less clearly distinguished between a "transaction" and an "exchange." This conforms to the distinction made in courts of law, which, after all, are closer to business practices every day than are the economists. A bargaining transaction is the negotiations and agreement which transfer *ownerships* under the "operation of law." An "exchange" is reduced to the mechanical and labor process that physically delivers the object under commands of the owner.

The accepted formula of early economists that "goods exchange for goods" fits only a primitive "barter economy." They omitted the bank credit system and the decisions of courts. Shoes are not exchanged for wheat, but both shoes and wheat are today sold for a checking account at a bank, known as a "bank deposit." Even bank "deposit" is a misnomer. It is a bank debt owed by the bank, payable on demand to the "depositor" who, in turn, is not a depositor, but a creditor. By drawing a check on that account he who has sold the shoes in "exchange" for somebody else's check on a bank goes out into other markets and buys with his own check whatever he wishes and can command in exchange. The banking and credit system of the world has destroyed the simplified barter economy of traditional economics. "Goods" do not exchange for "goods"; they are generally sold for a checking account, which is a creditor-debtor relation of contracts enforced by the courts.

The obsolete formula of a barter economy stumbled on this double meaning of the word "commodity"—the double meaning of ownership and the thing owned—assets and wealth. When the manufacturer sells his shoes, or the farmer sells his wheat, it becomes a "commodity," meaning anything that is bought and sold. But he does not sell the shoes, he alienates his ownership of the shoes, and he does not sell the wheat, he transfers its ownership.

The term "price" thus also has a double meaning. It meant, in ordinary language, the amount of physical money paid for a physical thing, as the price of a pair of shoes or a bushel of wheat. But it means, in the legal economics of the courts, the "consideration," that is, the service which the owner of the money rendered to the owner of the shoes by alienating his ownership of money in consideration of the service rendered by alienation of the ownership of the shoes. Each owner alienates his ownership, and each owner acquires another ownership. Prices are paid, not for physical objects, but for *ownership* of those objects.

This is a hard saying, and not ordinary language. For example, I buy a pair of shoes for five dollars. I physically transfer five dollars, and the merchant physically hands me the shoes. The price of the shoes is five dollars in actual money. This is so-called "common sense." But it is much more important that I go away with the ownership of the shoes, and the merchant goes to the bank with the ownership of the money and transfers its ownership to the bank. There has been the alienation and acquisition of two ownerships. Critical economists have declared that ours is an "acquisitive" economy and not a "producing economy." It is both. It is also an "alienation economy." We acquire ownership of money by alienating ownership of things that are produced.

When the merchant sells his shoes to me in exchange for a bank check, which is approximately nine-tenths of modern money, he does not get merely a piece of paper, he gets lawful ownership of a debt owed by my banker to me as a depositor, and I transfer to the merchant my ownership of that much of my deposits at the bank. That banker's debt, owed to me and now owed to the merchant, was, strangely enough, also considered to be a "commodity" like the wheat or shoes, simply because it also could be bought and sold.

This remarkable fact by which a debt becomes a "commodity," like wheat or shoes, is an invention of the lawyers and courts, beginning only as late as the seventeenth century in England, but continuing to the present day by new additions under the general name "negotiability," and the debt owned by the creditor of the bank is a "negotiable instrument," not wheat or shoes. It serves as money, or general purchasing power, and modern "money" is mainly negotiable debts owed by bankers. The barter economy knew nothing of such a "commodity" as bankers' debts, but the early economists treated these negotiable instruments as if they were wheat and shoes, although they were not the products of labor, but were the products of sovereignty.

There was another kind of commodity, the "precious metals," which were a product of labor, like shoes and wheat. The early economists carried their formula of a barter economy over to the exchange value of the precious metals, gold or silver, which were also commodities. But there is a difference between "bullion" and "coin." Bullion is a commodity, but coin is lawful money, made so by sovereigns as the means of paying debts, both the compulsory debts of taxes owed to the sovereign and the voluntary debts owed to individuals whose payment was also compulsorily enforced by the courts. Coin and bullion were eventually made equivalent in value by "free and unlimited" coinage, whereby the owner of bullion could convert it into lawful money without expense to himself but at the expense of the government. Silver was "demonetized" in some countries and not in others, which meant that silver was reduced to a commodity and could not be converted, without expense or in unlimited quantities, into lawful money that would pay debts enforced by sovereignty. Finally, gold itself is substantially demonetized in all countries by withdrawing from individuals the privilege of "free and unlimited coinage." Governments become even the sole and monopolistic owners of gold bullion, and do not bother to coin it. The American government owns more than half of the world's supply, which it locks up underground and issues "certificates" of ownership, which are themselves legal tender. Governments buy and sell gold bullion at prices stated in terms of something else. That "something else," strangely enough, is not metallic money, and is not paper money nor even bank checks. It is a "money of account," meaning, thereby, a "unit of account" on the books, the dollar, or the franc, established by law as legal tender in payment of debts. It measures the amount of metallic bullion as well as the amount of paper money, of bank debts, and of all debts and the monetary value of all commodities. This unit of account is maintained by custom and law, in the language of weight of gold or silver coin, although the metal itself has long since been taken out of circulation.

These highly complicated interferences with the simplified barter economy may be summarized in the distinction between a *transaction* and an *exchange*. A bargaining transaction is a double transfer of ownerships. The word "exchange" had, and continues to have, the double meaning of the legal transfers of ownership and the labor transfer of things owned. A bargaining transaction, as readily understood in business affairs, is the legal transfer of two ownerships, to be followed by two physical transfers of the things owned, whether the "thing" be a physical object like shoes and wheat, or a negotiable debt, like a bank check or a government debt.

The physical and labor transfers have come to be comprehended in modern economics under the name of managerial transactions, while the legal transfers are the bargaining transactions and the rationing transactions. Bargaining transactions transfer ownerships in the familiar open or free markets; the terms of the transfers, including both price and the amounts to be sold, are arrived at by negotiation. Rationing transactions transfer ownerships where either the quantity or the price, or both, are determined by some authorized superior power. Ownerships are transferred by rationing in two principal fields: in the controlled markets of dictatorships and now in wartime economies; and within the integrated industrial concerns or combinations where ownerships of goods or services pass from one company to another without market bids.

Historically, bargaining transactions come latest, but for convenience, we consider them first. According to economists, a "market" consists of a number of "exchangers" making offers and bids to each other for the physical delivery of commodities. But, according to lawful economics these "exchangers" are sellers for money and buyers with money, and the accurate name of their dealings is alienation and acquisition of the two ownerships. This ownership is "property," meaning the "rights" of property. They are alienating and acquiring property rights in a commodity. What they offer to sell and buy are the *ownerships* of the commodities, and not directly the objects owned. *After* they have acquired ownership, then they are in position to do as they lawfully please with the objects which they now legally own. But, according to legal economics, the owners of the wheat or pigs, for example, or even of one's own labor, offer to sell their ownerships, and the buyers are owners of gold or owners of bank debts (deposits) payable on demand, who offer to sell their ownerships of gold or of bankers' negotiable debts to the sellers in consideration of the release of their ownerships of wheat, pigs, or labor. Owners offer to alienate their ownerships through exchange.

If we further examine the word "commodity," as used by economists and common sense, we can see these two meanings before us every day. A commodity is not merely a physical thing like a horse, or an automobile, or a loaf of bread. It is also the lawful ownership of the horse, automobile, or bread. Of what use is an automobile to me if I steal it? I can, indeed, use it at seventy miles per hour, but I have my eye on sovereignty in the shape of every policeman ahead, or on the sheriffs and deputies who are following and lawfully shooting at me or at my rubber tires. All this is done to me because I have not acquired ownership by previously inducing the lawful owner willingly to alienate his ownership to me. I might have bought the *use* of the car without acquiring its ownership, as when I rent a car. This use also is a "commodity," but with a legal time limit, whereas if I bought the car, there is no time limit except my own will and the wearing out of the car. It is sovereignty that makes things lawfully useful.

It was not until recent years that the Federal Reserve Board recognized, in its statistics, that the demand and supply of money in the United States is the demand and supply of *ownerships* in this country. The Board introduced the item of "earmarked" gold, to indicate metallic money owned abroad and not entering into the supply of gold on the American markets. It is *physically* here, but not *legally* nor *economically* here.

One of the legal technicalities of economic significance is what may be named the negotiational psychology of the law, by means of which the intentions of the participants are discovered. These intentions may require actual investigation in cases of criminal law, usually by circumstantial evidence, but in cases of proprietary law it is sufficient to read into the minds of bargaining participants the intention to do what was right and lawful under the circumstances of time and place, as similar participants who were lawful men would have intended to do. This comparative behavioristic psychology is investigated or assumed under the name of custom, or usage.

When we reduce all of the prospective buyers and sellers upon a given market to those who participate in one bargaining transaction as our smallest unit of investigation, then they are the "best" two buyers and the "best" two sellers, meaning the two buyers who offer the highest prices and the two sellers who offer to accept the lowest prices, in consideration of transfers of ownership. All others are, for the moment, excluded as "potential" competitors. The best two sellers are those able to sell at the lowest price. They compete for choice of alternatives offered by the best two buyers, those able to buy at the highest prices, while, in turn, the best two buyers are competing for choice of alternatives offered by the best two sellers. The actual transfer of ownership by sovereignty, in that one transaction, is made by reading "purpose" or "intention" into the minds of one actual buyer and one actual seller. When they are "off the market," by "closing the negotiations," then, for the next transaction, the best pair of those who were potential now become actual, until all are off the market.

Thus, instead of the "exchange" of physical things between two parties as contemplated in the former physical economics, there are five parties, all of whom are "potential" and then they are successively "actual" participants in the lawful alienation and acquisition of ownerships. I use the term "futurity" instead of the physical term "potential." Consequently there are four expectant economic relations on the market. There are two expectant buyers who are competitors, and two expectant sellers who are competitors. But the two buyers are offering opportunities to sell for the two sellers; and the two sellers are offering opportunities to buy for the two buyers. Then the actual seller and actual buyer, whose intentions lead sovereignty actually to transfer ownerships at a price or "consideration," are the two who actually close the negotiations by agreeing upon the terms of the transaction. But throughout the negotiations, there is a future judge ready to issue commands to any of the buyers or sellers in the name of sovereignty, if any dispute arises. Eventually there is a future Supreme Court to which appeal may be made on any alleged act of injustice by the trial court, or by the legislature or executive which has given directions to the trial court.

In order to make visible this complex relationship in one hypothetical transaction of five parties we may construct a formula somewhat as follows:

$$\text{Trial Judge—Supreme Court}$$

| B | $B^1$ | buyers |
|---|---|---|
| \$100 | \$ 90 | |
| S | $S^1$ | sellers |
| \$110 | \$120 | |

In this one supposed transaction there are four possible grounds of dispute regarding the transfers of ownership by those who may turn out to be the actual seller and buyer, and each of these disputes may finally be decided by the Supreme Court, and thereafter taken for granted, that is, "customary."

First is the issue of *competition,* as to whether the competitors have acted fairly toward each other.

Second is the issue of *equal opportunity,* as to whether the actual buyer discriminates unfairly between the sellers, or the actual seller discriminates unfairly between the buyers, by charging or paying different prices under similar circumstances.

Third is the issue of *bargaining power,* as to whether the price, or consideration, agreed upon by the actual buyer and seller was determined with or without duress, coercion, unfair competition, or unequal opportunity, known as a fair or reasonable price or value. These, as we have said, are treated technically as the "law of fair and unfair competition."

Fourth is the constitutional issue of *"due process* of law," which might be named the due "operation of law," as to whether the trial court, the executive, or legislature, unjustifiably deprived any one of the participants of his liberty or property.

The issues over these four relations involved in the transfers of ownership are all inextricably dependent on each other, such that a change in one will probably change the other three.

Thus the unit of investigation in economics is not an individual, it is a transaction involving, in this bargaining transaction, five individuals. This complicated transaction is short-circuited by economists and laymen who call it an "exchange." The difference is between individualistic economics and institutional economics, and between static economics and dynamic economics. The individual is important enough, but *economic science investigates what he is confronted with and what he does* in getting a living and getting rich by transfers of ownership. He is confronted by sovereignty which does the creating and transferring of ownerships. Sovereignty imposes the duties of avoidance and forbearance which create ownership, and the duties of performance and payment which transfer ownerships. The individual is confronted by competitors who are trying to take from him his living or riches by fair or unfair methods. He is confronted by discriminations which may unfairly deprive him of equal opportunity with others in getting a living or getting rich. He is confronted by the bargaining power of others compared with his own bargaining power. He is tied into an expected repetition of transactions within which he must find as much liberty and property as he can.

Finally, the closing of the negotiations between the actual buyer and actual seller creates two lawful debts, a debt of performance owed by the seller and a debt of payment owed by the buyer. The seller is under obligation to deliver the commodity to the buyer at a certain place within a specified time. The buyer is under similar obligation to make the payment immediately or at a future designated place and time.

These debts of payment also can be bought and sold, on what is known as the "money market" or the "capital market." Indeed it may rightly be said, as it has been said in effect, that the greatest of all inventions in the field of economics was the discovery that a debt could be bought and sold like a physical commodity. Debts were originally only debts of honor or a personal obligation, not imposed by sovereignty, and it seemed at that time to be preposterous that such a moral or personal duty could be sold by the creditor to a stranger, just as it now would seem preposterous to sell to a stranger a woman's promise to marry. That was the very prejudice which lawyers had to overcome when they invented the "negotiability" of debts in the seventeenth century. The nobility, indeed, did claim that their debts were not merchants' debts but were debts of honor which could not be sold to strangers. The matter was settled nearly two hundred years ago in England, when the court refused to listen to a grandee who argued that he was not a merchant.

Thus, besides the four grounds of dispute in bargaining transactions, there are four economic facts which are inseparable, namely, transfers of ownership by sovereignty, the monetary prices to be paid in acquiring ownerships, and the two debts of performance and payment created by the transaction. These debts may be named "rules of action" or "working rules" agreed upon by the participants and enforceable by the courts in case of dispute. Each participant must arrange his business so as to fulfill his debts of performance and payment when due. These four facts constitute the modern credit system, the foundation of capitalism. Briefly, they are alienations, prices, debts, performances, and payments, inseparately tied together in a bargaining transaction.

In point of time sequence, the bargaining transaction has three stages: first, the negotiations, which are closed when the agreement on intentions is reached; then the contract or "commitment," which imposes the obligations of performance and payment upon the parties in future time; finally the administration or performance of the obligations agreed upon, which, when completed by both parties, closes the transaction.

In point of time duration, bargaining transactions are cash, short-time and long-time transactions. In cash transactions the negotiations, the transaction, and the performance and payment are all begun and closed together, without a measurable interval of time. In the short-time and long-time debts of hours, days, and years there are measurable lapses of time between the closing of the negotiations which originate the transaction and the final closing of the transaction itself by execution of the duties of performance and payment, during which lapse of time interest is paid.

The kinds of debts, above mentioned, are simply economic duties arising at law from the acquisition of ownerships. The fulfillment of these duties is effected by an entirely different transaction, which, in recent time, has come to be known as a managerial transaction, such as the dealings between a foreman and a laborer, a master and servant. This also has a legal foundation. Before a managerial transaction can lawfully be carried through, legal ownership must be obtained. This is obtained by lawful bargaining transactions. With legal ownership thus obtained, the owner has the legal power to issue commands and require obedience of laborers. While the law of bargaining transactions sets up an ethical ideal of persuasion between individuals who are equally free, the law of managerial transactions rests on the legal right of the owner to issue commands to laborers and on the correlative duty of obedience by the laborers to the commands of owners.

This is because the law of managerial transactions runs back into antiquity beyond the law of bargaining transactions, which, in our jurisprudence, has a history of only about three hundred years. The law of managerial transactions is plainly a law of inequality compared with the assumptions of equality in bargaining transactions. The present day assumption is that when the free laborer enters upon the premises of the owner, not as a visitor or a thief, but with the joint intention of owner and laborer to become a producer of wealth, he thereby accepts the obligation to obey the commands of the owner, delegated perhaps to foremen. He is, in law, a "servant," as was literally the *servus* or slave. But he differs from the slave in that the court will not compel him to work, that is, will not compel him to fulfill his obligation of contract, because he has now acquired both the right to run away from his job without penalty, and the right to refuse to enter upon the premises without a previous understanding of what the job will be.

It is these rights to withhold his services that give to him bargaining power. They were denied, in the American history of slavery, by the Dred Scott decision of the Supreme Court (1857), but reversed by the Civil War and the Thirteenth and Fourteenth Amendments to the Constitution. But there still remain, during the period of time while the laborer is on the premises of the owner, the ancient obligations arising from the law of command and obedience. This is violated by the "sit-down" stike. The owner is free to "hire and fire" at will, an economic inducement, and the laborer is free to serve or quit at will, the reciprocal economic inducement. These are the preceding bargaining transactions. But these do not give him freedom while he is on the owner's premises.

By this law of managerial transactions the seller of property rights is placed in a position to fulfill his duty of *performance,* and the buyer his duty of *payment,* by "hiring and firing" laborers and by commanding their obedience.

Rationing transactions, the third type of transactions, are even more primitive than bargaining and managerial transactions. They were the decrees of sovereignty apportioning among subordinates, without their consent, and without bargaining, which in recent times would be bribery, the benefits and burdens of the joint production of wealth by the joint action of all producers of wealth. The historical example is taxation, and a modern example is taxation for the support of education. The burden of taxes is apportioned by sovereignty without consent or bargaining on the part of individual taxpayers. So with the children who are sent to school by commands of sovereignty. The parents, without their individual consent or bargaining, are deprived of their physical control over their children during specified hours, days, and ages. A fascist or communist dictatorship extends this economics of domestic law to all the transactions of economics. Modern totalitarianism is rationing transactions imposed by those in power, the "superiors," upon those deprived of power, the "inferiors."

A fiction has long prevailed that in countries of legislative sovereignty these same taxpayers and parents have given their consent through their representatives in the legislature. But taxpayers and parents have not individually or voluntarily given their consent, as they are supposed to do in bargaining transactions. The false analogy is a confusion of collective action with individual action. Sovereignty is the collective action which has monopolized powers extending to violence, and there cannot be found any individual taxpayer or parent who by bargaining has consented to be compelled by threat of violence to pay the specified taxes or give

up the specified control of his children. If he tried to bargain with
the policeman, one or both would go to jail on a charge of bribery.
The appropriate statement, avoiding fictions, is collective action
in control of individual action. This kind of collective action has,
by economists and usage, been given the name of "rationing." But
we need to know the method by which sovereignty acts in its
process of rationing. Such activity may be distinguished as rationing transactions.

Such transactions may be seen in any legislative assembly,
depending upon the constitutional organization of the legislature.
The members are arguing, debating, exchanging views, and finally
closing the negotiations by majority vote. They may, by fictitious
analogy, be said to be "trading votes," but they are not lawfully
alienating or acquiring ownerships as they do in bargaining transactions. Trading votes is lawful negotiation, and not bribery,
within a legislative assembly.

Dictatorship is only another and more primitive form of rationing transactions. No dictator can arbitrarily impose his sole will
upon a nation. He consults his associates, or his monopolistic
party, or his military chiefs, as to what shall be the particular
rationing of benefits and burdens among those individuals who
are subject to this dictatorial form of sovereignty. The rationing
negotiation is perhaps closed by his one vote instead of by a
majority vote. And it is probable that a majority vote in a democracy is, at times, as dictatorial over minorities as is the vote of a
dictator over majorities. Indeed, historical analysis reveals that the
judicial sovereignty in America was created and is now sustained
by the combined religious, political, and economic *minorities* as
their protection against the democracy of majority rule.

Interestingly enough these rationing transactions are discoverable in all collective action, as may be seen in the board of directors
of a corporation, or in a cooperative association, in making up its
budget for the coming year. The board apportions, without individual consent or bargaining with subordinates, the expected
benefits and burdens of the concern. The execution of this rationing, within the budget limits, is carried out by means of managerial
transactions. Collective action in control of individuals becomes

a hierarchy of collective action in control of the bargaining, managerial, and rationing transactions of individuals.

One of the main advantages of the modern large corporations is in the elimination of bargaining transactions by enlarging the scope of managerial and rationing transactions. It is carried furthest by a so-called "integrated" industry. The substance of this elimination of bargaining transactions is in the consolidation of ownerships with a coordinated legal control by a board of directors at the top. In the United States Steel Corporation, a hundred, or perhaps several hundred, formerly separate ownerships are consolidated under a so-called "holding company," meaning an owning company. Its activity, within its own jurisdiction of ownership, is exercised by rationing and managerial transactions.

Since I make transactions the units of economic science, it is well at this point to offer a diagrammatic presentation of the scope of transactions. Its detailed application will appear at many points. Of course, facts do not thus neatly assort themselves in boxes, but the boxes help to arrange our ideas.

SCOPE OF TRANSACTIONS

| Time Sequence | Kinds of Transactions (status of participants) | | | Kinds of Economics |
|---|---|---|---|---|
| | Bargaining (Legal equals) | Managerial (Legal superior & inferior) | Rationing (Legal superior & inferior) | |
| 1. *Negotiational psychology* (inducements, intentions, purpose) | Persuasion or Coercion | Command and Obedience | Command and Obedience | Qualitative (not measured) |
| 2. *Commitments for future action* (agreement, contracts, obligations, rules of action) | Debts of Performance and Payment | Production of **Wealth** | Distribution of Wealth | Qualitative (not measured) |
| 3. *Execution of the commitments* (administration, management, sovereignty) | **Prices** and Quantities | **Input and** Output | Budgets Taxes Price-fixing Wage-fixing | Qualitative (measured) |

# Chapter iv

## CAPITALISM

———◆———

The hierarchy of collective action has reached different peaks of power, the communism of Russia, the fascism of Italy, the national socialism of Germany, or the capitalism of the British Empire and the United States. We place the United States at the peak of capitalism, and summarize its dominant forms of collective action as limited liability corporations, labor unions, and political parties.

Whichever nation is considered, collective action is organized by a small number of leaders, scarcely 5 to 10 per cent of the membership. In the United States it is known as "the management" of the corporations, the "leaders" of the labor unions, "the machine" of the political parties.

The investigators who have most completely summarized the situation in the United States as between the corporations and the political parties are the lawyer, A. A. Berle, and the economist, Gardiner C. Means, who wrote in the year 1931 as follows: [1]

The rise of the modern corporation has brought a concentration of economic power which can cope on equal terms with the modern state—economic power versus political power, each strong in its own field. The state seeks in some aspects to regulate the corporation, while the corporation, steadily becoming more powerful, seeks independence and not infrequently endeavors to avail itself, through indirect influence, of governmental power. Not impossibly the economic organism, now typified by the corporation, may win equality with the state and perhaps even supersede it as the dominant institution of

[1] *Encyclopedia of the Social Sciences,* New York, The Macmillan Co., 1931, Vol. IV, p. 423. Copyright, 1931, by The Macmillan Company. Similarly at a later date, A. A. Berle and G. C. Means, *Modern Corporation and Private Property,* New York, The Macmillan Co., 1932, p. 357.

[ 58 ]

social organization. The law of corporations, accordingly, might well be considered as a potential constitutional law for the new economic state; while business practise assumes many of the aspects of administrative government.

These authors speak of "the modern state" as "political power." But if we consider the state as an activity rather than an abstraction, then it is the collective action of political parties in control of physical force; and the political parties themselves are the management of the physical force of sovereignty which bestows the rights of existence on corporations and labor unions. Economic power grows out of the exercise of these privileges of incorporation or organization. The totalitarian nations have suppressed or subordinated by physical force the former self-governing corporations, labor unions, and political parties, but in the United States the threefold economic activity of these forms of collective action is becoming the dominant aspect of capitalism at its peak.

The other kind of capitalistic action, the cartel [1] is similar to a stock exchange or a labor union. Its purpose is the regulation of output and the activities of its members, including collective bargaining with labor unions. The cartel has no stockholders or bondholders. In this, it differs from the joint-stock corporation. The cartel may be an agreement between corporations to restrict output; [2] but the corporation is a creditor-debtor organization for the conduct of business, the debtors being stockholders with limited liability, the creditors being bondholders.

The creditor-debtor relationship is strategic in making the modern corporation dominant, with this "limited liability" of the stockholder. While he is the debtor of the corporation, the share holder is not liable for the debts of the corporation, beyond losing the amounts already paid for shares of stock. In this respect he is like a bondholder. The partner, or individual, in the older forms of organization with unlimited liability, was liable, in case of

---

[1] See A. A. Berle and G. C. Means, *Modern Corporation and Private Property*, New York, The Macmillan Co., 1932, Chap. I, pp. 13–15.

[2] See my report, written in 1904, on *Regulation and Restriction of Output, Eleventh Special Report of the U. S. Commissioner of Labor* (1904), *H. R. Document No. 734*, 58th Congress, 2d Session; also testimony of Thurman Arnold before Senate Committee on Cartels, in newspapers, March 26, 1942.

bankruptcy, to lose all his property, including that not invested in the corporation.

These limited liability corporations were not opposed by Adam Smith and the other classical economists, because such corporations were created for the production of wealth and the conduct of business. But the modern great size of many of these corporations, including railway, telegraph and telephone, banking, merchandising, under control of "the management" with limited liability, has developed them into the equivalent of cartels for the restriction of output, as well as corporations for the production of wealth.

It is to counteract these activities of cartels and corporations for regulation of output and restraint of trade that the American states and the federal government have established the new administrative commissions, culminating in the Federal Securities and Exchange Commission.

It is also these huge creditor-debtor corporations that have changed the meanings of old terms in the sciences of economics, such as "profit" and "interest," and have brought in new terms such as "venture" capital and "investment" capital.

"Venture capital" is the shares of stock with limited liability, and gives to its owners control of the corporation by election of "the management," and such risky returns of income as have the name of dividends, the now dominant meaning of "profit."

"Investment capital" is the corporate bonds, which are legal contracts between bondholders and stockholders, the bondholders expecting a more secure income in terms of money, known as "interest," enforced by the courts.

Formerly, no clear distinction existed between profit and interest, but now profit is the reward obtained by "management" for the stockholders, seldom reaching, on the average, more than a margin of 6 per cent of the total corporate income, and falling to zero, or *loss* instead of *profit*.[1] Evidently, the shares of stock, or venture capital, are owned, not because they yield *interest*, but because they yield *control* of the corporation, and, indeed, control of the whole capitalist system, including control of the interest paid to bondholders and the wages paid to laborers.

[1] See my calculations in *Institutional Economics*, p. 560 ff.

This means that such former terms in economic science as "active" and "passive," "dynamic" and "static," are now separated in the capitalist system. The active or dynamic participants are the stockholders and management; the passive or static participants are the bondholders who are the investors. Here also is the great opportunity for manipulation, known as "financial capitalism" as described by Berle and Means in 1931, the kind of finance that precipitated the collapse of the system in 1929.

The significance of the foregoing distinctions, newly developed under capitalism, is in contrast with the totalitarian governments, which have taken over the "cartellization" activities of regulating output, of fixing prices and wages, and of controlling credit and foreign exchange. In doing so they have eliminated the capitalistic self-governing corporations, labor unions, and political parties, so that what remains of "capitalism" is found in a nation like the United States, which is struggling against complete totalitarianism in order to preserve its corporations, labor unions, and political parties, in spite of their own excesses, through the method of administrative commissions.

The term "financial capitalism" is used to indicate a third stage of the capitalist system. It followed "merchant capitalism" and "industrial capitalism." The above three terms indicate, not clear-cut historical divisions between one and the other, but indicate the relative predominance of the merchant, the industrialist, or the banker in the evolution of capitalism. These three stages all exist at the same time in different American industries, but their historical development grows out of the capitalistic evolution of western civilization.

First was the stage of discovery of new lands and new markets pioneered by the "merchant adventurers," but with simple and crude tools and hand processes. Second was the stage of scientific invention and technology when the steam engine, electricity, gasoline, and machinery of all kinds were being utilized to produce, on the large scale of so-called "mass production," the huge quantities of products to be shipped to the previously expanded markets. Third was the stage that followed the "closing of the frontier" against further expansion, the period of world-wide market scarcity, when mass production had to be curtailed in order to maintain both prices and the values of the investments needed to finance the amazing scientific inventions for overproduction beyond demand in this new age of mechanical power. This latter financial stage is as yet incomplete in the case of American farmers, who still remain in the merchant-capitalist stage.

The beginning of the twentieth century (1900) brought a great legal invention, the "holding company," that made possible the financial capitalism in the United States, which expanded and then collapsed in 1929. The holding company was invented in the offices of my lawyer friend, James B. Dill, in the financial district of New York. The problem of Dill's clients, the great financiers J. P. Morgan and partners, was how to eliminate Andrew Carnegie, the outstanding industrial capitalist, from competing with Morgan's steel industry in the United States, yet without violating the antitrust laws. Dill devised the holding company for the use of J. P. Morgan & Co., and induced the legislature of New Jersey to legalize it. Corporations had previously, indeed, bought and owned the stocks of other corporations, for the purpose of investment of their own surplus savings not immediately useful in expanding their own business. But Dill invented the scheme of expanding these investment holdings into control holdings of competing corporations without the expenditure of any additional cash by the holding company. The holding company thereby became the financial company. The invention consisted in creating shares of stock of the holding company, with the familiar limited liability, and then exchanging these created shares for at least a majority of the shares of each of the industrial corporations in order to vote the stock and elect the board of directors of each industrial corporation by the management of the financial company. The scheme, as was intended by the Morgan company, brought under the management of the financial corporations, organized as the holding company, all the competitors of the Carnegie company.

But Carnegie demanded cash, or its equivalent, if he were to accept the "dismissal wage" which would eliminate him from the steel industry. This cash equivalent was, therefore, arranged in the form of bonds, to be sold to the general public, obligating the holding company to pay *future cash* upon termination of the bonds. The bonds became, in fact, an obligation of the entire steel industry to Carnegie. It was estimated and reported afterwards that Carnegie was paid three hundred million dollars in bonds for his properties whose cost of reproduction was estimated not to exceed seventy-five million dollars. Since these are estimates, they indicate the "order of magnitude" rather than the exact measurements. And this was somewhat the order of magnitude in the exchange of holding company stock for the industrial corporation stock, a ratio, in some cases, of three shares of holding stock for one share of industrial corporation stock.

Thus the holding company stock was "watered stock" legalized by the legislature of New Jersey, but it had the financial solidity of a legalized cartel. By controlling the industry as a whole and maintaining prices of steel, it was able eventually to build up physical extensions to the production plant by "plowing back" excess profits into the plant. Other states copied and expanded the legislation of New Jersey, in view of the high fees paid to the state for incorporation of holding companies by the state governments. This profitable union of corporate and political management in an entirely legal enlargement of both state revenues and corporation revenues, during the years 1900 to 1929, indicates what I mean by the peak of capitalism in the United States.[1]

Adam Smith, in 1776, made his *Wealth of Nations* an attack on merchant capitalism, the so-called "mercantilism," that dominated the "commercial policy" of governments at that time. His attack was made in the interest of individual liberty and was similar to the attack made in the American Declaration of Independence, the same year 1776, and again, in 1789, in the Declaration of the Rights of Man at the beginning of the French Revolution. These two "declarations" were the practical application of Smith's *Wealth of Nations*. They declared all men created equal, en-

---

[1] See hearings and reports of *Temporary National Economic Committee*, 1940, 1941. The Committee was organized by the Congress and the several administrative departments of the federal government. See *Amer. Econ. Review*, Vol. XXXII, June 1942, No. 2, Pt. 2, Appendix B, p. 129.

dowed by their Creator with inalienable rights to life, liberty, the pursuit of happiness, rights of property, and resistance to oppression, as stated somewhat differently in the two declarations.

Smith's attack on merchant capitalism as a violation of economic liberty reads almost like a description of present-day capitalism, which has adopted nearly everything that Smith opposed. He specified at length his opposition to protective tariffs, bounties on exports, navigation laws, exploitation of colonies by prohibiting colonial manufactures, and he opposed combinations of employers against laborers, exclusive corporations and guilds, and low prices on exports in order to defeat competition and to import large quantities of metallic money. Smith attacked the merchant capitalists in theory; the American and French revolutionists, by their declarations of the rights of individuals, attacked them in practice.

After the French Revolution the neglected "right of association" began to be demanded in Europe and America. The word "socialism" first appeared in the year 1833, and the word meant, during the next two decades, different kinds of "voluntary cooperation," nowadays named consumers' cooperation, producers' cooperation, credit unions, and the like. These "socialisms" were denounced in 1848 as "utopian" by Karl Marx, one of Germany's refugees in England, and indeed they were utopian as advocated at the time. He advocated socialism through the physical force of dictatorship of the "proletariat."

But it was the joint stock, limited liability corporation that actually survived. The American economist, Henry C. Carey, contemporary of Marx in the middle of the nineteenth century, advocated the right of association, by which he meant this limited liability corporation. Carey thus laid the foundations for a policy of protective tariffs which should build up large-scale manufactures in America and other backward countries. These countries were handicapped and even exploited, as his wide investigations showed, by the free competition of the powerful established industries of England. His philosophy, which he called "association," was limited liability corporations against the socialisms and communisms of Europe.

The individualism of the eighteenth century had made Adam

Smith the first economist to work out the principle of "division of labor." If a trade were free between individuals, between nations, between city and country, or between occupations, then division of labor among individuals would promote, more than all else, an increase in the wealth of nations. Each individual in each nation, or section of a nation, would devote himself to that kind of product wherein his labor was *more* efficient, and then would obtain, by free exchange with others, the kinds of product wherein his own labor was *less* efficient, and that of others more efficient. Each side would gain, as is quite evident, if efficiency were the only thing to be considered. But it meant, according to Carey, as between nations, that England would be the manufacturing and shipping nation of the world, and all others would be reduced perpetually to agriculture. This meant, as Carey maintained, that England would be the dominant nation of the world and the oppressor of all other peoples.

This was because manufacturing on a large scale, as required by modern inventions, especially inventions of the steam engine and laborsaving machinery, could be succesful only by mass employment of wage-labor.[1] This kind of associated labor is far more efficient than individual labor, as Carey took pains to show. Division of labor within a single establishment is really associated labor, and Carey extended the idea to a nation. Division of labor within a nation between agriculture and manufactures is associated labor within the nation, and makes that nation more prosperous because it is more efficient in both agriculture and manufactures. But it was an unequal contest if the long-established associations of labor in British manufacturing industries, with their large equipment of machinery, were able to prevent by free competition the organization and equipment of associated labor in America and in the less industrialized countries.

As matters turned out, Carey's limited liability corporations

[1] It was this large-scale associated labor with machinery that indicated Carey's advance of the protective tariff argument beyond that of Alexander Hamilton a half century before. Carey was followed by Friedrich List, in Germany, who got his ideas while an exile in America. Carey's first book, *Essay on The Rate of Wages,* Philadelphia, 1935, had merely copied the classical free-trade doctrines. His later doctrines were against free trade.

were less utopian than other forms of organization. Carey was, in fact, the pioneer economist of industrial capitalism, which had a free field for development after the American Civil War. It was in the preceding decade of the 1850's, both in America and in England, that the enactment of general incorporation laws, with limited liability, was rounded out. Before such laws were enacted, an association of capitalists, desiring to incorporate, was required to obtain a special act of authority from the state legislature. This practice of special legislation for each corporation led to astounding abuses, the corruption of politics, and the evils of lobbying. Only Democrats could obtain charters from a Democratic legislature, and only Whigs from a Whig legislature. But with a "general incorporation" law the association merely filed articles with the Secretary of State and automatically it was thereby incorporated. Corporations were no longer monopolies, because all competitors could incorporate and compete as corporations. The "right of association" thus became one of the "rights of man." Adam Smith's violation of natural liberty became an institutional right of liberty. If the revolutions of the eighteenth century established individualism, the revolutions of the nineteenth century established corporationalism.

These corporations themselves were treated by economists and courts as though they were big individuals with all the rights previously acquired by natural individuals. A corporation acted as a unit like an individual, notwithstanding it was "immortal" and endowed with limited liability of stockholders.

Carey's philosophy of limited liability corporations and a protective tariff triumped after 1861 in the American Civil War. This war was a second American revolution. It, too, was an individualistic revolution, comparable to revolutions of the eighteenth century. Yet, there remained much for the philosophy of individualism to accomplish. The slaves were granted individually the rights of life, liberty, and property. The Homestead Act of 1862 opened up "free land" to individual ownership without payment. This unoccupied empire westward to the Pacific called for the limited liability action of railway and telegraph companies. A population of the most industrious pioneers from the east and from all nations filled the middle west and the far west. They were the "rugged individualists" of the world. The limited liability manufacturing corporations, protected against England, now had a free market within the United States greater in area and purchasing power than anything known in the history of the world.

Not until the frontier was being rapidly closed by land speculation in advance of population, and settlers could no longer go west in droves, did a different angle of associated action come into view.[1] This was a shift from producing power to bargaining power. The farmers associated themselves in the 1870's to control railway corporations through politics and through the so-called "Granger laws," and in 1890 the farmers joined with others to dissolve manufacturing corporations through the "antitrust" laws. The laborers made attempts at control by nation-wide strikes in the 1870's, the 1880's and 1890's. Carey's limited liability associations of labor for increasing the large-scale production of wealth had split into two opposing associations, of capital and labor, for control of the distribution of wealth. They had become what Adam Smith had opposed, collective action to deprive individuals of what he considered to be everyone's natural liberty.

And their large-scale organization is astonishing. Collective action in a single corporation, the American Telephone and Telegraph Corporation, has reached the total of a half million stockholders and bondholders. A single labor union, the United Automobile Workers, has reached 1,100,000 members. The Federal Reserve system is a union of many thousands of banking corporations. Limited liability corporations now control an estimated 90 per cent of the manufacturing output in the United States, besides controlling practically the whole of the services of transportation and communication.

Evidently collective action had by no means reached, at the time of Carey, its national or world-wide control of individuals. Carey had only steam power to build upon. The twentieth century is the Power Age.

The main characteristic of this twentieth century economics and

[1] See John Steinbeck, *The Grapes of Wrath*, New York, The Viking Press, 1939.

the reasons why it can be distinguished as banker capitalism are the large amounts of savings of millions of investors that must be brought together in order to finance these huge aggregations of machinery, and armies of employees, made feasible by science, invention, and world-wide markets.

This is the reason, too, why the transition is being made from individualistic economics of the eighteenth and nineteenth centuries to what is coming to be named the "institutional" economics of corporations, unions, and political parties. And since these institutions turn on the institution of money controlled by bankers rather than on the production of wealth created by labor, the transition is also made from the creation of wealth measured by man-hours to the accumulation of assets measured by dollars.

# Summary

## *PART ONE*

———◆———

The peak of financial capitalism in the United States may be said to have been reached in November 1929, when the financial system collapsed. This culmination and collapse of financial capitalism, leading to revolutionary and even bloody measures for recovery in Europe and America, we have outlined in the preceding chapters, and shall consider more in detail in later chapters. The outstanding characteristics have been the incoming of mass production by greatly enlarged corporations financed by investment bankers by means of the new framework of holding companies; and the incoming of similar large "industrial" unions on top of the older forms of "craft" unions, along with the depression of agriculture, which is not yet organized.

The science of political economy, following these institutional changes, has slowly shifted, as we have seen, from its early individualism and antimonopoly attitude to the analysis of collective action, bargaining and rationing transactions, and governmental agencies seeking to control, regulate, or even to eliminate the corporations, labor unions, and the political parties. It is to the development of these findings in the science of political economy that we turn for further investigations.

# PART TWO

---

## Simplified Assumptions

# Introduction

Economic investigations in the twentieth century, with its revolutions, credit cycles, unemployment, and repeated wars, must take into account many different aspects of activity. Otherwise research and investigation cannot be brought to full use in the collective effort to control the great and violent "forces" of today.

Out of our experience in collective action, including administration and conciliation of conflicts, and through study of the development of economics, including the economics of the courts, I find five assumptions or hypotheses to be primary in interpreting modern economic activity. These five simplified assumptions—sovereignty, scarcity, efficiency, futurity, and custom—are logical assumptions, made for the purpose of attaining systematic interpretation and understanding in a world of diversity. They are devices for investigation. The validity of such assumptions is found through the fruitfulness of their uses.

# Chapter v

## SOVEREIGNTY

————◆————

The first collective action that helps and restrains everybody in getting a living or getting rich is his own and other governments. This kind of action is sovereignty. If we separate the idea of sovereignty from our ideas of right and wrong, of ought and ought not, of kings and despots, then sovereignty is collective action in control of violence. We usually think of violence as wrong. But it was not always wrong. It was the honorable profession of the feudal nobility, by which they obtained wealth. It is honorable today in the military profession. It is honorable in prize fights. The difference is in the collective effort to take violence out of private initiative by regulating it. The process of regulation is "the State." Sovereignty is monopolization of violence. If individuals start something violent and contrary to the rules, then a procedure is set in motion, simplest formula for which is the relation between plaintiff, defendant, and an official of sovereignty who decides the point and commands obedience.[1]

Curiously enough, this formula is identical with that used in labor arbitration, commercial arbitration, a stock exchange or other market exchange, and in ecclesiastical trials for heresy. There thus occurs a hierarchy of governments, which has led recent writers to speak of a "pluralism"[2] of governments, instead of the

[1] As formulated by the Austrian jurist Hans Kelsen, who drafted the republican constitution of Austria after the war on this simplified formula. Kelsen moved to Switzerland. See his *Allgemeine Staatslehre*, Berlin, J. Springer, 1925. The argument of this chapter was developed in my articles on "A Sociological View of Sovereignty," *Amer. Jour. of Sociology*, Vol. 5 and 6. (Published in 7 articles, July 1899 to July 1900.) Described by a sociologist as an "economic interpretation of sovereignty."

[2] See "Pluralism," *Encyclopedia of the Social Sciences*, New York, The Macmillan Co., 1932–35, Vol. XII, p. 170.

traditional idea of sovereignty superior to the others. By pluralism is meant, not the American scheme of federal and state sovereignty, but the sovereignty of occupational groups over their members, such as labor organizations, capitalistic organizations, or ecclesiastical organizations. They are, indeed, governments, since they are collective action in control of individual action through the use of sanctions. They may be named, in the case of employers and employees, industrial government,[1] or preferably "economic government." They have their legislative, executive, and judicial departments; yet, instead of using the general term pluralism, we can classify these governments according to the kind and degree of power which they use to enforce their decisions upon their members. Three *kinds* of power may be used—moral power, economic power, and physical power. The difference is not in the formula of plaintiff, defendant, and official but in the kind of *sanction*, or collective inducement, which each employs to enforce obedience. In our American system, since the separation of church and state by depriving churches and monasteries of landed property and taxing power, the ecclesiastical government has only the sanction of collective opinion, to which the name "moral power," or "propaganda," seems best fitted. In the case of economic government the term "economic power," or power of scarcity, seems appropriate, being the power of withholding property rights from others as a means of commanding obedience. But in the case of sovereignty proper the sanction is the "physical power" of organized violence, for which the term "duress" is usually employed.

Thus, we have a hierarchy of superior and subordinate governments, instead of a pluralism of equal governments. Each is similar in that it determines for individuals their rights, duties, and liberties within its own organization and in view of expected obedience to its own collective commands. In the case of sovereignty this is public purpose, or public policy. In the other organizations it is private purpose. But each is different in the kind and degree of power used to enforce the rights and duties of individuals. Since the power of ecclesiastical organizations nowadays

[1] See J. R. Commons, *Industrial Government*, New York, The Macmillan Co., 1921.

in America is not much different from that of social clubs and the like, the general name of common opinion, or propaganda, which is moral power, indicates the weakest power within the hierarchy. More powerful are the collective economic regulations based on scarcity of jobs and materials; and most powerful of all is the sovereign power of bodily compulsion, life, and death. For this reason sovereignty is not equal to, but superior to, moral and economic collective action.

This hierarchy does not work automatically. There are heretics, rebels, hypocrites, criminals. All of the governments must have moral power whose most familiar name is propaganda. The most dictatorial sovereigns are today the best-organized propagandists. The American government is highly propagandist, mainly through political parties and newspapers. Capitalistic corporations have their "public relations" departments, which are their propaganda departments, designed to back up their economic power by moral power; labor unions and farmers' organizations have learned the need of propaganda, which the labor organizations have long since named their "moral power," designed to strengthen their economic power. Religious organizations, having only moral power, live only by propaganda. Propaganda is the first essential of collective action. It is not logic or reason, it is inducement, incitement. It can be and has been investigated.[1] The name "moral power" distinguishes this kind of power from economic and physical power.

We may attempt to give precision to the three kinds of power, physical, economic, and moral, by adopting from the science of jurisprudence the terms duress, coercion, and persuasion. Duress is the physical power of violence; coercion is the economic power of scarcity and ownership; persuasion is the moral power of propaganda. The term "power" indicates, not the actual use of power, but the preliminary use of a language of promises or threats, indicating an intention to use that power. In the case of individuals endeavoring to influence one another, this language of duress, coercion, or persuasion may be distinguished as "inducements." But in the case of collective action the term "sanction"

---

[1] See "Propaganda," *Encyclopedia of the Social Sciences*, New York, The Macmillan Co., 1932–35, Vol. XII, p. 521.

has achieved considerable usage as the language of a purpose to use collective power of duress, coercion, or persuasion, as the case may be, if the plaintiff or defendant does not obey the commands. Sanctions are collective inducements.

Thus, the word "power" indicates an influence addressed to the human will, and this distinguishes economics and politics from the physical sciences. The early economists treated economics by analogy to the physical sciences, and thus practically eliminated the human will except as exercised in sovereignty and propaganda, which, for them, did not pertain to economics. Adam Smith, indeed, allowed for "higgling" of the market, which we translate into the legal term "negotiations." Thus, the term "power" signifies physical, economic, or moral inducements exercised by human beings who act volitionally upon each other. These "volitions" signify a purpose, as distinguished from the different kinds of "energy" evidenced in the forces of nature, from gravity and chemistry to electricity and light, which are nonvolitional, or purposeless. By rhetorical analogy to the physical sciences, the word "pressure" has been borrowed to mean collective action of "pressure groups."

This is the first simplification needed—the distinction between "nature" and "human nature." One is blind pressure, the other is purposeful power. The three kinds of power are each economic in their effects, but they can be separated mentally for separate investigation by distinguishing moral power as a kind of power, like public opinion or any other collective opinion, which operates without the use of economic or physical sanctions; economic power as the power of scarcity and private property, like scarcity of jobs or scarcity of food, which operates merely by withholding supply or demand, without moral or physical sanctions; physical power, like war, taxation, imprisonment, which operates by the sanction of violence, without economic or moral sanctions.

These three kinds of power, moral, economic, and physical, are inseparable in fact, but can be distinguished by analysis. They are used both individually as inducements and collectively as sanctions, but the historical tendency has been, as indicated by the words "law and order," to extract the inducement of violence from private action and to concentrate and stabilize it as the collective action of sovereignty.

Historically there is justification for this mental separation of sovereign power from economic and moral power. In our Anglo-American political economy, beginning with William the Conqueror in 1066, there was no distinction made between sovereignty, which is physical power, and property, which is economic power. William was both the sole sovereign over his subjects and the sole proprietor of all the land which his tenants needed for their living or riches. His subjects owed to him military service in maintaining his sovereignty, and they owed it to him as a rent for the lands which they were permitted to use. In the course of time, beginning with Magna Carta in 1215, and ending with the Revolution of 1689, the sovereign was ingeniously divided into two personalities, a sovereign and a proprietor. The sovereign now became the legislature, representing the tenants who became landed and business proprietors. This revolution made the historical sovereign a figurehead, and also made the judiciary independent of the sovereign by giving the judges tenure for life or good behavior, thus depriving the sovereign of his former power to control their decisions by removing them at will. Finally, amendments to the American Constitution made the judiciary superior to both the executive and legislative officials of sovereignty, by the simple device of authorizing citizens to bring suit against officials on the ground of deprivation of life, liberty, or property without due process of law, to be decided by the judiciary.

This separation of personalities finally separated sovereignty from property, and not merely the king but all officials have two personalities, that of sovereignty, indicated usually by an oath of office, and that of an ordinary proprietor, similar to the ownership by all others who are not officials. Those not taking an oath of office are simply "employees," working for the officials as they do for private employers.

This historical separation of property from sovereignty took on, for a time, the fascistic dictatorship of Oliver Cromwell, spokesman for the large and small property owners, in opposition to the claims of divine right of the hereditary sovereign to dictate the grants and transfers of private ownership. Other fascistic dictators have appeared in other countries, like Napoleon I and Napoleon III in France; or like the many historic dictators in other countries, and the so-called "tyrants" of ancient Greece. The recurrence of proprietary dictatorships in modern economics, and the significance of an independent judiciary in safeguarding life, liberty, and property were indicated to me by an American jurist who interviewed a fascist judge in Italy. The latter replied confidentially that he could not, like American judges, decide cases as he might conclude from his own reasoning, because he was liable to be dismissed without notice or hearing by the executive head of the government.

At the time of Cromwell or Napoleon the nonproperty owners, known from the time of the Roman Empire as the "proletariat," or the slaves, were not considered as participants in sovereignty, simply because, without property, they were not deemed to have a permanent interest in the stability of the commonwealth. They took this status as matter of course without successful rebellion. The modern fascist dictators need not abolish hereditary sovereigns, who have already been exterminated or converted into decorations. The fascist dictators of today busy themselves with suppressing legislatures, as well as the independent judiciary, political parties, trade unions, corporations, and cooperatives managed by nonproperty, or small-property, owners.

Throughout this historic shifting back and forth of sovereignty and property, with the related executive, legislative, and judicial branches of sovereignty, has occurred, as seen especially in America, a succession of changes in the meaning of the word property. These changes were not merely "verbal." They had economic effects. In earlier times there was substantially but one kind of property, "corporeal" property, meaning thereby the ownership of a physical body or "corpus," such as lands, cattle, or slaves. Ownerships consisted mainly in the expectation that the sovereign, by physical power, would prevent physical trespass upon the "corpus" by those not deemed to be its owners. The rules adopted by the courts of England and America for preventing this trespass, and thereby permitting the owner to exercise his own free will upon the "corpus," came to be known as "the common law."

Then, when the former peddlers and merchants came to have political influence, a new kind of property, a property in debts, came to be recognized and enforced by the courts under the name of "incorporeal" property. Incorporeal property is simply the duty of the debtor to pay money, known either as a credit or its equivalent debt. It does not become a debt, for economic science, unless the judicial branch of sovereignty is in position to exercise control of the body or property of the debtor and compel him, by physical power, to pay money or perform what the courts recognize as his legal duty. This duty, in the American Constitution, is known as "the obligation of contracts."

Finally, beginning with the time, in the last quarter of the nineteenth century, when legislatures essayed to reduce the freight and passenger rates charged by railway corporations for the use of their corporeal properties, the meaning of property, as protected in the Constitution, was further enlarged by the Court in the United States to include what was named "intangible" property, or the economic power of sellers, buyers, or competitors, in charging against others or paying to others such prices as they wished or could enforce for commodities or services. Typical cases of intangible property are patents, the goodwill of a business, the right to do business, the right to earn a living or get rich, good reputation, trade marks, trade secrets, and going value. They are not the "incorporeal" property of debts; they are the "intangible" property of liberty and scarcity. In economics they are "purchasing power."

It may seem strange that such "intangible things" as these can be "owned." The early economists did not include them in economics. They included only "tangible" things, "corporeal" things, like horses or slaves. But ownership consists in being permitted to do as you please with yourself or with things that you claim for yourself, without interference from other people. It is created by enforcing duties of avoidance and forbearance on others. For example, a chemist of my acquaintance invented a process for storing electricity, which was not patented. He tried to keep it a secret. But one of his employees, entrusted with the secret, went to work for a competitor at higher wages. The competitor then began to use the secret process. The inventor brought suit against the competitor. The court awarded the inventor several thousand dollars in damages—in fact, all of the profits which the competitor had made by using the secret. Besides, the court issued an injunction prohibiting the competitor and his employees from further use of the secret, on penalty of contempt of court and imprisonment. The court enforced the duty of avoidance by its physical sanctions. It created a right of property in secrets. The true inventor became rich, the competitor became nearly bankrupt. The secret became his "intangible property." He could sell or lease it if he wished. So with good will, good reputation, trade marks, and other "intangibles." They are worth money; money is purchasing power; purchasing power is bargaining power; bargaining power is property; property is assets, and the assets are means of getting rich. Property is created by sovereignty, by keeping other people off, by preventing robbery, trespass, stealing secrets, or preventing "infringement" upon one's opportunities to buy, sell, or compete. The creation of intangible property is usually named the "law of unfair competition." It is created by creating duties of forbearance and avoidance.

Evidently these enlargements of the meaning of property followed the historical economic change in methods of getting a living or getting rich, from ownership of physical things to ownership of debts; then to ownership of opportunities to buy, sell, and compete. Each of these methods of acquiring and alienating ownership is practiced today, and has extended from primitive local communities to the circuit of the globe. The separation of their meanings by mental analysis can be understood only by understanding the historical economic and political changes which occasioned them, known in biology as "evolution."

But the word property, as thus analyzed in its unfolding meanings, carries the idea of something passive or stationary, usually named "statics." Its active or "dynamic" content which makes property what it really is in human affairs is transactions, which we have already described. These are also the creations of sovereignty within such limits as individuals are permitted or required to act by the courts. The older economists eliminated sovereignty from economics by way of the meanings they gave to the terms *"laissez faire"* and *"exchange."*

The term *laissez faire* indicated the purpose of economists, expressed as an advice addressed to the officials of sovereignty, meaning "let us alone, let us do as we please," keep your hands off all economic transactions of landlords, business men, and laboring men. Sovereignty seemed to them to be artificial and arbitrary, like a king, such that, if once eliminated, economic activity would take its "natural" course, like the motions of planets and stars and the multiplication of animals and plants which satisfy human wants. They assumed, apparently, that property owners should be left to protect their ownership individually by violence against trespassers upon their lands and machines, or against impairment of the obligation of contracts, or against infringement upon their markets.

These property rights are indeed artificial. Nothing like them is found among planets, stars, plants, or animals. They are the artificial creations by those who, in the exercise of sovereignty, endeavor to monopolize the use of violence. The officials and courts got their ideas of property from the customs of merchants and landlords. By *laissez faire* was really meant a maxim of advice to these officials of sovereignty recommending the use of physical force against persons who interfered with ownership, but alternatively recommending the use of physical force in favor of the owners themselves.

The businessmen and economists did not really mean all that they said about *laissez faire*. They were speaking to England and France, the most powerful governments in the world. Those governments had already conquered other nations, had opened up foreign markets, and had created property rights. The capitalists were also, through use of standing armies, police, and courts of law, powerful enough at home to prevent insurrections, strikes, or other interference by dissatisfied people against themselves while they were doing what they pleased with their own property rights. What businessmen and economists really meant by *laissez faire* was: prevent everybody else at home and abroad from doing as *they* please, in order that we may do as we please with what we claim as our own.

But governments differ greatly in what they consider to be private property, and also in what degree of power they use in permitting owners to do as they please with their own. Also, the same governments differ within themselves at different times, a kind of difference which, whether good or bad, is known as evolution.

The other term, "exchange," when followed consistently in its meanings, led also to the exclusion of sovereignty from economics. Exchange meant the transfers among individuals of physical things or the uses of physical things, whether materials or laborers. It meant, in fact, a physical process of delivering to other individuals certain physical "commodities," which might be slaves. But the word "commodity" had a double meaning, ownership and the thing owned. And, in course of time, the thing owned acquired the three meanings of corporeal, incorporeal, and intangible property—a physical thing, a debt, and a market opportunity. Consequently the word "exchange" also carried the double meaning of a labor process of transporting and delivering a physical object, and a legal process of transferring the ownership of either a physical thing, a debt, or a market opportunity. Only by historical investigation can the circumstances be discovered, in contemplation of which this double meaning of exchange and this treble meaning of property came to be recognized. The labor process was the meaning given by the classical, communistic, syndicalist, and the early technological economists. But this meaning we have distinguished from the legal process of transferring ownership, by distinguishing an "exchange" from a "transaction." Only sovereignty transfers ownership, while labor, aided by machinery, transfers and delivers the thing owned, under commands of the owner.

What we have previously said regarding "money" and "cash" will illustrate the changed historical meanings of the word property. Gold and silver are corporeal property. A banker's debt, or deposit, is incorporeal property. The purchasing power of that debt, which is the modern "cash," is intangible property. It is still called money, by the force of habit, but it is the purchasing power of credit.

It was quite consistent, therefore, while excluding sovereignty, that the early economists should consider exchange a part of the labor process of producing wealth. Labor—including machinery dramatized as "embodied labor"—moves things in three directions, each of which has the purpose of giving to them a greater value. One direction is toward "form utility," such as the change from iron ore to knives, forks, and machinery; another is toward "place utility," the transportation from the mines to the factories, then to the ultimate consumers; inseparable from this is "time utility," the accumulation and storage of things until they are needed.

None of these creations of utility by labor and machinery has necessarily anything to do with transfers of ownership. Adam Smith identified division of labor with division of ownership. But they are separate. Labor creates and exchanges useful things, but in doing so the laborers may be commanded by an owner, like the United States Steel Corporation, or by a sovereign owner like the communist state of Russia. Hence, starting with the division of ownerships, it is needful, first of all, to transfer ownership before the labor transfer is permitted by sovereignty. A laborer takes my apples from my orchard. Is he a laborer or is he a thief? The labor process is the same, but I may call in sovereignty in the shape of a policeman. The economists assumed that the ownership process was the same as the labor process. The many technicalities of law required to define ownership may be summarized, for economic purposes, as transfers of legal control by sovereignty, distinguished from transfers of physical control by labor. The early English economists, habituated to the Revolution of 1689, took for granted that the transfers of ownership were made by individuals, like the exchange of commodities, and, therefore, that sovereignty could be eliminated from economic theory. But recent revolutions do not permit us to take the economic behavior of sovereignty for granted, and both the law books and observations reveal that only sovereignty transfers ownership. Sovereignty had not been eliminated—it had been changed from arbitrary to stabilized sovereignty, from feudal to capitalistic sovereignty. Rather should we investigate all of the different kinds of economic transactions through which the expected succession of officials of sovereignty transfers legal control at the requests of subordinate individuals. In this book we have distinguished these economic transactions as bargaining, managerial, and rationing transactions.

A peculiarity of the American system of sovereignty is the separation of sovereign powers along many different lines. There are territorial divisions of municipal and local governments, state governments, and a national government. Within these territorial divisions are separations into legislative, executive, and judicial powers, and, in recent years, a further separation of administrative powers. Over all is a federal Constitution interpreted by a Supreme Court, designed to protect citizens against abuse of sovereign powers by this multitude of sovereigns. The main protection of economic significance is the protection against depriving citizens of life, liberty, or property without "due process of law," which in its later development, is protection against depriving them of their economic power of collective action.

This "due process of law" comes to us from the Revolution of 1689 in England. It has been the most admirable of all protections which has made America the outstanding capitalistic nation of the world. Individuals and corporations may be deprived of liberty and property by these sovereigns, whom we name politicians and political parties, *with* due process of law, but *not without* due process of law. Since sovereignty creates both liberty and private property, the most extreme deprivation of property or liberty is permitted under the so-called power of eminent domain. But if one of the many sovereigns exercises this supereminent domain power, the Constitution provides that the private owner must be compensated by payment of the full value of the property taken.

Yet there are many ways in which the sovereigns may deprive individuals or corporations of property and liberty *without* compensation. When the government changes the standard of money from silver to gold or to paper money, it deprives some individuals and corporations of their property without compensation, and transfers the ownership of that property to other individuals. Yet this deprivation and transfer of ownership is done *with* due process of law. The power of taxation is another process of depriving individuals and corporations of property and transferring its ownership to other individuals or corporations. Yet this is done *without* compensation, but *with* due process of law.

There has arisen, in the American system, a peculiar power, known as the "police power," by which also the sovereign officials may deprive individuals and corporations of their rights of property and liberty *without* compensation and transfer it to other individuals or corporations. This police power is usually described as limited to state and local governments, but a similar power is permitted to the federal government under the name of the "commerce power." By the extension of the commerce power, the federal government has invaded the "police power" of the states and municipalities.

Considering all of these sovereign powers of depriving individuals and corporations of property, and transferring its ownership to other individuals and corporations, there are just two main divisions of economic importance in the exercise of sovereign powers over deprivation and transfer of ownership of private property without consent of the private owners. They are the power of deprivation and transfer *with* compensation, and *without* compensation. The power of deprivation and transfer *with* compensation is the power of eminent domain. The power of deprivation and transfer *without* compensation is the great variety of powers distinguishable as the money power, the tax power, the police power, the commerce power, the postal power, the emergency war power, and others.

Eminent domain applies historically and mainly to ownership of corporeal property. The other powers apply to the transactions which enlarge or diminish values and valuations, which, in turn, are the economic dimensions of assets and incomes.

The failure to recognize and investigate this *due process* feature of the American economic system is one of the many tragic conflicts in American politics. We may contrast the public utility legislation of Wisconsin in 1907 with the Tennessee Valley Authority legislation in 1934.

The Wisconsin legislation was based on recognition of the

economic waste in permitting competition in the ownership and operation of "public utilities." In reference to monopolies the legislature provided, therefore, that if a municipality decided in favor of public ownership and operation of a street railway, the water works, gas, or an electric utility, the city should not build a competing plant but must purchase the existing private plant at a valuation—the principle of eminent domain. But instead of a local jury or a local court of law establishing this valuation, the law set up its State Railroad Commission as the valuation authority. The municipality should pay to the private corporation the value established by the State Railroad Commission with a review based on "due process" by the Supreme Court of the state. Under this provision a number of waterworks properties were transferred from private ownership and operation to municipal ownership and operation, without any serious uprisings or revolutions.

But the federal legislation omitted all of these administrative provisions in the case of the water power development of the Tennessee Valley Authority. Instead of setting up the Interstate Commerce Commission, or a similar administrative authority, as the valuation authority under the eminent domain rule of "fair value," Congress provided for duplication of power plants, and competition of the public versus the private plants throughout the states. The result was an unseemly political struggle over a valuation claimed to be approximately $100,000,000 by the private corporation and about $50,000,000, said to have been offered by the officials of the TVA. The final settlement was a compromise valuation of $78,000,000 made by the lawyer of the private corporation who, after negotiating it, became the Republican candidate for President of the United States. That or a different valuation might have been made by the Interstate Commerce Commission, with review by the federal court, after investigations and hearings, without precipitation of a tragic political conflict in the face of an impending world conflict.[1]

---

[1] See my article on the TVA in *Survey Graphic*, "What I Saw in the Tennessee Valley," *Survey Graphic*, May 1938, Vol. XXVII, p. 279; also M. G. Glaser, *Outlines of Public Utility Economics*, New York, The Macmillan Co., 1927.

It is, indeed, these struggles over economic valuations that are the immediate issues in the totalitarian revolutions of Europe, as they already are threatening to become similar issues in America. The American Constitution provides an administrative means of meeting the issues by "due process of law," that is, by economic investigation, without dictatorship, civil war, or conquest.

# Chapter vi

## SCARCITY

———◆———

Scarcity in economics is property in jurisprudence, and the rights and duties of property are the working rules of sovereignty in control of scarcity. Nobody would ask his government to protect him against others in getting exclusive ownership of what is as abundant as pure air in the United States of America. He asks protection in getting legal control of strategic land sites that are blessed with pure air. He has evidently, in times past, used physical force to push weaker people into the cold air of the arctics or the hot air of the tropics. When he learned to manufacture warm air in the winter and cool air in the summer, he claimed and acquired private property in the patents, the instruments, tools, materials, and buildings which were scarce and needed in the process.

Pure air is the most valuable of all natural resources, but it has no scarcity value. Its value is its "use value." It is useful but abundant. Scarcity value adheres to property rights in what is scarce or expected to be scarce. So with other natural resources. Weaker peoples are pushed into the Indian reservations of America or into the slums, and the flags of conquering nations are planted on expectedly scarce land sites.

Scarcity and property came piecemeal into the theories of economics, usually in order to counteract anarchistic, communistic, idealistic, or other revolutionary programs. Adam Smith had assumed abundance to be the natural state of man, on account of divine beneficence, but his common sense assumed also that private property was natural, and this restrained him from carrying out logically his idea of efficiency to such an extreme limit that, like air, useful things would have no value. He opposed monopoly, which was artificial scarcity, but he did not investigate natural scarcity, or property rights, because they were self-evident.

But his followers of the French Revolution were not restrained by common sense. They were logical. They exalted the same God of Reason but carried to the extreme Smith's idea of reason by assuming logically that, if earthly institutions like the state and the church were abolished, then there would be abundance of everything as divinely ordained. But when Thomas Malthus, also rated as a "classical economist," wrote his *Essay on Population* in 1798, twenty-two years after Smith's *Wealth of Nations*, Malthus had the very practical purpose of replying to William Godwin, the first so-called "anarchist," who, in his essay, *Enquiry Concerning Political Justice*, written in 1793, had carried out the logic of abundance to extremes by proposing to bring into England the principles of the French Revolution, by abolishing both private property and the existing government. Malthus replied that mankind was not governed by logic but by passion, and, therefore, even if Godwin should succeed, the result would be merely more population which would again press upon the means of subsistence and would compel England to restore substantially the existing institutions of private property and government. The overpopulation predicted by Malthus was not logical, like anarchism; it was biological and proprietary.

Sixty years after Malthus, Charles Darwin, in his *Origin of Species* (1859), took his cue from Malthus to whom he acknowledged the idea. But Darwin went further and developed a universal principle of biological scarcity for all living creatures. For scarcity first came into the world with the emergence of life. It becomes a principle of economics, not perhaps more fundamental, but more primordial, than the property and sovereignty which Malthus had derived from it. Darwin worked out the formula of scarcity in great detail, during a period of twenty years or more, after getting the idea from Malthus. Scarcity involved the investigation and correlation by Darwin of five simplified assumptions, namely, heredity, variability, multiplication, struggle for life, and survival of those best fitted to survive.

These Darwin named "natural selection." But natural selection was quite different from the Malthusian "moral selection." The latter was provided for by Darwin in what he named "artificial selection." But Darwin regretted afterwards the use of these terms. He should have said purposeless and purposeful selection. Natural selection is just as purposeless when it lets wolves and liars survive as when it lets gazelles and George Washington survive. Success is its only measure of fitness. But artificial, or rather purposeful, selection introduces ethical ideas of fitness—the ethical ideas of right and duty, goodness and badness, justice and injustice—and these ideas are limits set by sovereignty and other collective action on the methods of success. Political economy belongs to the field of artificial selection, because it deals with human purposes.

It was the Malthusian idea that the moral virtues of thrift and enterprise are developed by the "middle classes" in the struggle to avoid poverty by acquiring riches, and that this was the divine plan in contrast to Adam Smith's idea of divine beneficence and earthly abundance. The two contrasted divine plans are carried over in modern arguments for and against legislation by government. The Malthusian theology, with the aid of Darwin, is used against legislation which provides old-age pensions and unemployment insurance, as when President Cutten, of Colgate University, says to a convention of teachers, "Now comes social security to guarantee us soft living from the cradle to the grave, to beg the unfit to become more unfit, and to beg the fit to give up the struggle and vegetate." [1] This is Malthusian and Darwinian economics of struggle for life, combined with a theology that identifies sin with scarcity and virtue with abundance.

Indeed, from the time of Malthus a troublesome problem in economic science has been the separation of scarcity from sin. Were Adam and Eve expelled from the Garden of Eden on account of sin or on account of overpopulation? Since the time of Malthus and Darwin, economists have reasoned that the expulsion was on account of scarcity. Prior to Malthus, in a world of divine beneficence, the expulsion was ascribed to sin. The issue was debated one hundred years ago in the effort to abolish imprisonment for debt. That practice was ultimately prohibited by distinguishing

[1] *Wisconsin State Journal,* Madison, Wisconsin, February 14, 1936.

scarcity from sin, and misfortune from fraud.[1] Fraudulent debtors were thenceforth punished for fraud, but unfortunate debtors were set free by bankruptcy laws, by laws against peonage, and by laws against imprisonment for debt. Previously, in England, the bankrupts were imprisoned for their bankruptcy.

On a similar line of argument of divine government, if anyone was poor in a world of divine beneficence, his poverty came from disobedience to God's laws. This was the theology expounded by Senator Carter Glass, of Virginia, in 1935, against changes proposed in the federal banking laws. Economists had usually considered that the excessive prosperity and inflation of 1927 to 1929 was the cause of the depression after 1929, but Senator Glass said, "God Almighty penalizes everybody who disobeys His law; and there is no reason why everybody should not be penalized who disobeys the laws of sound economics and the laws of the country. . . . Theology teaches that if you do not punish sin, a fellow is going to keep on sinning; and that is just as true applied to economics as it is to theology."[2]

The difficulty with this line of argument in economics, as in religion, is that both prosperity and depression fall upon the just and the unjust, upon those who caused it and upon those who neither caused prosperity nor were responsible for the depression. The Congress was endeavoring, through the Banking Act and through the regulation of the stock exchanges, to prevent another period of artificial scarcity by preventing the overspeculation in stocks and bonds, whether the speculators were innocent or guilty. This overspeculation was known to have been the main abuse during periods of abundance, and to be the main cause of succeeding depressions.

Malthus predicted correctly about the return to private property. The French Revolution swept away a multitude of injustices practiced under the old regime, but private property remained stronger than before the Revolution, because the peasants now

[1] See Commons and Associates, *History of Labor in the United States*, New York, The Macmillan Co., 1918, Vol. I, pp. 221 ff.

[2] *Hearings, Banking Act of 1935:* Subcommittee of the Committee on Banking and Currency, U. S. Senate, 74th Congress, 1st Session, May 24, 1935, p. 686.

became owners by dividing up the estates of landlords and the church. Even the industrial revolution of steam, electricity, machinery, and the physical sciences, which promised, as never before, a world of abundance, made room for more population and more scarcity, more war, and more misery. The population of western Europe more than doubled within a hundred years after Malthus, notwithstanding the emigration of millions to America and to other parts of the earth.

The next piecemeal introduction of scarcity into economics came in the last quarter of the nineteenth century. It injected scarcity into the very soul of the individual, and its originators are known as the psychological, or hedonistic, school of economists, especially the Austrian economists, Menger, Wieser, and Böhm-Bawerk. It spread to other countries and furnished the strongest arguments in favor of individualism as against the rising tide of theoretical communism.[1] For it was based on the most intimate and continuously felt force within the individual, the familiar fact, which can be observed at every dinner, that the feeling of pleasure accompanying the satisfaction of wants diminishes in degree of intensity with each added unit of meat, or butter, or bread consumed, until such time as intensity disappears, and the individual then turns to something else. This diminishing intensity of pleasure was named "diminishing utility," but it should have been named "diminishing scarcity," and the point where the consumer changes to something else was named "marginal utility," but should be "marginal scarcity." This universal fact of psychology underlies the "law of supply and demand," and is the foundation of the principle of scarcity. Diminishing satisfaction with increasing abundance supports the conviction that "you cannot go against the law of supply and demand," that is, against "economic law." The pleasure of consumption is most intense when the object wanted is scarce, like water on a waterless desert, and the pleasure is least intense when there is an oversupply, and the excess becomes a "nuisance," as water in a Mississippi flood.

It is possible, then, to classify three aspects of the principle of

[1] See Eugen V. Böhm-Bawerk, *Karl Marx and the Close of His System* (translated by A. M. McDonald), London, T. Fisher Unwin, 1898.

scarcity, coming piecemeal into economics, as the *biological* scarcity of Malthus and Darwin, the *psychological* scarcity of the pleasure-pain economists, and the *proprietary* scarcity enforced by working rules of government and by the collective action of corporations and labor unions.

The recognition of proprietary scarcity came with the recognition of "intangible property" in law and economics by the courts. The idea of "corporeal property," which prevailed from the early common law and was the idea of Smith and Malthus, contemplated exclusive possession of one's own use of objects that were wanted but were scarce. It was an idea of "holding" for self. But the idea of "intangible property" is the idea of "withholding" from others what they need but do not own. Both turn on the principle of scarcity, but one is the individualistic idea of preventing trespass by nonowners, while the other is the bargaining idea of two owners withholding release of ownership until a price or ratio of exchange is agreed upon in the negotiations of a transaction. The older idea fitted the notion of individuals producing wealth each for his own individual use, an idea of the self-sufficient or isolated individual. The other idea fits the notion of economic interdependence where the individual earns a living or gets rich by acquiring ownership of things produced by others. What was "corporeal property" becomes "intangible property," when the purpose of production becomes production for sale upon a market.

The distinction underlies the difference in economics and law between "wealth" and "assets," and the difference between "use value" and "scarcity value." The distinctions are not made by customary common sense, but a science of economics should make the distinction. "Wealth," thus distinguished, is increased by increasing the abundance of things useful to mankind, even going so far as to reduce their exchange value to zero, like pure air, the most useful of all. The "assets" of an individual or association of individuals are increased by limiting their supply so that they will have exchange value, or bargaining power, in commanding other things in exchange, and especially, in modern life, commanding "money" in exchange. Modern business is conducted on the basis of assets, that is, scarcity of wealth, and not on the abundance of wealth according to Smith. With assets one can give security for loans of money, but the security is worthless if the supply of "wealth" is increased so greatly that assets have little or no scarcity value when sold upon the markets for money.

This paradox of wealth and assets is confusing to common sense. But common sense has previously injected unconsciously something that restricts the supply and maintains scarcity value. Common sense injects private property, which is the sovereign power granted to individuals to withhold supply if the exchange value—that is, the scarcity value in terms of money—falls below the cost of production or some other standard deemed reasonable or compensatory. Smith and the classical economists injected "labor" which restricts supply, because the laborer gets tired or his labor power gets exhausted if he tries to produce wealth beyond his limited capacity of performance. But modern machinery, or technology, "produces" far more wealth than ever could have been imagined possible with the limited powers of manual labor which had set the limits to quantity of production at the time of the classical economists. Machinery eliminates fatigue. Smith and early economists thought that the only forces besides labor that restricted supply was monopoly, and monopoly was artificial, whereas the limited capacity of labor owing to fatigue was something quite natural. But private individual property has become private collective property, and too, this seems quite natural in restricting supply, because corporations are personified as big individuals.

The twentieth century economics of collective action practically begins with the closing of the frontiers at the end of the nineteenth century. Malthus and the economists considered that the closing of the frontiers was merely a matter of migration of population into new lands. But the frontier is closed by ownership and land speculation in advance of population. Formerly labor leaders, like John Mitchell, when their unions were defeated, could move west and find employment or could take up "free land" under the homestead acts. Mitchell tried it when his miners' unions were defeated in Illinois. But he found the western land occupied and labor unemployed. He had to return to the east and then became the organizer of nearly half a million workers throughout the whole nation.

I, myself, saw the closing of the western frontier in the year 1894 by land ownership when I stopped overnight at Indianapolis with "Kelly's Army," from California, of high-grade mechanics who were then on the way to the capitol at Washington to appeal for unemployment relief. I compare this visit in 1894 with the effort of the unemployed from Oklahoma to move to California in 1937, as pictured in Steinbeck's *The Grapes of Wrath*.

In a similar way the large corporations of the twentieth century are the outcome of increased bargaining power that comes with this closing of the frontier. These corporations were formerly approved because they promoted efficiency; with closed frontiers, now they promote scarcity. Even the world frontiers were closed by conquest and private ownership in Africa at the end of the nineteenth century.

# Chapter vii

## *EFFICIENCY*

———◆———

Abundance and efficiency are the opposites of scarcity and assets, but the distinctions may be covered up in the dubious meanings of common words. The word "labor," for example, had three different meanings, according to its different relations, not distinguished by Adam Smith but distinguished by later economists. Does the word mean the quantity of human labor which the owner of money or property can *command* in exchange, that is, the purchasing power of money or property over labor? Or does it mean the quantity of labor *embodied* in the product which labor creates out of the materials and forces of nature, that is, a metaphysical idea of output or efficiency? Adam Smith in 1770 used both interpretations. In addition, he offered a third meaning, the amount of one's own labor which a person can "save" by imposing the labor upon somebody else, termed *opportunity,* or choice of alternatives. Smith described and used the three meanings as though they were the same, and the three are in use today. Various schools of economists, such as the capitalists, communists, anarchists, fascists, unionists, and protectionists, in succeeding years, have split on these different meanings or combinations of them.

These three meanings of labor were different meanings of value. In the present century they may be distinguished as *efficiency, scarcity* and *opportunity*; which, in terms of *value*, are known as "use value," "scarcity value," and "opportunity value" or "opportunity cost."

These several splits in meanings of both labor and value occurred at the time of, or immediately preceding, revolutionary wars, which seem to have been the germinating periods of origin and revision of the science of political economy. The first was the French Revolution, 1789 to 1815, the period of the classical economists, Smith, Ricardo, and Malthus. The next period included the revolutionary wars of 1848 in Europe, and 1861 in the United States, the period of Karl Marx, the communist, and Henry C. Carey, the American protectionist. The third period includes the revolutionary wars of the present century, the era of Mussolini, Hitler, American corporations, and labor unions.

The first split on meanings of labor and value occurred between Malthus and Ricardo, forty years after Smith, although all three were known as "classical economists." Malthus used the meaning of "commanded labor," which, for him, was the exchange value, or money value, of labor and labor's products on the markets. Ricardo rejected that meaning on the ground that "money wages," or monetary prices, were only a "nominal value" of labor and labor's products. It turns out today that this "nominal value," in terms of money, is the very *real* value of prices and wages, which is the "scarcity value" about which the conflicts of "capital' and "labor" are focused.

But for Ricardo, who was followed by Marx, the communist, "real value" was "embodied labor," the amount of value which the exertions and fatigue of labor bestowed upon the materials and forces of nature in producing useful commodities. This amount of value was the amount of "use value" of commodities, measured not by money, but by tons, pounds, gallons, or other physical units of measurement, all of which were only different units for measuring the *one real value*, the quantity of labor embodied in the different commodities or the efficiency of labor.

This efficiency meaning of labor, taken over by Karl Marx in 1848, is today the official meaning of labor in Russia. The same meaning of "embodied labor" was taken over in America in 1911 by the mechanical engineer Frederick W. Taylor, the founder of so-called "scientific management." [1] Taylor created what I consider the correct or at least the most usable of all the different meanings of "efficiency," that is, output per man-hour regardless

[1] See his *Principles of Scientific Management,* New York and London, Harper and Brothers, 1911; also R. F. Hoxie, *Scientific Management and Labor,* New York and London, D. Appleton and Company, 1915.

of money value. I, with him and his followers, visited many of the establishments where his system had been installed, and I made use of it in installing the program of unemployment compensation in the Chicago clothing market in 1925. I had claimed that the prevention of unemployment by the employers would increase both profit and wages by increasing the efficiency of the industry, without cost to anybody. The auditor of the largest firm compiled for me from his records, over a period of years, the "output" of clothing compared with the "input" of labor, that is, the total number of hours worked by the four or five thousand employees of the firm. The record showed that, in the course of five years, including one year of the unemployment prevention plan, the output per average man-hour of men and women workers had increased 100 per cent.

The representatives of the employers claimed that the increase in efficiency was due to management. They had introduced all of the short cuts in shop organization and machinery advocated by Taylor and more. The employers' claim was true. Fatigue had actually been reduced, partly by shortening the hours of labor by the day and week, while increasing the rate of wages per hour. The representatives of the union claimed that these laborsaving schemes could not have been introduced or made effective had not the union cooperated with management in the investigation and elimination of all the various restrictions of output which the laborers or the management had previously been practicing. This also was true. They cooperated because they now recognized that they were "citizens of the concern," and the success of the firm in meeting competition meant more steady employment and more annual earnings for them.

I concluded that any effort to measure the amount of "merit" to be assigned to management, compared with the amount of merit to be assigned to the labor union, for bringing about that increase of efficiency was not worth while, and indeed would tend invidiously to defeat the main purpose of increasing the joint efficiency of management and labor, that of increasing both profits and wages. A part of the efficiency of management had been the adoption of this very scheme of unemployment prevention at the request of the union.

Since efficiency is joint efficiency, I proceeded to develop, with the help of Taylor's disciples, the foregoing idea of a "managerial transaction," instead of the isolated idea of "management," and to tie it up with the whole legal and economic situation which, with the growth of huge industry, had apparently separated management from labor. Efficiency itself can be measured, as Taylor had demonstrated. It is a ratio of output to input, which I name *man-hour* efficiency, to distinguish it from the *dollar* efficiency, which is not efficiency but is the relative scarcity of bargaining transactions.

How do we distinguish and measure this double meaning of efficiency, which goes back to the dispute between Malthus and Ricardo? [1] The distinction between man-hour efficiency and dollar efficiency is maintained by new terms of activity introduced into the science, namely, the ratio of *input* to *output*, an idea taken from the mechanical engineers like Frederick W. Taylor. This is contrasted with the ratio of *income* to *outgo*, that is the money income relative to the *money outgo*, which measures relative alienations of scarcities, that is, relative bargaining power, or purchasing power.

The distinctions of output and income are related to that between wealth and assets. An increase of efficiency, that is, an increase of output per man-hour, is an increase of *wealth* in the form of *use value*; but an increase of money *prices* or decreases of money *wages* is an increase of assets for the employer and may be a decrease of wealth by restriction of output. To beat down wages paid, and to uphold prices received, often described as "business efficiency," is an increase of profits and assets, but is not an increase of real wealth for the nation.

These distinctions indicate the century-old confusion that arose from the two meanings of labor as efficiency and scarcity, or output and income, used but not distinguished by Adam Smith in 1776. Business efficiency, the increase of assets by bargaining power, was given the same meaning as technological, or engineer-

---

[1] This argument was developed in greater detail in my *Legal Foundations of Capitalism*, New York, The Macmillan Co., 1924; and *Institutional Economics*, New York, The Macmillan Co., 1934.

ing, efficiency, the increase of wealth by productive efficiency, the one measured by dollars, the other by man-hours. Yet the two meanings were made identical by the long line of classical economists who followed Ricardo, unmindful of the distinction already emphasized by Malthus at the beginning of the century.

The third meaning of labor, as "labor saved," made identical by Smith with the other two, did not get its independent significance until developed by Henry C. Carey, the American economist, contemporary of Karl Marx in 1848. It became the foundation of the protective tariff policy adopted by the victors in the American Civil War of 1861, and also the meaning adopted by Hitler when he started his nazistic revolution in 1933 on the banner of *brot und arbeit*, food and employment, for the people of Germany.

This third meaning of "saved" labor, made identical by Smith with "embodied" labor and "commanded" labor, was the labor saved for self by imposing it upon others, as when I hire a laborer to dig a ditch instead of digging it myself.

But before the time of Carey, at the middle of the nineteenth century and seventy-five years after Adam Smith, the inventions of the steam engine and machinery had greatly increased the efficiency output of British labor. The British capitalists, by underselling, could prevent the introduction of machinery into America, if America retained the free trade doctrines of the British classical economists.

Carey, therefore, used the "labor saved" meaning of Smith as the meaning of value, but instead of labor saved for one individual by imposing it on another individual, it was the labor that would be saved for the American people by imposing it upon machinery and steam power, if protected by a tariff tax against British imports. This meaning caused a decided change in the meaning of value as now defined by Carey. Instead of Ricardo's "real value" determined by the amount of labor exertion "embodied" at the *preceding* time of actual production, the value of all products becomes the much less but present "cost of *reproduction*," by substituting machinery and steam power for labor in the present.

This was a decidedly optimistic turn to the meaning of labor and the meaning of value because of increased productivity of machinery and, on this account was opposed by the followers of the classical economics of Ricardo. This became the official meaning of labor and value in the United States, for it was the meaning intended by the advocates of the protective tariff, and also by the courts of the United States, in all calculations of the present value of public utilities, such as railways and similar enterprises requiring large amounts of physical equipment. The value of these properties would be, not their cost of *production* in the past, but their cost of *reproduction* in the present.

Now it was not *labor cost,* as measured by man-hours, the meaning retained by the communists—it had become *money cost,* the very different scarcity meaning of business *assets* instead of *wealth* of nations.

Lastly, the much larger increase of fixed capital, or "durable goods," and the use of other forces of nature, such as electricity and chemistry, made apparent that it was the "embodied" forces of physical nature, rather than the embodied human labor power, that determined the whole capitalist system and the change from individuals to corporations, labor unions, and political parties. New changes of words and their meanings came to the front. The "real" meaning of labor became the opportunity to get employment in face of the ownership of these huge capital equipments by corporations. While Carey and the protectionists had meant an increase of efficiency by the substitution of machinery, the miserable paradox of wealth and assets came to be the political and economic issue, and with it the problem of obtaining employment by equality of opportunity in times of prosperity and depression, rather than the problem of efficiency or the problem of bargaining power over prices or wages. Efficiency was no longer a problem, if the man-hour output of labor since the beginning of the nineteenth century had increased eightfold as estimated by Carl Snyder, and the equally probable increase of fourfold in efficiency rate of output in the 40 years since 1900. This is, of course, the paradox of the capitalist system. The optimism of enormously increased opportunities, when output per man-hour is now probably ten times as great as it was a hundred years ago, is frustrated by the unemployment and part-time employment that forbids access to this magnified equipment and tenfold greater efficiency.

Perhaps it is because another great change in the labor theories of value has occurred, the change from the labor of the past, embodied and projected *forward* into present commodities, to the labor and efficiency and bargaining of the future, capitalized *backward* into a present worth of stocks and bonds. This is the credit system taking the place of the primitive labor system. We name it "futurity."

# Chapter viii

## *FUTURITY*

———◆———

Economic science began with the study of what had happened in the past, then moved to what is now happening in the present; finally it is concerned with the hopes and fears of what may be expected to happen in future time.

Mathematically defined, "the present" is a moving *point* of time between the outgoing past and the incoming future. Psychologically, "the present" is an *instant* of time when feelings of pleasure and pain occur, modified by memory of the past and expectations of the future. Institutionally considered, however, the present is limited by the dates of concluding the negotiations of the several transactions which commit participants and subordinates to a line of behavior in the future.

The three stages of time are embraced in three different theories of value constructed by different schools of economists. The classical economists, followed by the communists, began with the exertions of labor in the production of *wealth* in past time, which gave "embodied" value to the products in the present. The hedonistic, or pleasure-pain economists, began with the pleasures of consumption of wealth in the present, which create the *demand* without which the products would not have their present market value. The institutional economists begin with the legislative, administrative, and judicial decisions of both governmental and private collective action on which depend the *security* of present expectations of future profits, investments, jobs, and contracts. Without this security of expectations, there would be little or no present value, present enterprise, present transactions, or present employment. Value is *present worth* of future net income.

No school of economists was clear cut on these time dimensions.

All of them took past, present, and future for granted, without investigation, just as time was taken for granted in the physical sciences before the incoming of recent theories of "relativity." One reason why early economists did not separate out future time for special investigation in their theories of value was the assumption, taken from the physical sciences, that cause *precedes* effect. Labor precedes its product; sensations precede action; scarcity and want precede effort and satisfaction. But here is an *effect* that *precedes* its *cause*. Philosophers distinguish the two perhaps as "end purpose" and "instrumental purpose," "reason and consequence." Without too much philosophizing we investigate their transactions, instead of their individual pleasures and pains, as well as the expectations which they offer to each other in order to induce each other to act. This is negotiational psychology.

Furthermore, early economists were *laissez faire* as regards government. They thought government was repressive and obnoxious. We also investigate how government acts to lead people into a supposedly better economic administration. We find that people act in exactly opposite ways during periods of depression and prosperity. Not logic, but fear and hope are fundamental. People act to enlarge valuations in periods of hope and to depress valuations in periods of fear.

Their reasons are expected consequences and the immediate alternative opportunities. This, again, is negotiational psychology instead of rational or hedonistic psychology—it is "volitional psychology," or "will power." Its instrument is signs and language. It is the psychology of persuasion, coercion, duress, command, obedience, fear or hope; the truly behavioristic psychology of business, of labor, of politicians, of propagandists, of legislatures, of executives, or courts. Its simplification in one general term is futurity. The credit system is its institutional creation.

Different features of futurity may be mentioned and also the dates of their introduction into economic science. Debts and credits are aspects of futurity. Clement Juglar of France was the first, in 1862,[1] to investigate debt exhaustively; his investigation was in

[1] See *Encyclopedia of the Social Sciences*, New York, The Macmillan Co., 1932–35, Vol. VIII, p. 469.

terms of speculative activity, not in terms of the physical analogy of a manufactured commodity. A debt, in British and American law, is "incorporeal property," which was made "negotiable" in the seventeenth century so that it could be bought and sold like the physical commodity, metallic money. Juglar made debt the economic base of the optimism and pessimism of the English economists. For them, however, the allowance for time was not economics but psychology. But now it is economics, through the inclusion of debts. A debt has two stages in time, distinguishable as the date of "closing of negotiations," and the date of "closing the transaction."

The negotiations are closed at a definite point of time in law, say, September 1, 1936, 3 p.m., which is "the present." At that date the rights and duties of the contract begin, which are "the future." These are to continue until the transaction itself is closed by the performance of the last of all the obligations created by closing the negotiations. Two obligations, or "commitments," are created: a duty of performance and a duty of payment, which in economics and law are debts. The seller of the commodity undertakes to deliver it within an immediate or deferred future, a debt of performance. The buyer undertakes to "deliver" the money, or other customary equivalent, at a future date or dates, a debt of payment. When the last of these obligations is fulfilled, the transaction is closed. Until they are closed they constitute each a rule of action, in view of which the debtors must hire laborers and must subordinate their other economic activities. Within that period, which may be one day or a hundred years, the two debts are negotiable or assignable, whereby the rights and duties are transferred by negotiation to others.

The negotiability or assignability of these rights and obligations means their salability, and this attribute gives to them exchange-value, which has come to be distinguished, in American decisions, as a special case of "intangible property." Other intangible properties, whose present value depends on their expected exchange value or expected income, are such as patents, good will, trade-marks, corporate franchises, various rights "to do business." All are "intangible," because all are cases of futurity. Even the so-called "corporeal property"—the ownership of a tangible thing, like land or an auto—is also "intangible" because it means a present right to sell or rent the thing in the future for money or its equivalent in exchange, which could not be done if one did not have "the right." In all cases the present value depends on expected scarcity, which is economic futurity, and this is property.

Other aspects of futurity may be mentioned, such as risk, security, profit, interest, savings, or investment. Risk had always been assumed in economic science as true for everybody, whether manufacturer, laborer, or investor. But it was not separated out for investigation until corporation finance had made the distinction between stocks and bonds.

This separation required a distinction to be made between two dimensions of time, a "flow" of time and a "lapse" of time. Each has practical significance only with reference to future time. A "flow" is an expected *succession* of events, the expectation of *profits*; a "lapse" is an expected *interval* between two events, the expectation of *interest* on investments. All future events are risky because they are unknown, but the stockholder takes more risks than the bondholder, and names it profit or loss, because he takes what is left after the bondholder is paid. His are the risks of the "equity." He gets "profit" in the form of dividends; the bondholder gets "interest," secured by contract as a prior claim upon the assets. The distinction is between "venture," or equity capital, and "secured," or privileged capital. Each is savings; each is "investment" of savings. Stockholders and bondholders are both capitalists, and both invest their savings. Both take risks, but the stockholders insure the risk of the bondholders to the extent of their investments as stockholders. Were it not for the governmental scheme of "limited liability" for stockholders, there would be no investments of savings in corporations adequate for large-scale industry.

The same is true of a farm or other business, not incorporated. The mortgagee has a prior claim on the farm; the owner has the "equity"—whatever is left. The owner's "profit" depends on the "margins" of what is left in the succession of risky transactions. The lender's "interest" is guaranteed during the interval between a present and a future event.

Having analyzed the matter in the intricacies of corporation-finance, the modern economist shifts the analysis back to the primitive farmer or manufacturer for whom the early economists did not find it necessary to make the distinctions. But the time factor is exactly opposite to that of the older economists. Early economists began with the past and traced the origins of the present out of the past. Economists now begin with the future and read it back into the present.

One of the facts for economics is the past intentions of the parties to the transaction. What did they agree to do or not to do? Courts of law have developed methods of investigating this negotiational psychology. One of their devices is in the distinction between "law" and "fact." The facts are ascertained by a jury who are ordinary humble men and therefore "reasonable." What would a reasonable man have intended to do in assenting to that agreement under the "then" circumstances? It is a method of comparative psychology. The economist makes similar investigations of negotiational psychology in general. I have sometimes made similar investigations in interpreting collective bargaining agreements and in the negotiations themselves leading up to such an agreement. I formulate certain "psychologies," the business man's psychology, the socialistic psychology, the trade unionist psychology. What do they want to do? Why do they differ in their psychologies? How can they negotiate an agreement under the circumstances? It is a "technique" of negotiational psychology which I investigate in successful arbitrators, mediators, business managers, executives, and in politicians.

Negotiational psychology is often mistaken in its calculations of the future. It may be too optimistic, too pessimistic, or too ignorant. Yet it is controlling and controllable. In feudal times domination was the psychology of physical force. At the opposite extreme in the highly developed credit system of voluntary agreements, with the modern emerging monopolistic central bank or reserve system and its variety of "controls," it is through the negotiational psychology of sellers, buyers, bankers, that their transactions, prices, and voluntary rules of action for the future are controlled, more or less, for good or ill.

Thus I make negotiational psychology a part of the foundation of economics. It always has been "social psychology." But that term is too broad for use in economics. When reduced to a mental tool of investigation usable in economics, it is negotiational psychology which is the psychology of transactions. There is difficulty in constructing the idea for those brought up on the individualistic psychology of pains, pleasures, wants, satisfactions, or dreams and psychoanalysis. Yet negotiational psychology is the psychology of courts of law, of business men, of legislative bodies, of all collective action where it is necessary to agree upon prices or wages that will be paid in the future, upon deliveries that will be performed, or upon future rules of action that will be followed.

Negotiational psychology can be seen actively at work and can be investigated in any bargaining, managerial, or rationing transaction. I name it *objective* psychology instead of the subjective psychology of pleasure and pain. It is the psychology of language, of duress, coercion, persuasion, command, obedience, propaganda. It is the psychology of physical, economic, and moral "power," the truly "behavioristic" psychology of economics in preparing for the unknown future.

# Chapter ix

## *CUSTOM*

———◆———

Custom is such similarity of behavior as may be expected to continue almost unchanged in the future. Individuals must adjust themselves to that similarity, simply because it has become habitual and not because it is logical, rational, or intelligent. This is the distinction which we make between "simplified" logical assumptions and "habitual" customary assumptions. The two kinds of assumptions are distinguished in our analysis, but they are united by further analysis under the name of "relativities." When collective action in the form of corporations, unions, or political parties becomes habitual, it becomes a custom, and any logical analysis that leads to the elimination of custom is likely to lead to a revolutionary breakup of the ties that hold society together, and to be unenforceable.

The attempt to establish, for example, a minimum wage by law for women higher than, or even as high as, the customary level for women, or to establish a universal prohibitive liquor law against practices that are customary, breaks down because juries will not convict, or witnesses will not testify. Even a sovereign dictatorship would hesitate to introduce revolutionary changes in custom.

In the nineteenth century, along with the idea that "society" was a myth and had no actual existence because only individuals lived and existed, came the related doctrine that society had passed from the Age of Custom to the Age of Contract. But contract is also a custom—for example the "custom of merchants" in enforcing agreements between individuals through their guild courts; and the modern joint stock corporations exist only because the necessary contracts are habitually enforced by the courts in cases of dispute. The fact that disputes are not brought before the courts on points where the expected decisions are known beforehand is itself an adjustment to the custom of the judicial branch of government.

Customs change in the course of repetition of practices, which thereby become habitual. The modern meaning of "money" for example, as bank checks payable on demand, not in metallic money, or bullion, but in a bookkeeping unit of account enforceable at a court of law, is a new custom, and now becomes habitual under the new meaning of money. The whole of the new credit system is administered upon the acceptance of this custom of bank checks to a point of compulsion. Today no person can continue in business who always demands metallic money or habitually refuses to accept lawful bank checks as full payment and release of debts, as was formerly customary.

The compulsory character of custom differs at times in extent of area, and in the degree, or kind, of compulsion upon individuals. These differences have required distinctions to be made between practices, usages, customs, and common law. In all cases these differences have the similar significance that individuals must adjust themselves to what others are doing, regardless of logic, reason, or self-interest. But they differ in other respects.

The term "practices" is usually restricted to the customs of a particular establishment, different from those of other establishments. One who patronizes a particular establishment, say a cafeteria, must adopt the practices of that establishment, or pay an extra cost for additional or for unaccustomed services of the cafeteria. The employees must likewise adjust themselves to the practices of the establishment or work elsewhere. The courts, in cases of dispute, would enforce reasonable practices, as found on investigation, and so these private practices, if deemed reasonable, become a part of the common law.

"Usages" are similar practices of all competing establishments, such that individual customers or employees have no worth-while alternatives by going elsewhere. These usages, if enforced by some kind of a tribunal, such as the arbitration committee of a stock exchange, become compulsory and add significance to the word "custom," which takes the place of practices or mere usages. It was this "custom of merchants," enforced by the merchants' guilds of the Middle Ages, that were taken over and enforced by the courts of law. This enforcement of "customs" constituted the "common law" of negotiable instruments in its early stages. A similar common law method of creating "judge made" law by "finding" it already in existence, as a custom, converts the customs of chambers of commerce, and the like, if deemed reasonable, into the common law enforced by the courts. The same practice goes on in arbitration boards, which are constantly establishing new customs by new decisions in settling disputes in the field of employment.

Eventually this creation of new law may be taken over by the legislature, but even then the legislature entrusts the administration to courts or commissions which go on to modify the statutes through decisions in settlement of disputes. When these decisions are accepted generally, they become the still further extension of custom and the common law.

# Summary

## PART TWO

———◆———

We have considered five so-called "simplified assumptions" as starting points in the investigation of economic problems. These assumptions would usually be called "fundamental principles," or "elementary principles," or "fundamentals." They are named assumptions because they are mental tools for purposes of investigation. But even if called "principles," they do not exist in the world about. A "principle" is only an assumed similarity of activities and has no existence except in the mind of him who constructs or borrows the principle as an instrument with which he selects what he considers to be the facts worth while.

These presuppositions become universal in the minds of all who contemplate the economic complexities which confront themselves and others. If economics is approached as a science of human beings, instead of a physical or biological science, then these very presuppositions, and even obsessions, are the first subject matter of investigation. Let them be considered, however, as elementary assumptions with which human beings unconsciously or habitually guide their economic activities. Then it is possible to treat them as mere similarities and to use them as our own consciously constructed mental tools, simplified as much as possible, and then recombined into thousands of special cases which we are called upon to investigate.

The first observation to make is that the simplification of an assumption is wholly artificial and designedly so, just as a spade or a mowing machine is artificial. Being artificial, the similarities do not exist independently, but are picked out for separate investigation as though they did exist independently. Furthermore, even though we have five similarities, each is in itself a complexity having several divergent applications according to the points of contact where they infringe on other simplifications. Scarcity, in one of its diversities, is property, and property is one of the diversities of sovereignty. Efficiency counteracts scarcity. Futurity applies mainly to the credit system and to contracts. Custom signifies futurity coupled with security of expectations.

Each individual, each race of individuals, each corporation or labor union is a special case where only special investigation can ascertain and explain the relative predominance of the several simplified assumptions which serve as clues or mental tools to enable the investigator to find his way. About as far as an assumption can go is to correlate things by various "relativities," and then to expect that there may be individuals, races, or peoples who will remain primitive, like oysters, and others who will acquire understanding and initiative to move forward and formulate ideas that may work in the future. No method of investigation, however scientific, can have the answers to the puzzles of human progress. Ultimately progress rests with the human will.

# PART THREE

## Relativities

# Introduction

The modern theory of relativity has superseded the older ideas in physics of the absolute distinctions between time and space, and between the investigator and the materials investigated; it is also urgent that we see the relativities in social action and investigations. This does not require that we abandon the insights of earlier economists who have worked with absolute or nonrelative definitions and categories. But it does require that we broaden our analysis to incorporate the study of the relativities of individuality, ownership, time, and judgment.

The individual is a different person according to the nature of the concerns or transactions in which he participates. Paul Waring transformed the street cleaners of New York City from dirty, slovenly, Tammany Hall "ward heelers" into upright, independent, respected "sanitary" workers through organizing them into a union and providing them with white uniforms. The individual is a system of relations, and changes with the collective action of which he is part and product.

As with individuals, so with things, instead of assuming that all valuable things are owned we need to study the processes of ownership as well as of production, that is, private property and economic power. Again this is a field of degrees of power, of the relative equality or inequality of the participants in economic transactions. Public policy and administration in America proceed by "reasonable" conciliation of interests in terms of a multiplicity of purposes, rather than by the dictatorial triumph of one interest or purpose over all others.

Social affairs are also relative to time. Everything I have taken up in my investigations seems to have had its character determined by what went before or by something that came after.

The human mind is an active participating mind—with the power of giving direction to events, within limits, by turning its ability to the strategic or controlling factor. Consequently the thoughts, ideas, and investigations of social scientists are a part of the materials of their own investigations. This determines the necessity both for investigating the similarities and differences within experience, and for devising ways of checking upon the habitual assumptions of the investigator.

It follows too that the unit of investigation depends both upon the purpose of the investigation and the nature of the probem.

Out of the requirements of these relativities we have found the going concern with its constituent transactions to be fruitful units of investigations. We conclude that the going concern, as developed by the courts, is an adequate and relevant unit of investigation in economics. We were searching for a unit that would be more appropriate than the mechanistic, atomistic, or organic analogies from the physical sciences. For Adam Smith, individuals were like atoms; Karl Marx made the whole of society his unit of investigation. Others followed out mechanical or organic analogies. But what is needed in economics is some unit which has parts and can be analyzed; one that has been the deliberate construction of the human mind and will. It is also necessary to be able to show the combination of degrees of power exercised by the human will in relations among persons and in the choice of alternatives. This permits the analysis of judgment of valuation, wherein the various factors are given their due weights, rather than the acceptance of a determination even with multiple causation.

As I have studied practical problems it has always seemed to me that the life-and-death struggle of making a living and trying to get rich was at the bottom of all other problems. Out of this basic struggle come political parties, constitutional governments, labor unions, corporations, and so on. Always I worked out some administrative task, but the administration grew out of the underlying struggle for making a living. Consequently I have never been able to think of the various social sciences as separate fields of history, political science, law, economics, ethics, and administration. What we need is some way of working through the whole complex of problems that grow out of this fundamental struggle.

For these reasons I have worked out over the years the analysis of the three transactions. This is the smallest unit we can find which permits the analysis of all dimensions of the human will in action, with the correlated social relations. In distinguishing the various transactions, we have attempted to correlate the similarities and differences found in analyses of pricing (bargaining) with those discovered in the analyses of industrial efficiency, in ways which also permit correlative investigation of the rationing practiced by industrial and political governments.

The study of discretionary human activity in making a living must be as broad as the whole field of the adult, sane, legally recognized human will—both individual and collective. Within this broad field we need analytical tools for investigating the whole array of relativities which find their most inclusive integration in judgments of value.

# Chapter x

## *METHODS OF INVESTIGATION*

———◆———

### 1. SIMILARITIES AND DIFFERENCES

Isaac Newton, nearly three hundred years ago, conceived a possible similarity between objects falling to the ground and the moon swinging around the earth. He spent twenty-five years investigating that supposed similarity, thereby inventing a new mathematics and a method of investigation by comparisons. Millions of people had seen the two motions but had not thought of inquiring whether they were similar, much less had persisted in such an investigation. For this reason their observations were "empirical," instead of theoretical or even practical. They did not set up an hypothesis of similarity for investigation and agreement in the midst of the differences plainly visible.

Newton's similarity was the simple hypothesis that both the objects and the moon were falling toward the earth. His twenty-five years were filled with guesses, theories, hypotheses, mathematics, and ended with the laws of motion. These so-called "laws" were simply similarities of motion amid diversities, and as such, became the method of the physical sciences and of the inventions of mechanical engineers.

The modern practical scientific process of the engineer can be resolved into three main components discovered by successive generations of theoretical scientists, inventors, patentees, mechanics, and business executives, all of them on a search for similarities in the midst of nature's millions of diversities. These three components are *facts, purpose,* and *theory.*

The *facts* are activities whose relations to other events have been established by investigation. Facts are the outcomes of settled questions, such as statistics. The *purpose* is control of nature's apparently blind activities. These blind forces or activities are to be directed for the purpose of constructing aids and substitutes for human labor, for other natural materials, and for increasing profits. The *theories* are the hypotheses which guide the search for similarities of activities. The theories are tested or proved by control of the diversities through control of a few similar activities.

Indeed, under the name efficiency, in Chapter VII, we have included the materials of the whole of the physical sciences started by Sir Isaac Newton, in so far as promoted or obstructed by modern governments, corporations, and labor unions. These operate by laws of property, by profit-seeking, and by regulations and restrictions of output.

It is this very commonplace principle of similarity and difference that leads to both the separation and the correlation of all the sciences in their practical applications for human activity and understanding. There is a big difference whether the participants are able to recognize and discern the similarities or are confused by the multitude of differences; likewise, whether the participants are able to discern differences and distinctions when and where they exist, or are blindly accepting alleged similarities. The rather small number of individuals who search for similarities and for significant differences are the active, constructive, inventive leaders. The large number befuddled by differences, unable to discover the similarities, or unable to recognize real differences, become the passive subservient followers.

In 1901 I was invited to sit in with a joint conference of mine owners and union representatives of four midwestern states who were negotiating a labor contract for the central soft coal field.[1] They were bargaining over the terms of the contract, and the conference became deadlocked. Each side then appointed an equal number of representatives to a committee of sixteen which was instructed to reach an agreement. This committee of sixteen in turn appointed two operators and two miners who worked out the terms of the agreement which was later submitted to the large

[1] For an analysis in terms of constitutional government in industry, see J. R. Commons, "A New Way of Settling Labor Disputes," *American Monthly Review of Reviews,* March 1901, Vol. 23, p. 328.

committee and then to the joint conference as a whole. The report of the small subcommittee was adopted by both groups. Subsequently, during the life of this agreement, laborers were hired by the mine operators in the four states only according to the working rules adopted at the conference. I then called this procedure "collective bargaining," but following out the distinctions made in transactions, I found that there were significant differences within the transactions which followed.

The original agreement reached by the joint conference was a collectively bargained transaction. It was a bargaining transaction with the participants meeting as legal equals; their wills met in the terms agreed upon. But the object of their agreement was really the working rules that bound both operators and laborers in their dealings over the terms of employment for the entire coal field during the life of this contract. Both the mine owners and the labor union bound themselves to follow the joint or collective will of this agreement.

Subsequently, all the particular labor contracts with individual mine operators made throughout the central field were partially rationed transactions. The joint conference had agreed upon rates of pay, hours of work, volume of work allowed each miner, and so on. These agreements were in the form of working rules, but they were rules enforced upon the whole field for the purpose of equalizing competition. Actually the head of the miners' union, John Mitchell, was authorized to ration out the economic opportunities by differential terms of employment according to the agreement of the joint conference. The conferees agreed upon working rules for the rationing transactions. These working rules are quantitative in the sense that they refer to the relevant performance in measurable terms—man-hours, rates of pay, wages per ton, and so forth.

In similar fashion, I see bargaining transactions giving way at every turn to rationing transactions in our modern American capitalism of corporations, holding companies, and labor unions. In these great integrated concerns, materials in all states of fabrication pass from one "company" to another without bargaining—that is, by rationing.

Whatever bargaining occurred at the individual mines was carried on within the terms of the joint conference agreement. Actually, then, the bargaining and rationing transactions were simultaneous and complementary in the hiring of the workers. Neither aspect of the complex problem can be ignored without omitting an essential part of the activity. The similarity is the transaction, the meeting of the wills. The difference between these transactions and strictly bargaining transactions was that the local union representatives and operators were free to negotiate only within narrow limits. In the broader limits and terms the local participants only executed the will of the superior body whose creation they had previously authorized. This significant difference is almost inevitably overlooked if the transaction is looked upon solely as a "price" in a price system, and there is a vast difference between a "bargained" price and a "rationed" price. The difference rests in the way the human wills meet, and in the working rules that make up the respective implied social organizations.

In like manner, viewing the whole economy, we may conclude that the profit motive is the strategic "similarity" in all production relations under capitalism. The differences in size, capital holdings, negotiation, etc. are ever present between one employer and the next. One may hire a dozen employees, another a thousand or more employees; but both depend upon the labor power. Both produce for the market, where each negotiates and transacts for his own commodities and interests. Both are opposed to dictatorships, and both the small and the large producer are opposed to coercion or any interference on the part of outsiders, be it the state or the labor union. Both seek profits. Yet to understand profits we need to recognize differences in profits—differences in the meaning and use of the term. Thus, we find a *rate* of profit, a profit *yield*, a *margin* of profit, and a profit *share*.

The same principle of similarity is applicable to the labor unions. Though each labor union may differ in some respects from all others, labor unions as a whole serve a utilitarian purpose for their members, as the corporations have a purpose in serving their owners. It is the labor union that negotiates and engages in transactions with the corporation employer. One desires a space in this world as much as the other. It is both in the broad and in the narrow field of activity where we must seek the similarities among the myriad of differences.

The differences must also be sought for. Not all factors are reconcilable, and differences between one activity and another are many. Wages and profits are not identical. Neither is large-scale mass production similar in all respects to domestic hand-tool production. A farmer is just as much a producer and desires as high a standard of living as the wage worker, but the tools, the resources, and the skills that each employ are different.

Various differences exist between labor unions and corporations, but the differences in each do not necessarily mean that the corporations must resort to coercive methods to impose their will on the labor unions, or vice versa. The employment of persuasion would sometimes eliminate the friction often created by coercion, and win the support of those groups and interests whose services are essential in productive enterprise.

This method of searching for significant similarities and differences in activities may be properly called the comparative method of reasoning. This is in contrast with the deductive methods usually employed in orthodox economic theorizing. The first is the method of investigation to isolate similarities. The second is the method of generalizing—arriving at universals.

The beginnings of all science consist in a few universal similarities from which by deductive reasoning all special cases are derived. Then follows the discovery of differences which accumulate until the science splits into specialized details; or multiplies its complexities until it becomes unmanageable in its verification of facts, or in its practical application as a whole. At this stage a new formulation of general principles, or universal similarities, becomes imperative.

The deductive method is characteristic of the classical or orthodox economics which rested upon the isolated assumption of self-interest. Complexities are eliminated because a single assumption is isolated. This method finds the single cause in the assumption regardless of the time factor.

The conflict between deductive and comparative reasoning becomes evident when economists are required to work with public administrators—in the administrative commissions or action agencies. The economist and the administrator may be speaking different languages—each may be appropriate in its own field, but the economist may start with a single assumption and reason deductively that all individual cases are similar. The administrator starts with all circumstances and must give appropriate weights to each in the volitional result. The economist's similarities may be only analogies, i.e., incomplete similarities. In recognizing similarities and differences, it is primarily the purpose of administrators to formulate rules and laws that will benefit all parties concerned. The investigation of similarities and differences in public administration and public policy results in directing attention to particular conflicts and problems. This gives a limited purpose in administration instead of a general purpose covering the unlimited variety of industries, individuals, and collective acts. In this way the tasks become more favorable for the limited capacities and limited factual knowledge of either theorists or participants. An adequate theory simplifies the problem by focusing attention upon the strategic similarities.

In my own experience, I have studied not only the available relevant facts and statistics, but also the divergent points of view of the individuals who collect and report the facts and statistics. Then by getting the parties together in conference, I have found they were forced by necessity of action to reach an agreement. In this way they reached a kind of "weighted average" or balanced emphasis of individual viewpoints. The theories of the participants served as guides to workable rules of action for the circumstances of time and place, but in the negotiations the progress was made by the comparative method of searching for similar or common ground amid the multitude of differences.

## 2. WORKING RULES

Working rules are the way in which the management or administration of collective action guides the acts of subordinate individuals. There is a hierarchy of collective action, and history reveals how it came about. If economic science had started with corporations and unions instead of individuals, it might have started with the rules of action which apportion to each of the associated individuals the kind and amount of work which each should do, the kind and limits of transactions upon which each should enter, and the shares of the joint product to be apportioned to each. These apportionments are made by the working rules of the concern.

All economic activity goes through the three stages—negotiation, transaction, and administration. A housewife examines the potatoes in the grocer's bin. She is thinking of the qualities, the possible substitutes, her stock on hand, her confidence in what the grocer says. The grocer considers whether she will pay cash or ask for credit until Saturday, and states his price. That is the *negotiational* stage, the stage when valuations are being made.

Then she finally agrees with him on the price, the quantity and quality which she will take. This is the *transactional* stage, when "the wills meet." The meeting of wills lays down a rule of action for each. It is a "commitment," a "contract." Forthwith the grocer packs a peck of potatoes, and she hands him fifty cents. This is the *administrative* stage when the rules of action are carried into effect.

Bargaining is also collective bargaining of various kinds. Representatives of the two sides are arguing, persuading, threatening, talking, evaluating the alternatives—that is, negotiating. Then they either directly, or indirectly through the aid of a mediator, or arbitrator, agree on the terms such as wages, prices, quantities, or qualities—this is the *transactional* stage of economic activity in laying down rules of action for all parties concerned. Then the parties proceed to carry out the agreement by giving orders to subordinates, buying materials, paying the amounts agreed upon, and otherwise administering whatever is needed to execute the agreement. When this *administrative* stage is reached in economic activity, it becomes quantitative and measurable. It is here that the working rules specify measurable performance, just because there must be some way to ascertain whether the commitments made in the transaction are actually carried out. The three stages, negotiation, transaction, and administration, are united being made continuous and consistent by the working rules.

A steel corporation agrees to sell 1,000 tons of rolled steel of specified shapes and qualities at $50 per ton, totaling $50,000. The steel is to be delivered thirty days later at a designated place. The payment is to be made sixty days later at the office of the corporation by means of a check on the purchaser's bank. Two rules of action are laid down by the agreement: one is executed when the corporation hires laborers, sets machinery in motion, employs quality inspectors, etc., in order to execute its debt of performance in thirty days; the other is executed when the purchaser sets his establishment to work, sells agricultural implements, collect funds, builds up an account at his bank, in order to execute his debt of payment in sixty days.

The three stages are separable, namely, the negotiations which are closed by a joint *valuation*; the *transaction* which lays down *rules of action* enforceable at law as to price and quantity, and published in the market reports; the *administration* of two enterprises so as to conform to the rules of action previously laid down at the consummation of the contract. The first is the joint valuation; the second is the transaction; the third is its administration.

A legislature debates a proposed measure of taxation. This is the negotiational or legislative state. It may vote a 2 per cent tax on all property—the transaction stage which is publicly laid out or published in the form of working rules for executives. The assessors value the properties and the treasurers collect the taxes when due. This last procedure is the administrative stage.

Having distinguished these negotiational, transactional, and administrative stages in the latest historical development of economics, we read them back into the activity of the housewife and the grocer, or any other simple transaction that requires only a minute or two of time of the participants.

Herein we may distinguish the hierarchy of parts in the whole activities and the similarity of working rules which make individual action a part of the whole activity. Even where only two individuals agree on a rule of action as to price, quantity, and quality, there are also the customs, the habits, the laws of the land, and the Constitution, all of which are tacitly setting the rules within which the two individuals deal with each other. A rule of action is not like a "law of nature," which supposedly cannot be violated by atoms or electrons. A rule of action often becomes habitual, but seldom is it permanent. More often, however, we find that individuals have that variability known as "free will" within which they operate. On account of the historical and changing economic conditions, a working rule holds true only for the time being or for the changing circumstances to which it happens to fit.

No individual can earn a living or get rich without regard to what other individuals and associations of individuals are doing. Each person is a participant, willingly or unwillingly, in many forms of collective control. He begins as a member of a family which controls minutely the kind and supply of milk, food, clothing, shelter. When family control relaxes, one finds himself participating in other collective controls. In earlier days an individual was, willingly or unwillingly, a member of an all-inclusive church which regulated the details of his individual activities and even was able, by the sanctions of physical power, to control his individual action in getting a living. Since the separation of church and state, beginning in America, the church is left without either physical power or the economic power of property rights, and must depend on its moral power to induce obedience to what the divines may set up as the rules the member is exhorted to observe in getting a living, getting rich, or allowing others to make a living.

Whatever occupation the individual follows, he finds he is subject to some of the rules of collective action. If he rushes violently to get to his job on time, a policeman may take him in charge and he is up against the rules of sovereignty. If he is in the banking business, he finds that the Federal Reserve system is regulating him and his conduct of business. If he is working in a factory, he soon learns that the rules made are strictly enforced, and must be obeyed if one desires to get along with the management or with his fellow workers. If he is a member, or even a nonmember, of a labor union, a farmers' association, a cooperative association, a stock exchange, or any association that might be mentioned, he discovers immediately that there are rules as to what he can, cannot, may or may not, must or must not do, in getting a living or in getting rich. He may think he is free, but he is free within the working rules of some sort of associated action for the time being. Even if he is outside any organized collective action, he is up against the seemingly unorganized collective action of custom, habits, and traditions.

Rules of action, or working rules, and their changes apply to all fields of human activity—through to legislative statutes, judicial decisions, and administrative orders. The meaning of "working rules," as here used, is substantially equivalent to the historic meaning of "institutes," but the collective action which "institutes" the rules is here named an "institution." An institution might be a corporation, a labor union, an insane asylum, a university, a business concern, a church, a political party, a fascist, communist, or militaristic government, all of which can be grouped under the general name "going concerns" as long as they are going. Any associated action, or even a similarity of action like a custom, if it exercises a greater or less degree of control over individual action is an "institution," but the rules themselves are "institutes"—to go back historically to the Roman law where the word originated.

What are called "monopolies" or "monopolistic competition" are references to the working rules of collective action. But "free competition" itself is also another kind or degree of collective action.

Formerly only governments were empowered to create these rules of action in the form of laws and executive orders or judicial decrees. But nowadays corporations and labor unions are undertaking the task of creating the bulk of working rules, and governments merely take sides, in an attempt to hold a balance between corporations and unions. These working rules are the main subject matter of twentieth century economics. They constitute the issue between free competition, regulated competition, and monopoly; between the legislative, administrative, and judicial branches of government, on the one side, and the collective action of corporations, unions, and political parties on the other side. Instead of taking for granted a beneficent providence that makes the rules, as did the early economists, the rules themselves are investigated as adopted and enforced on individuals by different kinds of collective action. It is through knowledge of working rules that modern administrative economics learns its mechanism of control by collective action.

### 3. PART-WHOLE RELATIONS

Ten years after World War I, I asked Sidney Hillman, leader of the Amalgamated Clothing Workers, why his members were less revolutionary than they had been when I knew them twenty-five years before in the sweatshop. They were even less revolutionary than they had been after the war when they had been telling me that they would not be hard on the owners of the big corporation they worked for, after they had taken over the establishment by confiscation—as was then being done by the syndicalists of Italy—but would pension the owners and managers. Hillman replied, "They know now that they are citizens of the industry. They know that they must make the corporation a success on account of their own jobs." They were citizens because they had an arbitration system which gave them security against arbitrary foremen. They had an unemployment system by agreement with the firm which gave them security of earnings. This is an illustration of the meaning of part-whole relations.

A similar relation is that of the individual to "society." An eminent statistical economist said that the unemployed should be left to religion. Other economists said that unemployment was the responsibility of "society." Karl Marx and his communists repudiated "society" and said that the unemployed are a "reserve army" created by the capitalists to beat down wages, and the whole capitalist system should be destroyed.

The Supreme Court had said, "there is responsibility without fault." It is not the responsibility of religion, nor of society, nor of taxpayers, nor of capitalism as a whole. It is the responsibility of specified corporations which had appealed to the Court against the enforcement of a social security law, on the argument that it deprived them of their liberty and property. They must be held responsible for the unemployed in the interest of the nation as a whole. Again, in the public utility and railway enterprises, the Court had further said that the owners had "devoted their property to a public use, and therefore must consent to be regulated by the legislature representing the public.

Thus, the American courts and American collective bargaining supported by the courts had overruled certain doctrines held by both the early economists as to the liberty and property of individuals, and by the communistic economists as to the "class war." This overruling was the recognition by the courts of *organized action* along with *individual action*. Organized collective action was the whole of which individual acts were the parts. The part-whole relations were relations of individuals to legislatures, corporations, unions, political parties, and to other collective action.

The early economists had built their system on the self-interest of the individual in pursuit of his own welfare, which he could accomplish better than could be done by legislatures. They held that the individual knew his own interest better than the government could know it. When this was extended to society, they asked, "What is society?" It turned out to be the *sum* of the individuals. Yet the courts had always held that "the public," their name for "society," had a "public interest" in the transactions of individuals, and had created the courts and the legislatures to discover and formulate that interest and impose it upon individuals who otherwise were guided only by their own individual self-interest.

Then the state legislatures and the Congress had created administrative commissions, which are subordinate legislatures always in session, like the Interstate Commerce Commission, the Federal Reserve Board, the Securities and Exchange Commission, and a dozen others, for the purpose of imposing specified responsibilities on specified parts of capitalism, in the public interest.

Thus, this "public interest" involved an *organization* of some kind, such as a legislature, an administrative commission, a labor union, or a corporation of capitalists. The communist plan of "class war" was not built upon recognition of either the organization of legislatures, the organization of corporations, or the organization of labor unions. It was a logical extension of the early economists' idea that "society," or any other organization, was only a *sum* of individuals.

But "society" is not a *sum* of isolated individuals, like a census of population; it is a *multiple* of cooperating individuals—to follow the mathematical analogy—each far more powerful for both the public interest and for the interest of participating individuals when organized than when added together as separate units. The corporations were organized in the public interest of increasing the production of wealth more than could be done by separated individuals. The unions and administrative commissions were organized to restrain corporations, also in the public interest, from abuse of their corporate power over individuals. Without these private organizations the state would itself adopt public ownership.

In this process of organization the whole is greater than the sum of its parts, and the *personality* of each organized individual is higher and more capable than the personality of unorganized individuals. Their individual activities are parts of the whole activity of all who are working together. Their economic activities are their transactions, and all of the transactions of each individual are his personality.

Big corporations are often denounced as merely a method of suppressing individuals. But consider what a big corporation can do for individuals if its management is guided in the public interest instead of solely in the private interest of its stockholders. A modern corporation specializes its transactions, and individuals develop personalities and abilities as they specialize, much different from what they were when society was individualistic.

Corporations are organized into several departments. In the employment department are the bargaining activities of hiring and firing, of individual or collective bargaining, of regulation of wages, hours of labor, and sometimes speed of work. I have observed some remarkable abilities in the employment departments of corporations.

In an investigation of two refinery plants belonging to the Standard Oil Company, I, with some of my students, found the difference between the individual system of management and the corporate system. The two plants were of equal size, each having about 5,000 employees. In one of the plants the general superintendent was an engineer, trained in the application of modern scientific methods of engineering to management. In the other the general superintendent had risen to his position by promotion from the ranks through the traditional grades of foremanship. The wage earners of both plants distinguished the one as "fair," and the other as "hard boiled." In the engineer's plant the employment department had a relatively independent position through an advisory committee of employees, called a "company union." In the foreman's plant this same company union was an unnecessary encumbrance, for the foreman claimed that each one of his 5,000 employees had direct access to himself, in his office, for remedying any of their complaints regarding employment. He combined in himself, according to his interpretation, the employment department and the production department, as had been the case in the "personal" relations of the primitive small establishment where the employer worked along in daily contact with all of his employees. One superintendent realized the value of organization, the other did not.

The production department handles the managerial transactions, from general manager, superintendents, foremen, down to the "straw boss." The grandest personality among those whom I knew was Frederick W. Taylor, the engineer and inventor of "scientific management." I attended the conventions of scientific management specialists and saw a high profession of strong personalities which had developed out of the work in large-scale corporations.

Then, in all corporations large enough there are other departments. There are the sales and credit departments. They develop a profession of salesmanship based on knowledge of markets and integrity of customers. The purchasing department develops its members in a knowledge of qualities, tensions, prices, sources, which would be impossible under the individual system of production. The financial department of a corporation deals with investors and bankers, and gives much time to the stock and bond markets. The public relations department, the legal department, and the lobbying department of a corporation each becomes expert in dealings with pressure groups, courts, legislatures, and administrative departments of government. Corporations also develop safety and health departments. Finally there is the rationing department—the board of directors, making up the budget and apportioning expenditures to all subordinate departments—by whose actions all participants are brought together in their activities toward the common purpose of an enduring concern. These several departments of any corporation are compelled to work together for the sake of efficiency. The production department becomes demoralized if rush orders are not followed by new orders, so that layoffs occur. The salesmen must plan deliveries ahead so as to keep the flow of work as steady as possible. I saw the beginnings of this planning by the United States Steel Corporation, and I also talked with the customers.

The customers, reciprocally, learned to send in their orders systematically instead of rushing ahead of other customers, knowing that by the new rationing transactions of the corporation they would get deliveries when needed. Thus, they did something toward preventing unemployment. I thought these customers' character and consideration of others had also improved, though they were irritated by the Pittsburgh-plus discriminations practiced by the United States Steel Corporation and had appealed to a higher organization, the Federal Trade Commission, to remedy this abuse of power.

My idea is that most of the individuals under corporations must be better men and women than they would have been under the petty higgling of small individual employers. The better-organized corporations have one characteristic not true of mere self-interest: they work by means of general rules which require them to treat all individuals alike in the interest of the corporation as a whole and regardless of personal likes and dislikes. They work under a merit system, instead of under an unorganized self-interest. Individual workmen are often proud of the corporation they work for.

Even wealth and assets are not particular pieces of wealth

added together to make the "wealth of nations," as Adam Smith figured it out. They are the organizations of transactions in a world of getting a living and getting rich.

This is the economic meaning of such modern terms as "holism" and "emergent evolution," [1] whereby philosophers embracing both physical and economic science, see physical nature and economic society not as atoms but as organizations within atoms and across a universe; who see economic society, not as did the early economists as a census of population, but as a hierarchy of organized managerial, bargaining, and rationing transactions from the family to a hundred sovereignties. Individuals may rise within an organization, their personalities may thus be enlarged, or they may be coerced, their personalities depressed; but nevertheless they are organized as members one of another. If not "citizens" of a nation, or a corporation, or a labor union, then they are atoms, animals, aliens, tools, or machines without rights, duties, or liberties.

So it is with other relationships. Every individual is shaped by and learns to shape himself to each relationship. If he enters upon the premises of an employer and the foreman sets him to work, the courts have established the rule that, even though no written or verbal contract was made between worker and foreman, the sovereignty makes a master-servant contract between them. This implicit contract provides for work at the wages, hours, discipline, efficiency, and liberty to quit without notice, that are customary or collectively agreed upon or stipulated by the legislature. Each gives up a portion of his liberty for the time being in the expectation of a greater liberty when the work is finished. All our preceding "simplified assumptions" and all our different "relativities" are read into this and into every other transaction, as occasion may require. The wage earner and the foreman are not merely added together to make up two individuals of the population, each seeking his own self-interest. Their joint activities are their part of the whole activity of a system coming out of the past and moving into the future.

---

[1] See J. C. Smuts, *Holism and Evolution*, New York, The Macmillan Co., 1926, and his article "Holism" in *Encyclopedia Britannica*.

Recommendations and investigations for public policies and programs need especially to avoid the fallacies which result from the failure to see the part-whole relationships. A national economy is an extremely complex going concern. In analysis, and especially in our theoretical reasoning, we simplify by selecting similarities which we consider significant. From these we generalize. This is logical, but economic logic is not equivalent to economic law.

Professor W. I. King, a logical mathematical economist, has written of "economic law" which is really "economic logic" and is only a part of the whole.

He said, typical of others:

Ignorance of economic laws makes them work no less inexorably. The fact is well illustrated by the results produced by the increases in wage rates brought about by the National Industrial Recovery Act. The clothing industry furnishes an excellent example. In this field, wage rates per piece were moved up sharply. The employers, of course, advanced the prices of clothing to offset the increased wage costs. The higher prices charged for clothing caused sales in this line to fall off sharply. Thereafter, fewer clothing workers were required. Thousands of those who were discharged soon found places on the public relief rolls. The reduction in the buying ability both of the unemployed erstwhile clothing workers, and of the taxpayers who were now supporting them, naturally produced a shrinkage in the demand for other types of goods, and this shrinkage doubtless threw out of work thousands of men and women living in localities where there were no clothing factories and concerning whose very existence the clothing workers were entirely ignorant. Furthermore, these workers in other industries who lost their jobs probably never suspected that the action of the N.R.A., in raising the wages of the clothing workers, was responsible for their misfortunes.[1]

Evidently this ignorance of "economic law" was ignorance of "economic logic," like 2 and 2 equals 4. King's logic is "inexorable." This meaning of "law" as logic gives to the one who believes it a confidence of infallibility which cannot be reached by contradictory facts. I know from my own trade of typesetting

[1] Willford I. King, *The Causes of Economic Fluctuations*, New York, The Ronald Press Co., 1938, p. 201. Revised Printing. Copyright, 1941, by The Ronald Press Co.

during the 1890's that, with the recovery of business and the invention of machinery, this logic was not true. We shortened hours by one-half and increased output fivefold per hour. The logic depends on timeliness. So with King's clothing trade. There was being promoted at the same time (1934) a combination of several other measures directed toward an all-round recovery from the trough of the depression of 1932, such as devaluation of gold, reduction of discount rates, reconstruction finance in aid of corporations and banks, and other measures which were beginning to send up prices, and to increase business activity and employment in general. If these or other measures should turn our partly successful, as was probable, then not all the logical consequences portrayed by King and others would have occurred. Their logic is not a "law"; it is a part-whole fallacy. Any one principle of similarity, when isolated from all others, such as the law of supply and demand, which should be named the principle of scarcity combined with other principles, can be carried out logically to its inevitable disaster. This is not economic law; it is economic logic, regardless of time and circumstances, like 4 minus 2 equals 2.

Interference with the law of supply and demand has always been the main objection raised against all collective action, whether against protective tariffs, against immigration restriction, against labor unions, or against corporations; but these interferences have nevertheless been repeated and cumulated for a hundred years, because the alternatives of noninterference under the circumstances were deemed worse than the interferences.

Public programs and policies can not be evaluated in terms of the logical consequences of isolated assumptions or similarities. They must be judged by the practical consequences of their operations. This requires a subtle balancing of many parts—some of which are *necessarily* contradictory. Administratively, it means continuous attention to the resolution of conflicts. For thought and analysis, it means that the full consequences can never be anticipated before programs are put into effect. Theoretically or logically, it requires that analysis must come to a focus upon judgments which evaluate the parts in relation to the whole and take account of the strategy and timeliness of action. Adherence to the analogies of physical causes leads to tyranny, revolution, or futility. An effective working whole is achieved only by constructive judgments and action.

To summarize the foregoing, the extremes investigated in modern institutional economics are "law and order" at one extreme, and "equality and liberty" at the other extreme, but "reasonableness" or "reasonable value" is somewhere between the extremes. The extreme that emphasizes "law and order" has at times actually meant and established perpetual oppression or slavery. The extreme that emphasized "equality and liberty" might actually result in anarchism or chaos. Reasonableness has meant something between the extremes which would be a complex according to circumstance of law, order, equality, and liberty.

These part-whole relations are not idealistic—they are the source of abuses as well as benefits, but they have been greatly improved over what they were in times past. Besides, figure out for yourself what are the alternatives if corporations, unions, and political parties are abolished altogether, as they are abolished in totalitarian countries.

The failure to take account of these relations of the parts to the whole leads to various "part-whole fallacies" in economic science. The way in which these fallacies occur is in the handy assumption that all other factors "remain the same" except this one that we are arguing about. We are always compelled to make this assumption in our logic and reasoning, else we could not carry out a line of reasoning to its logical conclusion along a single principle of similarity. But we cannot stop with that handy assumption. Nothing remains the same. When we are trying to tie together all the changing activities, we are at least trying to get away from our logical fallacies of taking only the part that we are interested in and neglecting the whole that concerns everybody. The problem is to attain a balance between the parts which recognizes the strategic and proportionate relations within the part-whole complex.

It is the "working rules" of each organization, governing

subordinates, that tie the individuals together and enlarge their personalities by loyalty to a "going concern." But it is the abuses that are embodied in these same working rules that require a hierarchy of superior working rules ultimately organized through the sovereign legislative, executive, judicial, and administrative departments of government.

### 4. HISTORICAL DEVELOPMENT

The early economists considered that economics was to be a logical, deductive science, to be built upon the one supposition of a rational self-interest of individuals. Hence they ruled out history as a part of the science because history brought in hundreds of conditions and causes, and thereby reduced the subject to a mere description, or a narrative, which could not claim to be a science.

Early economists had several meanings of self-interest beside their meanings of pleasure and pain, profit and loss. One of these meanings, the choice of alternatives, was not distinguished separately and made fundamental until the latter half of the nineteenth century. As we have noticed in the preceding chapter on "Transactions," the choice of alternative opportunities, according to changes in the external world, has become increasingly the meaning of individual self-interest. These alternatives have come about mainly through collective action of governments, corporations, unions, and political parties in times past, and have been selected and maintained largely by the courts as a kind of social environment surrounding the individual and setting for him the alternatives between which he is constrained to choose, if he is to make a living or to get rich.

This choice of alternatives by individuals is the foundation of the theory of value held by the courts and attorneys in the decision of disputes. "Opportunity cost" is, in fact, the legal theory of value. It is the sacrifice of foregoing an alternative. The courts or attorneys ask, what were the alternatives which the individual was "up against" when he made the contract? Were they "reasonable" alternatives at the time? Were they persuasive or coercive? Was the choice induced by hope or compelled by fear? Was it a free choice, or were the alternatives monopolized? Was advantage taken of the weakness or ignorance of the individual by those who were strong, or intelligent, or powerfully organized? Was the contract now asked to be enforced by the court made in a time of prosperity or in a time of depression, unemployment, or during other loss of alternatives?

Some of the dimensions of these alternative opportunities open to individuals were established many years ago and are still maintained, such as the distinction between property owners and nonproperty owners. Others have more recently been established, such as universal freedom from slavery. Others are being established from time to time. In fact, economics is as much a *history* of changes in the opportunities open to individuals, as it is in any other aspect of self-interest. How these free opportunities were brought about and may be influenced is a practical problem in economics, and can be investigated.

Thirty years ago when financed by the Russel Sage Foundation, I took three of my students on a two years' investigation of the United States Steel Corporation at Pittsburgh. I had been told by Florence Kelley, head of the Consumers' League, that employees of the United States Steel Corporation were working twenty-four hours on Sundays. To me this seemed incredible. The steel industry had been supported by political action through a protective tariff, on the argument for protection of American labor against the pauper labor of Europe, an argument which I accepted. This corporation, great beneficiary of the tariff, did not permit visitors to go through their plant unless accompanied by a guide furnished by the management, and that rule, properly enough, prevails today. I determined, however, to take my students without an official guide.

My friend, Mahlon Garland, formerly a labor leader in the Homestead strike of 1892, was then Collector of Customs at Pittsburgh, appointed by the Republican administration after his union had lost the strike. I thought he might have political influence. I asked him to get permission from the Carnegie management to take us, with himself as our guide, through the Homestead plant the next Sunday night. He did. He showed us the spot where he had harangued the strikers during their sit-down strike fifteen years before, in 1892. Several of the former strikers had been taken back and were then at work. They recognized him, and welcomed him and us.

We found one of the former strikers, a "heater," opening and shutting the doors of a fiery hot oven in which the huge steel bars were tempered for the subsequent rolling mills. He was about fifty years of age, stripped to the waist, his left arm blistered and bloody from the heat of the oven. It was now eleven o'clock Sunday night. He had come to work that Sunday morning at six o'clock, and would leave work at six o'clock the next morning. He had been on the day shift of twelve hours the preceding week and was then changing to the night shift of another twelve hours for the ensuing week. We saw the incredible. He talked freely to us, as to friends, during the intervals between opening and shuting the huge doors. Capable individuals, like Charles M. Schwab, had come out of that rugged individualism, but there were very few of them. This heater was an intelligent American citizen, not an immigrant pauper laborer. He was one of the high-paid wage earners.

We wanted to know how it came about that this intelligent worker was reduced to the alternative of working twelve hours per day or remaining unemployed. We discovered, from the convention reports of his labor union, that in the year 1889, the management, Andrew Carnegie, had offered the union an eight-hour day of three shifts, instead of the union rule of approximately ten hours, which had come down from the old puddling days of the iron industry. Carnegie had acquired the patent rights for the continuous twenty-four hour process of manufacturing steel. The labor union leaders had argued strongly for acceptance of the continuous process on the eight-hour shift, but the convention of the union rejected it. Three years later in 1892, H. C. Frick, Carnegie's partner, carried through as the policy of the corporation the annihilation of the union at Homestead, and then with the aid of armed forces, dictated the rule of the twelve-hour day, the seven-day week, with twenty-four hours off on one Sunday and with twenty-four hours on the next Sunday.

This rule continued until the year 1920, when the eight-hour day was installed by the Steel Corporation at the insistence, it was reported, of the Republican campaign managers in the midst of a political campaign. Fifteen years later, in 1935, a new industrial unionism arose and absorbed the remains of the older union, but this time it was the CIO, which negotiated an agreement with the Carnegie-Illinois Steel Company—constituent of the U. S. Steel and owner of that same Homestead plant. Thereupon new rules of action, which I name collective democracy, were agreed upon to set the alternative between which the successors of my Garland and my heater of thirty-five years before would make their choices. Such historical facts are essential to understand modern corporations, unions, and political parties.

It is often said that "history repeats itself." But the alternatives for individuals are not repeated. In America a hundred years ago, nine-tenths of the population were farmers dependent upon their own manual work and the weather. The farmer then invested his savings in more land, more slaves, more animals, or more houses. Today the bulk of savings is invested in stocks, bonds, or in urban land values. Investors cannot see their investments. The can read circulars, financial statements, and the names of financiers. They must depend on confidence in strategic individuals who control these investments. The real change is from private property to economic government by corporations, labor unions, and political parties. If a few managers or leaders turn out to be imposters, or their advice to be mistaken, the whole industry of the nation may suffer a collapse. Long-term savings for the immense quantity of "durable goods" required for modern industry—formerly named "fixed capital" by economists, because they could see it fixed to the ground—now depend on confidence in corporate management and political management of stocks and bonds. Investors seek "liquidity" so as to get their savings on demand, whereas formerly they sought "tangibility" like farms or property which they could see. These historical changes are a change from former theories of pure self-interest into institutional changes in the choice of opportunities.

Formerly manual laborers were a mere fraction of the population, without the franchise because they were not property owners. Now they are massed in cities, working for corporations, organized in unions, and voting for politicians through a secret ballot. With the margins of profit on sales reduced to a smaller rate than ever before, the "equity" of the stockholders, whose investments give security to the bondholders, can sometimes be wiped out by a meagre rise in wages or by a slight change in the general level of prices. So-called "venture capital," the capital invested in stocks of corporations, bears the whole risk of a rise in wages or a fall in prices. The ownership of stocks becomes, not only an opportunity for savings, but also an opportunity for financiers to get control of the corporations. Yet if people are afraid to invest in stocks, there is no security for those who invest in corporation bonds. When 90 per cent of modern manufacturing and transportation output has become the output of corporations on narrower margins of profit than formerly, history does not repeat itself. But history gives an understanding of how to cope with various situations.

Thus it is true, indeed, that history is not logical. Yet the history of economic conditions and the changing alternatives open to individuals is necessary for an understanding of present-day economics, and of the relative importance of hundreds of different factors that make up the facts, as well as the different proposals for the future. Even in the one illustration that we have narrated above from the steel industry, there is the history of many causes and conditions, such as protective tariffs, immigration laws, corporation law, labor unions, ignorance, passion, weakness, strength, and many others, which must be taken into account in present-day management and in administration. Instead of investigating a simple cause of self-interest, hundreds of causes and historical conditions must be weighed and balanced against each other in the endeavor to understand how to act on present day economic problems.

We have introduced a number of assumptions and relativities from different investigations. Of these relativities the four which deal particularly with the methods and the goals of economic investigations are the similarities and differences, the working rules of collective action, the goals to be reached in the part-whole relations, and the historical developments which create the modern conditions. Among these assumptions and relativities, the individual by comparison of similarities and differences must discover if he can, in his own circumstances, which are the strategic transactions on which others depend and which are the routine transactions which may be taken for granted.

This strategy of management and administration of corporations, of unions, of political parties, and indeed, of every individual in his choice of alternatives, depends upon the changing degrees of power, the velocity of transactions, and the wisdom of timely action under changing circumstances.

# Chapter xi

## *VALUATION:*
### *The Economists' Theory of Value*

———◆———

Two world wars have decomposed the economists' theory of value into its historical elements: an agricultural "cost of production" in the *past* as the cause of present use values; a consumer's present psychology as identical with *present* psychic value; a banker's expected enforcement of contracts as the *future* inducement of present negotiated value.

The theory of value as *past costs* came from the classical British economists and the German communists of the eighteenth and first half of the nineteenth centuries; the theory of value as *present pleasures* from the Austrian economists of the last quarter of the nineteenth century; the theory of value as *future enforcement of contracts* from the practices of American bankers and lawyers of the nineteenth and this twentieth century.

We distinguish the *participants* from the *professional* economists. The participants are farmers, laborers, consumers, bankers, lawyers, businessmen. The economists are the various schools of formal theorists. The participants' theories are their tacit acceptance of causes, purposes, circumstances, and plans of action, in their transactions and valuations, while "value" itself is the relative importance which they impute to the various factors involved. The economists' formal theories are elaborated from the participants' tacit theories at the particular period of time.

The classical economists had emerged, in the eighteenth century, from the French physiocrats who had made agricultural productivity the cause of value; but Adam Smith, in 1776, shifted to the productivity of labor as the prime cause. Ricardo and Malthus, in the nineteenth century, split on Smith's double meaning of labor.[1] Ricardo considered value to come from past labor "embodied" in present products as *"use-value"*; this is known today as technology. Malthus considered value to come from embodied labor also, but as labor had power to command an *exchange-value* with present owners of property through the medium of money.

Fifty years later, after 1848, when socialists and labor unions had begun to revolt against property and technology, these orthodox theories of cause and effect became the basis of Karl Marx's revolutionary theory of "exploitation" of labor embodied by laborers and commanded by capitalists.

Contemporary with Marx and the European revolutions of 1848, the American optimist, Henry C. Carey, avoided the pessimist exploitation theory by changing from a *past* cost of production to a *present* cost of reproduction by machinery at reduced costs. In his analysis, he shifted the time factor forward and injected machinery in order to support the protective tariff on behalf of infant American manufacturers against British free trade manufacturers and their exploited labor. The American Supreme Court, which after the Civil War had confiscated four billion dollars of property value "embodied" in slaves, accepted Carey's optimistic theory of triumphant democracy; but the American economists turned to the Austrians' psychological theory of consumers' diminishing intensity of pleasure. Yet, for the practical purpose of a measure of value, the American economists retained the metal, gold, as the classical embodied and commanded labor value, and thus avoided the "greenback" paper money and cheap silver theories.

The Austrian theory was a competitive theory of individual consumers. For Europeans, this psychological theory of value was sufficient to avoid the exploitation theories. But in America this conception of competitive choice culminated in the antitrust laws on behalf of consumers in 1890. Although the Austrian theory of value was widely discussed among American economists in the 1880's, Senator Sherman was, of course, not directly influenced by it in his fight for antitrust legislation. Yet this theory

[1] Mentioned by Hollander one hundred years later.

of value and the antimonopoly crusades of the 1890's are both outgrowths of, or expressions of, the "individualism" of the late nineteenth century.

The early theories of value were constructed from similarity to the various mechanistic theories of the physical sciences prevailing at the corresponding period of time. These mechanistic theories began with analogies to Galileo's and Newton's theories of the attraction of gravity and of action, reaction, and equilibrium; they were extended after 1810 by Lavoisier's theories of chemical affinities and repulsions; then, after 1830, by Faraday's conception of magnetic positive and negative poles; and after 1859 by the Malthusian theory of geometric rates of increase of population and Darwin's theory of the struggle for survival.

But the physical scientists had not investigated the value, or the processes of valuation, which are peculiar to the human will. They investigated so-called "facts" of physical forces but not "values." When it came to *values* they could think only of *subjective* feelings like sympathy, love, or conscience, as was done by Darwin in his *Descent of Man*, 1870. But these subjective "forces" were not measurable. Consequently, the physicists omitted economics from the list of sciences, although they included Freud's psychiatry, a mechanical and chemical reaction of diseased or abnormal human beings, leading up to medicine, but not to the legal economics of adult and sane human beings. It is a critical question, Why do physical scientists exclude economics from the list of sciences? [1]

In the meantime the American lawyers and bankers were working out a negotiational theory of value. For some three hundred years, in trials at court, the lawyers had been investigating the human will in all its different kinds and dimensions. Consequently, the courts through their decisions had constructed a history of human volitions which served as the foundation of the theory of value.

In the year 1900 the American banking house of J. P. Morgan

---

[1] See Harlow Shapley, Samuel Rapport and Helen Wright, editors, *A Treasury of Science*, New York and London, Harper and Brothers, 1943; also 1946 enlarged edition.

& Co. and their eminent lawyer, James B. Dill, avoided the anti-trust laws by means of the holding company which permitted inflated values. Dill, supported by the leading American economist, Jeremiah W. Jenks, lobbied this bill through the New Jersey legislature; this law was sustained twenty years afterward in 1920 by the Supreme Court of the United States. The theory of value in the holding company act was based on the credit system of expected enforcement of contracts, including corporate stocks and bonds.

The orthodox economists did not examine the work of the courts of law in investigating the behavioristic dimensions of the human will; so, it turns out that they could only imitate the explanations of mechanical and chemical forces. But when economists came finally to the study of the political theories of bankers and lawyers and their implicit theories of valuation, they discovered the foundation to be nothing less comprehensive than the whole of the *human will,* individual and organized, as it operated in politics, government, the enforcement of contracts, corporate charters, labor unions, cartels, and the Constitution of the United States.

When the lawyers, however, resolved the human will in their court decisions to its behavioristic dimensions in order to measure damages and enforce contracts regardless of subjective feelings, they made the will a "power." This power differs from the mechanical "forces" or "energies" of the physical sciences in that the human will has the power of self-control or self-command, which is totally lacking in physical forces. Instead of shifting over, as did the physical scientists, from physical forces to subjective feelings or to different physical organs of the human body—such as organs of digestion, action and reaction of the muscles and nerves, sexual reproduction of Malthus or Freud, or looking on the will as the pineal gland, like some philosophers—the courts took the human will to mean the whole of the human body as a unit of power, choosing, acting, or refraining. Their purpose in focusing on the will was *justice* instead of *love, sympathy,* or *conscience.*

Consequently, in what was really their experimental laboratory, a court of law in examining witnesses and documents, the lawyers had to discover and measure the behavioristic dimensions of the human will as a power of self-control, or self-command. The will was found acting either on the forces of nature, as individual laborers in agriculture and industry, or in rendering a negotiated service to owners and other individuals in their multitudes of transactions. Instead of imitating the physical sciences, by making human beings a complex of mechanical forces, they distinguished the adult and free human being as simply its outstanding attribute, *the human will in action.*

In going over their leading decisions in a search for these economic dimensions we find that they are reducible to practically four space-time dimensions of the will in action, to which the courts and legal commentators give names equivalent to *performance, forbearance, avoidance* and *timeliness.* All of these four dimensions are components of the power of self-control, or self-command, and are measurable according to the nature of the action or transaction in which the human will is engaged.

Performance is the 100 per cent positive act of self to the full extent of one's ability without any external command or restraint whatever. Forbearance is self-restraint, ranging in all degrees of power over self from zero restraint, or liberty, up to avoidance, which is 100 per cent self-restraint in that direction. And avoidance is therefore choice of the next best alternative performance—not "free will," which is subjective, but "free choice," which is objective and measurable. "Timing" or "timeliness," or the selection of the "right" time, "right" place, and "right" degree of power, is the fourth of the space-time dimensions of self-command.

Where the action is upon the physical forces of nature, the human will is engaged in production—the production of use values. The dimensions of this aspect of human activity are the space-time dimensions of the applied physical sciences. The measure of performance in these dimensions is the physical output per man-hour—named efficiency by engineers. Further, the human will has the power, by science and invention, to extend, enlarge, and make accurate these measurable dimensions, by means of tools, machines, clocks, and inventions to use the physical forces of gravity, electricity, etc.

Where the physical performance of the human will upon nature's forces occurs in organized or collective action there is also the transaction. I name this the managerial transaction. In this, two legally recognized wills meet in a superior-inferior, or command-obedience, relationship. The typical case is a foreman-employee relationship. This is the method by which the collective will of the going concern is made effective upon the materials or forces of nature.

The managerial transaction is a part of economics because it is the meeting place of human wills in the production of wealth—or useful things. The relations between human activity and physical (nonhuman) nature are also a part of economics, because they are the ways in which the human will controls or operates these forces of nature. There is also evaluation of alternatives and the choice of performance, avoidance, forbearance—at the right time, place, and intensity. The purpose is the production of wealth. The usefulness of the physical objects for future production is evaluated. This aspect of economics may be called engineering economics.

Thus the early economists were misled from the central problems in valuation by their imitation of the physical sciences. A more adequate theory of valuation turns to the analysis of human purposes and the human will in action. Such a theory must reject a simple mechanical theory of causation; also it must look toward the future rather than the past. Finally a theory of value, to be sufficient for the needs of modern action, must be relevant to collective action and conflicts of interest.

But the analysis of value must include the valuation of physical objects to which the early economists directed their attention so exclusively. We see now that we do not value the physical thing but the relation of physical things to human activity; that is, we value the use. This use value is in the broadest sense a civilization value. Things useful at one stage of civilization are outmoded at another. The nature of the physical objects has not changed, it is their usefulness that has changed.

These uses are futuristic and relative. Things are valued as useful according to the prospective service to human purposes, regardless of past cost or exertion. This requires, in turn, that the use value of any particular thing be judged in relation to the complex of human purposes. Consequently the "cause" of use value turns out to be the relative importance assigned by judgment, rather than a mechanical consequent to some antecedent action.

Thus the creation of use values, through action upon nature's forces, or through transactions which direct the human will in directing nature's forces to human purposes, is a part of the valuation process. But it is only a part and cannot be treated in complete isolation from the other aspects of valuation, as found in bargaining and rationing transactions. Or stated differently, a theory of valuation must embrace the whole will in action.

Under modern capitalism the rights to these future uses are valued in a market place. These markets are complex organizations wherein the expectations of future performances may be subtly valued. Although we speak of the price of commodities— or services—what we actually value in the market is the legal rights to these uses or services, namely property rights. Physical control follows legal control; legal control is strategic and valued.

In the bargaining transaction, participants meet as legal equals, negotiate with each other, arrive at a common or joint valuation, and agree upon the terms of mutual performances. Consequently, there arise the double duties of payment and performance, and the correlative and identical rights in the opposite parties. Payment is in dollars; this is the duty or debt of the purchaser and the right or credit of the seller. Performance is in whatever terms serve as the measure of the thing sold—pounds, tons, man-hours, time, or what not. Here too there is the duty of performance by the seller, with the correlative right in the purchaser.

This complex of rights and duties rests upon enforceable expectancies, expected stabilized social relations. They are property rights, which are created by the enforcement of duties upon correlative parties. Consequently property rights are expected stabilized human behavior; the behavior is stabilized by placing limits upon the arbitrariness of the wills of the various parties in the concern or state.

The duties of payment are made specific and measurable in our modern capitalism through money or a "unit of account." In this way the use values get commuted into, and become absorbed in, a fund of money values. This commutation occurs through the joint judgment or valuation of the parties in the countless bargaining transactions. Such money values are judgments of the future regarding both uses and the expected behavior of private persons and public officials with respect to the uses—including the rights to withhold from use. In this way physical things get caught up into intangible property relations. They are transformed into negotiated value, reducible simply to money value.

In an analogous manner, ownership may also be transferred through rationing transactions. Physical dimensions are similarly commuted to negotiated values, except that the relative importance of the parts is judged by authorized persons—perhaps arbitrarily or possibly through investigation. The values may be arrived at by some sort of collective judgment; but they are not achieved through the negotiation of rightful participants as legal equals agreeing upon the terms of the respective mutual performances. The will, judgment, and valuations of the authorized legally superior parties are made effective through such administrative devices as price or point rationing, dividend declaration, or tax levies. Nevertheless the whole performance may finally be "settled" in monetary terms. Again, the complex of anticipated future behavior is funded in the present as money value.

These processes of valuation are at once social and individual. Social valuation and activities are the matrix or data for individual valuation. Through collective action the alternatives and opportunities are made available to the individual. The measurements of performances and payments in the transactions are simultaneously the identical measurements of the individual's alternatives and opportunities. Through the working rules of collective action equality and liberty are made possible, or available, to the individual. In a sense, the purpose of social valuations is to make individual valuations secure and realizable. The objects of social valuations, the things valued, are the ways of human behavior—custom, practices, transactions. Social activities are appraised for their contribution to justice, order, security, liberty, equality, or whatever purpose. These public purposes are in turn embodied in the expected collective action of mankind and are thereby available to the individual.

But whether the purpose be public or private, and whether the object be the creation or the realization of opportunities, valuations look to the future—to expected behavior with respect to persons or things. The shift from past or present to futurity requires also a shift in the method of reasoning from the deductive method of a single efficient cause and its effect limited by *predetermined* "laws" and to a comparative method of seeking similarities and differences within a complex of *future indeterminate* causes, purposes, and events.

Something similar, indeed, but without the self-control of the human will, was true of the physical sciences when the scientists shifted, toward the middle of the nineteenth century, from a "philosophy" to a "science." Sir Isaac Newton looked upon his mathematical method of reasoning as a "philosophy," apparently because he considered his "attraction of gravity" as one of the divine purposes. But when, in the nineteenth century, both divine purpose and human purpose were dropped and the reasoning was reduced to only mechanical "causes," then the "philosophies" became the several "sciences" of physics, astronomy, chemistry, biology, psychiatry, and their multiple "forces" or "energies" of "nature" predetermined.

But it was found impossible to keep the many sciences separated with separate "causes" assigned to each, like gravity to physics and astronomy, affinity to chemistry, polarity to electromagnetism, and so on. Various efforts were made to unite them in one harmonious system. First was the theory of "multiple causation" in lieu of "divine purpose." But multiple causation, as summarized recently by Sorokin,[1] results in an "infinite regres-

---

[1] P. A. Sorokin, *Russia and the United States,* New York, Literary Classics, Inc., 1944, p. 214, and preceding books.

sion" leading either to a "prime mover" or to the vain proposition that "the whole world is the cause of everything." As an instrument of investigation, he says, it is impossible to describe these "countless antecedents," but an "incomplete catalogue" of causes leaves them unclarified; the selection of a few causes is "perfectly arbitrary"; the causes are "heterogeneous, incommensurable, non-comparable" and there is no "meaningful unity" and "no measure of relative causative power." This bewilderment of the investigator, he goes on, is even worse when "mathematical values" are given to the many causes. Consequently, Sorokin passes on to the new meaning of "value" given by sociologists who substitute subjective feelings or emotions for the former intellectual reasoning and the mathematics of value, and he gives to value the meaning of passions that drive individuals and peoples to action. But even so, he is compelled to distinguish the "main cause," which turns out to be a *main value,* from "supplementary factors." To a man up a tree it looks like a mere change of words with the same old meanings. Where formerly the issue was disputed whether our Civil War was "caused" by the southerners in rebellion or by the northerners invading the south on account of slavery, the Sorokin brand of sociologist would say "their value systems were incompatible."

The real difficulty with this multiple causation is that the physical scientists rest their case on the physical analogy of preceding causes in the past or present, whereas the human will is simply a name for a human being in command of the present with ability to influence the expectations of the future. The subject matter of the physical sciences, including medicine and psychiatry, namely, matter and force, has no self-originating performances, forbearances, avoidances, or notion that one time is better than any other time, and hence no self-command or command of other forces. Its future is in the plans of the scientific investigator himself. During the stages of economic science when the economists imitated the physical sciences, the individual was treated in economic theory like atoms, molecules, steam engines, horsepower, and the like, controlled by external forces and not self-controlled. This was, indeed, the business men's attitude, from whom the classical and hedonic economists, as well as the communists, took their analogies. Their science was founded on materialism, and when business men, as well as economists, came up against such facts as labor turnover, trade unions, secret ballot, and emancipation of slaves, where laborers had "wills of their own," they had to treat them either as dishonest and call in the army or begin to adopt methods of investigation and understanding based on purposes of the human will instead of the economic theory of causation by physical forces. The history of economic science for a hundred years has been a step-by-step approach toward investigations by a court of law under the Anglo-American system where the subject matter, an adult and sane human being, is presumed to have a will of his own which looks toward the future with purposes, instead of a physical force pushed from the past by "causes."

The valuation of all factors varies in *degree* as well as kind from the highest value imputed to the limiting or strategic factor and lesser degrees of value to the diminishing complementary or routine factors, which, again can be classified as immediate, proximate, potential, possible factors, in diminishing degrees of value. This is the legal method contrasted with the theories of multiple causation which take no account of differences in degree.

The courts state it in terms of "proportioning the factors" according to the "due weight" of each, that is, the due value of each, which, in turn is their meaning of "reasonable value." This again is the principle of "good judgment," "wisdom" or "public spirit" in the mind and soul of the judge or whoever is selected to manage the collective activity of the corporation, cartel, union, or nation. We cannot get away from these strategic virtues instead of predetermined causes as the determinants in any theory of value which passes judgment on relative importance, that is, *value*, whatever words may be used. It is not multiple causation but good judgment.

The latest effort to solve the enigma of multiple causation in the physical sciences goes under the names of "relativity" and "quanta," and includes also the enigma of transforming "matter" into "energy" brought to the front by the phenomena of "radioactivity." All of these terms are, in fact, not really something found in external nature but are mental constructions invented by the scientists themselves. They bring the scientists back to "philosophizing" about values much as the trade unionist says he is doing when he explains to you "the philosophy" of the "closed shop." For the scientist's "relativity" is his philosophy of the interdependence of all causes, effects, purposes, and their *dependence* upon the mental operations of the scientists themselves; and the "quanta" invented by the physicist, Planck, in the year 1900, and later adopted by Einstein to round out a theory of relativity, are merely the economists' "weighted statistical averages" invented by the economist, Jevons, forty years before.

The physicists' "quanta" and economists' "statistics" cover up the former disputes of deductive logic about cause and effect, as well as disputes about "free will," and they substitute "probability" instead of deduction, a kind of "logistics" instead of "logic," and tentativeness instead of dogmatism. Agreements may now be reached on probabilities by merely changing the "weights," that is, the "values," in place of the former unchangeable dogmatisms and dictatorships deduced from the theorists' predetermined single cause. Probability has indeed two meanings, the likelihood of truth and the likelihood of future happenings. "Truth" becomes an agreement of scientists on probability, say on evolution at the time of Darwin, or the Constitution at the time of Roosevelt; but future happenings are consequences of the practical agreements of business men, trade unions, politicians, on how to anticipate and plan for or avoid the probable future events and allow for risks. The deductive logicians took their stand on *truth,* "though the heavens fall"; but the pragmatists agree on probabilities when they try to prevent revolution and reaction afterwards. This is a difference between nature's energies which do not agree on the future, and the human will which does agree by, say, collective bargaining, not known to the classical or hedonist economists.

The deductive reasoning from a single cause goes in a circle, and its prevalence marks the dogmatisms of theorists and dictators instead of the investigations by scientists. "Man is mortal" is a major premise, and the second premise that "Socrates is a man" brings the logic back to the beginning where Socrates is also mortal. This was the circular reasoning of the classical, hedonic, and communistic economists, and prevails with their lineal descendants in economics and politics who do not have a sense of humor.

But the comparative method of similarities and differences is the method of the Anglo-American common-law courts, and is also the "scientific" method of investigating the apparent similarities themselves in each individual experiment as to whether it is really similar, and, if not, then treating these new cases differently by different similarities. In the case of legal science it is the search for valid precedents from preceding cases, or a method of starting a new precedent in time of revolution.

Here is where the scientist actually does his reasoning, and where the legal argument in court actually turns. Was the cited precedent really similar, or was it merely a poetic analogy, a figure of speech, a "double cross" perpetuated on the listener? These false similarities provoked the boisterous Theodore Roosevelt to speak of them as "weasel words." The weasel words in economics are value, equality, liberty.

We have tried above to avoid weasel words and to give precision to the historical meanings of value by separating three meanings, use value, psychic value, and negotiated value, thus reducing them from the hundred-year illusory embodied value and commanded value, which had been transformed to "money value." Gold and silver money, and latterly only gold, were held to be the only "true" money, for metallic money was real money in its own right of labor independent of government and the arbitrary human will. It was both the product of physical labor embodied in its use value and the owner's power to command labor which gave it exchange value. But, in the third historical stage, since bankers had made bank credit the universal purchasing power in all transactions, and the lawyers had made it binding by enforcement of contracts, money, too, becomes negotiated value resting on credit, politics, and control of courts. In this way all the other historical meanings of value, as "exploitation" value, "reproduction" value, "diminishing" value of pleasure, are also swallowed up in the complex behavioristic process of negotiated value, embodied in contracts and enforced by sheriffs or marshals, taking orders from the courts.

This meaning of value as negotiated value was modified still further in 1935,[1] when the Supreme Court rejected private negotiations in the "gold clause" in contracts as competent to agree upon the meaning of value unless previously authorized by Congress and the Supreme Court. The President had raised the price of the gold dollar 41 per cent in terms of the legal tender, "greenback" paper dollar, and the Supreme Court now sustained the President, on the ground that the Congress had previously created *two* standards of value, the gold in *weight* and the greenback in *value,* and the same political authority could therefore eliminate or change the gold weight, if desired, and could rest the standard unit of value on money as the valid standard in enforcing contracts. In the gold clause decisions [2] the Court upheld the Congress of the United States which had declared in a joint resolution on June 5, 1933, regarding monetary policy: "Every obligation, heretofore or hereafter incurred, whether or not any such provision is contained therein or made with respect thereto, shall be discharged upon payment, dollar for dollar, in any court on currency which at the time of payment is legal tender for public and private debts." [3] The Supreme Court's measure of *value* became simply money.

Thus even "money value" as metallic money disappears and all the different meanings of value become credit value as issued by thousands of banks in their negotiations with borrowers, and controlled immediately by the organized bankers of an administrative commission, the Federal Reserve system, but controlled ultimately by the politicians who select the President, the Congress, the Supreme Court and the member banks of the Reserve system.

---

[1] See Chapter XV.

[2] *Norman* v. *B & O RR*, 294 U. S. 240 (1935); *Nortz* v. *U. S.*, 294 U. S. 317 (1935); *Perry* v. *U. S.*, 294 U. S. 330 (1935).

[3] The joint resolution and the gold clause decisions have been published as *Senate Document 21,* 74th Congress, 1st Session, Washington 1935.

Thus it turns out that the measurement of value, in this respect, is influenced by all those activities of bankers, politicians, and courts, as well as the mass behaviour of millions of persons with their psychology of hope or fear, which influence the level of prices, the volume of purchasing power, or general prosperity or depression in an economy.

Even this is only a part of the valuation process in economic life, as will appear later. But this aspect of valuation, which is approximately equal to the usual field of price and market valuation in economics, is a part of collective action. Although we speak of the measurement of value or relative importance, actually we measure performance. Units of value are actually units for measuring what persons do in action. For this reason, the measures, even of prices, are working rules for the evaluation and comparisons of performances. In this way, the modern money value is simultaneously (1) a measure of relative importance to the individual, (2) a measure of relative performance agreed upon through negotiation in transactions, and (3) a working rule of the courts which measure one of the dimensions of opportunity.

But these modern money measures of performance, or relative importance, do not exhaust the meaning of value in economics. "Equality" and "liberty" are also necessary to the full meaning of value. These values too are institutional. Collectively they are the working rules which "institutionalize" or make these "values" accessible to the individuals as a part of their opportunities. Historically the actual content or meaning of these values, equality and liberty, also have greatly changed, especially after the Civil War of 1861 and the New Deal of 1933.

The American Civil War was the most revolutionary confiscation of property values since the French Revolution in that it both nullified four billion dollars of value without compensation to owners by the emancipation of the slaves, and it imposed finally by conquest the protective tariff values for northern manufacturers against the free trade values which had been taken over from the English economists by the southern slaveowners. The predominating theory of value was framed by the lawyers who substituted the laws of a stable government for the economists' "natural law," or "laws of nature." The lawyers did it by their authoritative position on the Supreme Court, and afterwards by a change in their theory of value based on the optimistic democracy of our revolutionary civil war. This theory continued to hold even into the destructive competition of farmers to the advantage of consumers and manufacturers; into the monopolistic valuation of railways and other "natural monopolies" known as "public utilities"; into the cases that had to do with the relative bargaining power of individual laborers and their corporate employers; into the "holding company" valuations of the decision in 1920 which validated the state legislation on behalf of bankers and stock speculators that had begun with New Jersey in the year 1900.

The Supreme Court also eliminated another double meaning when it nullified the double meaning of equality and liberty as previously adopted in the Coppage case of 1915.[1] A wage earner named Hodges and a railway corporation, acting through its foreman, Coppage, as employment agent, had been declared to be equals in their wage bargains. In this case, the U. S. Supreme Court, with three justices dissenting, held unconstitutional a Kansas statute, making it a criminal offense for an employer to coerce an employee to stay out of a labor union. Justice Holmes observed in dissent that: "In present conditions a workman not unnaturally may believe that only by belonging to a union can he secure a contract that shall be fair to him. . . . If that belief, whether right or wrong, may be held by a reasonable man, it seems to me that it may be enforced by law to establish the equality of position between the parties in which liberty of contract begins." [2] Within six years time the court was to declare that: "Union was essential to give laborers opportunity to deal on equality with their employer." [3] More recently, in 1937, the U. S. Supreme Court upheld the constitutionality of the National Labor Relations Act.[4] National policy, as declared by the U. S. Congress and upheld by the U. S. Supreme Court, now makes it

[1] *Coppage* v. *Kansas,* 236 U. S. 1, 1915.
[2] *Ibid.,* pp. 26–27.
[3] *American Steel Foundries* v. *Tri-City Central Trades Council,* 257 U. S. 209.
[4] *National Labor Relations Board* v. *Jones and Laughlin Steel Corp.,* 301 U. S. 1, 1937 is a leading case.

an unfair labor practice for an employer to interfere with the free choice of employees to belong to a labor union and to bargain collectively about conditions of their employment.

This later decision, in effect, substituted a labor union for Hodges as more nearly equal to a corporation of shareholders, and thus substituted, in effect, a rationing transaction under the name of collective bargaining as the negotiation of a working rule to regulate individual bargaining transactions and managerial foremen transactions. Thus a further double meaning of negotiated value was eliminated by distinguishing the processes of valuation as individual bargaining and collective bargaining.

The meaning of liberty was further clarified in the peonage cases [1] which brought up a danger of going to an opposite extreme of servitude in the enforcement of contracts. The security which the debtor gives to the creditor for the enforcement of the contract conceivably may be either the debtor's property or his body. If the body is the security offered, then the propertyless debtor is returned to slavery under the name of *peonage* and under the justification of enforcing the sacredness of a contract. The Supreme Court has consistently overruled statutes where the debtor's body was made the security.

Thus market value, equality, and liberty are the related meanings of value in economics which change when economists change from physical or hedonistic philosophies to legal and political philosophies, and when political government changes from slavery and peonage to New Era or New Deal, and the meaning of "capitalism" itself changes with new and revolutionary meanings of value.

We have noted that the physical sciences, when they extended themselves to human beings, could find the nexus between individuals only in subjective love, sympathy, conscience. But that direction went toward medicine and not economics. Medicine included Freud's psychiatry which rested on sexual love, the principle of population, uniting Freud to Darwin and Malthus.

But the science of economics arose from exactly the opposite

[1] Peonage cases 123 F. 671; *Clyatt* v. *United States*, 197 U. S. 207 (1905); *Bailey* v. *Alabama*, 211 U. S. 452 (1908) and 219 U. S. 219 (1911); *Taylor* v. *Georgia*, 315 U. S. 25 (1942); *Pollock* v. *Williams*, 322 U. S. 1 (1944).

social nexus, not love but conquest, not subjective conscience, but sovereignty and revolutionary civil war. It required two revolutions, following the original Norman conquest, in Anglo-American history, to prepare the way for the science of economics. First was the capitalistic property owners' revolution against feudalism, 1689 in England, 1789 in France. In England this revolution introduced the separation of secular lawyers from theological lawyers in courts of law for the enforcement of contracts and corporation law. In America, the revolution of 1861 overthrew the slave-owners and opened the way for government by corporations and labor unions.

In Russia, where the revolution was delayed two centuries, it took the extreme form of both a property owners' revolution against feudalism and a wage earners' revolution against property owners—a double revolution of capitalism and communism. The revolution against feudalism was the short Kerensky revolution by a cabinet of property owners, followed in a few months by the Marx-Lenin-Trotsky-Bolshevik revolution against the property owners.

This double revolution in the first world war took a further development by the time of the second world war, in a patriotic nationalism of the whole Russian people against the "Old Bolsheviks" of the first revolution and their banner of "World Revolution." The remnant of the property owners, as shown by Kerensky's exiled cabinet member in America, P. A. Sorokin,[1] took refuge in a despondent philosophy of perpetual gangsterism and world war on account of his experience—the overthrow of private property.[2]

This despondent philosophy is to be contrasted with the pragmatic theory of the American judiciary in the effort to retain capitalism and head off revolution by deciding disputes in detail as they arise in particular cases. The effort, summarized from the decisions, makes the distinction between three kinds of capitalistic competition and the three corresponding kinds of value. These

[1] P. A. Sorokin, *The Crisis of Our Age*, New York, E. P. Dutton & Co., 1942.
[2] Sorokin afterwards recognized the difference in the New Russia under Stalin. See above reference.

distinctions are the extremes of "monopolistic competition" and "destructive competition," with somewhere between these extremes the level of "fair competition," equivalent to "reasonable value." To prevent these extremes, the courts of law intervene to use the physical compulsions of sovereignty and eliminate, if possible, through analysis of precedents of reasonable value, both monopolistic and destructive competition, and sustain the intervening reasonable competition and reasonable value. The result is not perpetual anarchy, but a stable government of "law and order," where the courts are the actual sovereign and the executive sheriffs and marshals obey the orders of the lower courts which follow opinions of value laid down by the Supreme Court.

Applying the statistical tests of proportions to these legal results, subject to further verification, the marginal cases of monopolistic and destructive extremes in times of peaceful industry between wars or revolutions are unlikely to be more than 5 or 10 per cent of the total, but the reasonable competition and reasonable values between the extremes are probably 90 per cent of the total. This does not mean that 90 per cent of the billions of transactions are reasonable in any ideal meaning of the word "value," but reasonable in a pragmatic sense of attainable under the historical circumstances of the time and place. Even the courts are revamped by revolutions of political parties, as in the case of the New Deal, after their theories of value get unbearable in business depression. The traditional economics, following mainly the Austrian school, makes "marginal competition" the leverage on which the whole capitalist system vibrates, going down as far as "cutthroat" competition in times of depression. And this is quite the truth where there is no concerted effort by government, courts, unions, or cartels, to regulate or protect against that degree of competition.

Here always, however, is the danger of running to the opposite extreme of "monopolistic competition" and the necessity of having administrative commissions in many fields to assist the courts with expert statisticians and economists acquainted with the public purpose of establishing reasonable values in place of monopolistic or destructive values. It is quite certain that the bulk of economists, since the prevalence of statistical methods, as well as the American people on the whole, have these ideals of reasonable value in mind as warnings against extremes in destructive, coercive, revolutionary, and monopolistic values.

These judicial standards of reasonable value and fair competition originated in the "good will" and "trade mark" cases 300 years ago. They were later applied to the public utility cases and perhaps to patent right cases (where monopoly is avowedly substituted for competition by legislative policy). These standards of reasonable value are, in effect, a policy of outlawing both extremes of monopoly and cutthroat competition, including such practices as fraud, oppression, pauperization, and the more evident inequalities and deprivations of liberty, even though they are made plausible by the Austrian economists' theory of marginal value. Attention to only the marginal and extreme cases has a powerful leverage in raising or depressing the entire level of reasonable value. But without the long history of judicial efforts toward reasonable value, the Anglo-American civilization might well have become, as in the history of many republics, a history of swings between the anarchic gangsterism of destructive values and the dictatorship of monopolistic values.

With the economists' theory of statistical probability and the courts' fair competition between outlawed extremes, we have an economic theory, not of a narrow dictatorial logic deduced from antagonistic single causations, but a theory of reasonable value worked out from the proportioning of the complex factors of multiple opportunities and choice of alternatives in a system of stabilized values.

Two kinds of scarcity are to be distinguished as the biological scarcity discovered by the classical economist Malthus and adopted by Darwin, and the proprietary scarcity differently interpreted by Hitler, Togo, Churchill, the great corporations, world cartels, labor unions, and the Supreme Court of the United States. Each kind of scarcity involves the theory of valuation in a distinctive way. The biological principle of scarcity itself came from a revolutionary war, the French Revolution of 1789, for it was an argument invented by Malthus against Godwin's effort in 1794 to bring the French Revolution into England. The pressure of a geometrical increase of population against only an arithmetical increase of subsistence, argued Malthus, would soon override the French innovations of equality and liberty, and would restore the existing inequalities and restraints on liberty. But the proprietary principle, for which Malthus was really arguing, while on the staff of the East India Company, was the extension of ownership by conquest over weaker races of people and ended in the principle of sovereignty which granted or withheld rights of property, that is, rights of scarcity, to individuals, corporations, cartels, and unions.

Of these two origins of the principle of scarcity—a "principle" being a recognized similarity of action—the legal origin, culminating in the world wars over dividing up ownership of the world's limited natural and produced resources among individuals and collections of individuals, has become by far the more dominating power, specialized in by lawyers in individual cases, but commanding and rationing all individuals and professions into literally a world war of life and death. It is this proprietary aspect of scarcity, which, within the past half century, has forced economic science out of the hands of traditional classical and hedonistic theorists of value in their individualistic economics into the hands of organized banker and lawyer practitioners along the principles of sovereignty, corporations, unions, property, liberty, and futurity.

The classical and communistic economists specialized on the principle of efficiency, or use value, latterly technology, as the means of multiplying the man-hour output in order to override their biological principle of scarcity derived from Malthus, but the legal economists specialize in property, liberty, and equality of individuals and corporations, as their dogma of the truly great sources of value—not the physical use values of the classical economists but the expected legal scarcity values of the lawyers and bankers.

Since the enforcement of contracts and corporate charters is the enforcement upon individuals of reciprocal economic rights, duties, liberties, and exposures in the acquisition and alienation of property by means of the arguments and theories of the courts, stabilized for the future as custom, the so-called "science" of *ethics* is derived from conquest and not from love. Here is the scientific origin of ethics. The ethical aspect of economics was retained by the physiocrats and Adam Smith, the founders of physical economics, only by retaining divine beneficence as an overruling providence instead of human sovereignty by conquest, and, after the theological stage was dropped, the science became strictly materialistic without love, sympathy, justice, or ethics. Not until the transition is made to courts of justice as the dominant economists, and their analysis of economic behavior into self-controlled performance measured by money, does economics again become integrated with ethical science. It is an ethics progressing slowly over centuries, sometimes by revolutions.

Thus, while the arbitrary human will is not recognized by physical scientists as conforming to that "natural law and order" which is the goal of science, as inaugurated by Newton, yet the similar methods of analysis—investigation by observation and experiment, guided by theorizing—entitle economics to the rank of science. The theory of reasonable operation of the human will in view of foresight and consequences makes economic value turn on a science of ethics based on reasonable use of *economic power* instead of *love, sympathy* and *conscience*, as suggested by Darwin and the materialistic scientists.

If the nineteenth century is the culmination of three centuries of the scientific revolution," [1] the twentieth century, beginning with two world wars, is preeminently the century of an ethical revolution to correct the world massacres resulting from the triumphs of "science." For the scientific revolution consisted in dropping both the divine will and the human will from the restraints of ethical investigation, and reducing not only physical nature but also human nature to a blind war of atoms, molecules, protons, electrons, statistics, quanta, and a bloody struggle for existence and survival.

The changes in western civilization during the eighteenth, nineteenth, and twentieth centuries have been so rapid, world-wide

---

[1] See James Henry Robinson, *The Mind in Its Making,* New York and London, Harper & Bros., 1921, pp. 151 ff.

and overwhelming that they have been named "revolutions" by many scientists and historians. The most fundamental aspect of these revolutions is in the ways of thinking, philosophizing, and theorizing that culminate in wars, conquests, and violent over-turning of governments; all of them are grounded on revolutions in the theory and practice of economic value and valuations in the various prices, profits, rents, interest, wages, salaries, backed by the institutions of corporations, cartels, unions, and political parties. Four fundamental revolutions in thinking, philosophizing, and governing have been named the "scientific revolution" the "ethical revolution," the "legislative revolution," and the "admin-istrative revolution." We are in the midst of all of them, and the present writer has been sixty years off and on in the hot places of each of them.

Every one of these revolutions followed a period of compla-cency, senility, and exploitation of the poor and ignorant by the well-to-do and "intelligentsia." What started as a revolution in its awakening became a satisfied exploitation of the weak in its old age. It survived as long as its scheme of economic values con-tinued to be vested and to afford a living without provoking eco-nomic revolt by inferiors.

The scientific revolution began after organized religious institu-tions had suppressed inventiveness and personal innovation, and it culminated when science had utterly expelled notions of a divine or human will, as well as all philosophizing and theorizing about things that could not be felt and measured as hard realities unchangeable by human will or ethical purpose. This complacent stage was the stage of "facts" as dogmatically asserted, or "de-terminism" and "fatalism" in the language of philosophy.

The reaction came as a "revival," even an "ethical revolution," when the more pugnacious of the exploiters resting on mere "facts" of superiority would be bodily lifted out of their position, while something new and "empirical" would edge into their places. Yet an empirical ethics had been going on since the six-teenth century reign of Queen Elizabeth, when the courts of justice began making the innovation of "fair" competition and "reasonable value" in the judge-made law of good will and trade reputation cases, in contrast to the "free" competition theories of nature's unlimited struggle for existence by the classical and hedonistic economists in the nineteenth century. The courts, during the centuries, had to presuppose the facts of the human will as performance, forbearance, avoidance, and timeliness in order to do justice between conflicting parties in particular cases as they might come to the surface. Then, in the course of centuries, the doctrine of fair competition and reasonable value was spread to newly emerging cases under new conditions, including even the newly recognized but ancient evils of slavery and peonage. Until finally what had been only empirical stabs at justice, without a rounded out theory, became entitled to the name of all-around ethical science. This became incorporated by the justices in all cases of value and valuation, especially cases of unpreventable monopolies or monopolistic practices.

The "legislative" revolutions were the violent revolutions of the seventeenth, eighteenth, nineteenth, and twentieth centuries against superior executive or judicial power, mainly the English Revolution, 1689, the French Revolution, 1789, the American Revolutions, 1776 and 1861, whereby constitutions, codes, or statutes were changed without providing anything except the victorious military power of an army of occupation for the executive administration of the laws.

The "administrative" revolution came afterwards in the form of administrative bureaus such as the Interstate Commerce Commission state and federal health departments, and many others, after it was realized that laws and constitutions were not self-executing where military power was withdrawn from their execution, and reliance was placed only on the judiciary. The most astonishing extension of private administrative or managerial power came with the delegation of power to corporations, cartels, and labor unions, with thousands of participants who therefore had to confer on "management" the regulation of all details including the "rationing" transactions of fixing salaries, wages, dividends, and the new issues of stocks and bonds.

A further significant stage of this administrative revolution was the more recent admission of labor unions, along with the management of corporations, as the governing body of the huge corporations. This stage constituted a new system of representative government in the more revolutionary economic matters of conflict, such as prices, wages, salaries, and dividends—in short, economic values.

Through the centuries of these revolutions the contradiction between *use value* and *scarcity value* becomes intensified and extended until it reaches the two global wars of the twentieth century over the closing by conquest of the world's frontiers and the predominance of scarcity values leading to rationing transactions. The "use values" of the classical economists were the equivalent of a philosophy of abundance, of "efficiency," of increased man-hour output, of utopian cooperatives such as the Knights of Labor and Farmers' Grange of many decades ago.

The "scarcity values" of the twentieth century stage were equivalent to the property values of lawyers and bankers, the rationing transactions of corporations, cartels, and unions, the income values, instead of output values, of money and credit instead of labor, bargaining power instead of producing power. Underneath the conflicts of postwar peace plans is this basic contradiction of use value and scarcity value, of producing and bargaining.

# Chapter xii

## *STRATEGY OF MANAGEMENT AND ADMINISTRATION*

———◆———

### 1. Degrees of Power

The control of collective action within its various forms of corporations, unions, and political parties, as well as the control of other organizations and individuals outside, have brought into economic investigations certain ideas which go to make up the strategy of management or administration in economic activity. These ideas may be summarized as degrees of power, velocity of transactions, and timeliness of action.

We consider here the degrees of power, and we distinguish power from energy, following the distinction made by Bertrand Russell between the human sciences and the physical sciences.[1] The so-called "forces" investigated in physics, astronomy, and chemistry are the forces of energy, but the forces in the economics of human activity are the power of individuals, largely through collective action, in controlling the activity of other persons.

These powers differ greatly, both in kind and in degree. Differences in kind are moral power, or propaganda; economic power, or bargaining power through proprietary control of supply or demand;[2] and physical power through administration of violence, the foundation of sovereignty. These differences in kind merge into each other, and each kind differs in many *degrees* of power over individuals. Taken together they constitute the whole of power in economic activity and its use in the public and private administration of economic affairs.

[1] Bertrand Russell, *Power,* New York, W. W. Norton & Co., 1938.
[2] Russell omits economic power, which he reduces to either propaganda or physical force.

How these distinctions of degree came to be recognized is an inquiry toward understanding their present-day significance and the way in which collective action operates.

The degrees of power came into recognition through the distinctions gradually made in the later nineteenth century economics between *quantities* and *intensity*. It required a century of economic theorizing before the distinction came between *quantities* of objects and *degrees* of power in controlling the quantities. Jeremy Bentham, in 1776, the same year of Adam Smith's *Wealth of Nations*, asserted that mankind was governed by "two sovereign masters," pleasure and pain, different in *kind* and *quantity*.[1] These were his materialistic substitutes for the religious heaven and hell. A hundred years later came the "hedonistic" or pleasure-pain economists, who proposed that pleasure and pain differed in *degree*, like other forces of nature, such as *heat* or *steam* power.

These theories of degree came to America from Austria in the decade of the 1880's. They were highly individualistic, materialistic, and relativistic. To these economists pleasure was a diminishing degree of pain, and pain was a diminishing degree of pleasure. At the extremes they were poles apart from each other, like the north and south poles of magnetism. Hence to this principle of differences in degree was given the name "polarity." On the Mohave Desert in California the extreme scarcity of water means death by thirst, but in a Mississippi flood the extreme abundance of water means death by drowning.

It was a simple matter to turn this *pleasure-pain* economics into *proprietary* economics, and to identify degrees of the power of scarcity with the power of property owners to withhold from others what they need but do not own. This was done as early as 1874 by the famous Swiss economist, Leon Walras. He was followed by the equally famous Pareto, teacher of Mussolini at the same university of Lausanne, in Switzerland.[2] Proprietary scarcity

[1] Jeremy Bentham, *Fragment on Government*, 1776.

[2] See Étienne Antonelli, "Walras, Marie Esprit Léon," edited by Edwin R. A. Seligman and Alvin Johnson, *Encyclopedia of the Social Sciences*, New York, The Macmillan Co., 1934, Vol. 15, pp. 328–329; and Talcott Parsons, "Pareto, Vilfredo," *Encyclopedia of the Social Sciences*, New York, The Macmillan Co., 1933, pp. 576–578.

now became the social force in control of individuals according
to different degrees of power to withhold from others what they
need under different circumstances. Evidently the most powerful
of political parties to grant proprietary privileges to corporations
But this ownership was granted by sovereignty through the power
of political parties to grant proprietary privileges to corporations,
and to grant immunity from punishment to labor unions in organizing to contest this power of corporations and other proprietors.

Thus did the pleasure-pain economics, in the course of a century
and a half after 1776, pass from differences in *kind* and *quantity*
to differences in *degree* of intensity of feelings. Afterward it
shifted to institutional economics in the differences in degree of
power between individual owners to differences in degree of power
between collective ownership by corporations. Then came the
further shift to a contest or equilibrium between corporations
and labor unions, each struggling for control of the political parties
which grant or withhold the rights, duties, liberties, and immunities of private property. Collective bargaining, with its differences in degree of power by control of scarcity and abundance,
comes into economics through corporations, unions, and politics.

Fitted to this incoming of degrees of power is the shift from
"utility" to "opportunity." The terms "utility" and "marginal
utility" signified, in the nineteenth century economics, the diminishing pleasure or increasing pain of individuals in enjoying
through consumption the physical commodities that satisfy wants.
But present-day proprietary scarcity signifies the alternative
opportunities for employment at different wage rates, or opportunity for sale or purchase by transferring ownerships at different
prices, quantities, and monetary values. The prices or wages may
be falling or rising, may be extortionate or confiscatory, may be
controlled or may run wild. They differ greatly in the degree of
power to control the opportunities open to individuals, from extremes at either end of the scale to reasonable treatment somewhere between the extremes.[1]

Inseparable from the modern recognition of degrees of intensity
and degrees of power is the recognition of velocity of repetition

[1] See "Legislative and Administrative Reasoning," p. 213.

of the transactions through which these degrees of power over others are exercised.

## 2. VELOCITY OF TRANSACTIONS

A river flows toward the sea. The hydraulic engineer builds a water-power dam through a cross section of the flow. His selection of the spot for the dam is determined by investigation of the speed of the current, the volume of water, the height of the drop that generates power by the force of gravity. He takes both a cross section or a "transverse" view of the flow, and a "longitudinal" view of the flow.

The foregoing five simplified assumptions of Part II and their various degrees of polarity are a cross section, a transverse view of the flow of economic life. They are economic "statics." Velocity converts them into "dynamics"—a longitudinal view of the speed, volume, and energy of the various currents in the economic flow.

This analogy to hydraulic engineering is not too farfetched after all. The accountants follow a similar procedure for the business corporations. They set up at the end of the fiscal year a cross section of assets and liabilities at that point of time. They also set up an income and outgo statement of all the transactions during the preceding year. The first is "static," a cross section, as though everything were stopped at that point of time. The second is a summary of results of all the activities during the year. Yet, being a summary, it conceals the "dynamics." The economist makes it dynamic by investigating in detail the transactions themselves during the year, their velocities, degrees of power, volumes, timeliness, whose results are summarized by the accountant at the end of the year.

How difficult it was to bring the idea of velocity into economics may be seen in the experience of Henry Dunning MacLeod, the lawyer-economist and pioneer investigator of the banking system of England, 1858.[1] He had the idea of velocity but he named it "productivity," by which he meant the *speed* of production of wealth. He was attacked by the economists who charged him with

[1] Henry D. MacLeod, *Theory and Practice of Banking*, 2 vols., London, Longmans, Brown, Green & Longmans, 1855.

counting the same thing twice, once as *wealth* and once as a *debt* owed to a creditor by the owner of the wealth.[1]

But MacLeod was not interested in such technological questions as physics, chemistry, the invention of the steam engine, and so on, which increased the speed of production beyond what unaided human labor could accomplish. Being a lawyer he was interested in the *ownership* of wealth and the *transfers* of ownership by means of the credit system. What he meant by "productivity" was the increased speed of production brought about by the lawyer's "discovery" of the "negotiability" of debts. He asserted that the discovery by lawyers that a debt was a "salable commodity" had produced more wealth and affected the fortunes of mankind more than all the inventions and all the gold mines of the world.

He explained it as follows: the lawyers discovered negotiability of debts during the seventeenth century in the custom of merchants. The merchants were accustomed to buying and selling to each other their debts to pay money, and enforcing the payment of these debts in their own merchants' courts operated by the merchant guilds of the Middle Ages. But the common law, originating during the same period, recognized only *tangible* property, and considered debts as a personal promise, like a marriage contract, not salable to third parties who were strangers.

Prior to this discovery a merchant, when making a sale of commodities on credit, had to wait perhaps several months, especially in foreign trade, before he could receive the gold or silver in payment from his debtor. But when the debt itself was made negotiable, like the gold or silver itself, he could sell it to a banker in exchange for a banker's debt, known as a "deposit," a debt payable immediately on demand or salable on the money market. Being thus salable in exchange for commodities, it was as good as metallic money. Indeed, it became bank notes circulating like money.

Then, after MacLeod's time in the middle of the nineteenth

[1] Especially by Böhm-Bawerk in Austria, Knies in Germany and Sidgwick in England, in the 1870's and 1880's.

century, in both England and America, these bank notes became the modern bank checks, a money of account, drawn by depositors but not circulating at all. They were merely transferred from one deposit account to another deposit account in the same bank or any other bank through clearing houses in the entire banking system of the nation or world. Since the world wars have forced the nations to lock up the world's gold and take it out of circulation, it is this negotiability of banker's debts, payable on demand by transfers of book credits, that becomes practically the whole of the money system of the nation. Its velocity and its changes in velocity become the tragedy of the capitalist system.

Considering the ambiguity of MacLeod's notion of "productivity" as the *speed* of production, there are three different meanings of velocity used in present-day economics, stated briefly as follows:

1. Velocity of *output* in the production of wealth, a technological meaning, measured by man-hours;
2. Velocity of changes in *ownership* of commodities and securities, measured by dollars;
3. Velocity of *bank credit* creation and cancellation on the money market conducted by the bankers, measured by dollars.

These different velocities are not separable in actual practice, but they are measurable separately and have entirely different agencies for their conduct and administration. The differences between the three, and yet their correlation, may be illustrated by a shipment of shoes from Boston to New Orleans, reported in the newspapers during the period of business recovery in 1922. During the week or ten days required for the shipment on the railroad, the shoes were sold twelve times. They were the same shoes, and their transportation was the similar labor process of production of wealth as had been the manufacturing of the shoes. This was the technological process coming under managerial transaction and measured by man-hours.

But what was sold on the commodity market in Boston was not the shoes—it was the *ownership* of the shoes. These were the twelve alienations and acquisitions of ownership, to use the terminology of the law, coming under our definition of bargaining transactions, and our second meaning of velocity.

Each alienation and acquisition was presumably made by means of a check drawn against a deposit at a bank somewhere in the credit system of the United States. This was the money market conducted by the banks, our third meaning of velocity. This market was, in fact, a creation of *new money* at a different price or total value of the shoes, an increasing speculative *price* per pair of shoes, or increasing monetary *value* for the total shipment.

These alienations and acquisitions on the books of the banks appear in the statistics as "debits to accounts." They are debits to some accounts and credits to other accounts. The "debits to accounts" are the velocities of creation and cancellation of modern money, which is the creation and cancellation of purchasing power through the legal enforcement of contracts. And since each new price and new value, reflected in each new creation of bank money, is based on expectations of further increases in future prices and values during a general rise of prices, these are the record of credit transactions and therefore are the speculative aspect of the bargaining transactions—speculative because new money is created by the new debts in order to accomplish the purchases and transfers of ownership at increasing prices and values.

Other similarities and differences will appear. One is the distinction between the long-time trends in technology and the short-time cycles of prosperity and depression. During the more than a hundred years of mechanical inventions since the beginning of the nineteenth century, the speed of technological output per man-hour is estimated, on the average, to have increased eight-fold, and since the beginning of the twentieth century has increased probably fourfold. This is the technological meaning of MacLeod's "productivity."

On the other hand, the credit cycle increases the velocity of transfers of ownership in a period of recovery or prosperity as seen in our twelve transfers of ownership of the shoes, and greatly decreases the velocity of these transfers in a period of depression. This was MacLeod's real meaning of "productivity."

Moreover, since the product of a credit transaction is a negotiable debt, and since the accumulation of bankers' demand debts is the quantity of modern money under the name of deposits, and if these demand debts are *accumulating* faster than they are being paid and *cancelled,* then we have an *increase* in the quantity of money under the name of deposits. Inversely, if a part of the demand debts or modern money is paid and cancelled more rapidly than the other parts are created, then there is a *decrease* in the quantity of money under the name of deposits.[1]

### 3. TIMELINESS OF ACTION

In February, 1923, I visited Mr. Crissinger, Comptroller of the Currency and member of the Federal Reserve Board. I had come from New York where a confidential letter had been received from an official, stating that in the controlling circles at Washington everybody seemed to be dangerously committed to inflation. The statisticians in New York, who had been watching the inflation daily from the low point of depression in 1922, were alarmed at the velocity of the general rise in prices. They were rising at a rate even faster than they had risen in the disastrous inflation of April 1919 to June 1920. Mr. Crissinger said, "Yes, we all know about it; we know *what* to do, but we do not know *when* to do it, nor *how far* to go."

What the Reserve banks had been doing for several months was selling securities on the open market and they had just begun raising the rates of rediscount at Federal Reserve banks in different parts of the country. The inflation of wholesale prices stopped, within the next two months, and the average commodity price level remained fairly stable for the next five years. The Reserve Board then issued, in April 1923, its rather vague statement of a new policy based on this new experiment of timely control during 1922 and the early months of 1923.

I had been acquainted with the theory of what the Board was then doing from earlier writings of the Swedish economist, Knut

---

[1] For calculations of these quantities and velocities, see "Credit Administration," p. 239.

Wicksell.[1] But, although Wicksell, the economist, might tell *what* to do to prevent inflation and deflation, he did not tell the practical man entrusted with responsibility the other essentials he needed to know, just *when* to do it, *where, how much*, and with what *degree* of power to do it. This was my discovery of timeliness. It depended on the control of velocities. This control over human behavior depends on *doing* the "right" thing at the right *time*, the right *place*, with the right *degree of power*, and *always in advance*. The human activity here at issue was that of the bankers and business men of a nation, borrowing, lending, and actually creating bank credit, the modern money, with which to bid up all prices and call in the unemployed laborers, with the prospect of increasing business profits if they got there quick enough and ahead of their competitors. The administrative control over this kind of behavior consisted in making it more expensive to borrow and get into debt in a period of rising prices, not for any particular individual, but for *all* individuals, without the administration knowing whether it was acting too soon or too late, too aggressively or too cautiously, to get the results wanted in the unknown future.

The statisticians had worked out their theories of prices and equilibrium on a theory of probability. But probability had two meanings. It meant the law of averages, and it meant estimating what would happen to particular prices on the markets in the specified future. Both estimates were assumed to be based on statistics. But the statistics were collected upon what had happened in the past. There are no statistics of the future. Future probabilities can only be guessed with some aid from past relationships projected into the future.

A prosperous stock speculator once told me how he had become successful in predicting the future of stocks, but it was not only on statistics—it was on wisdom and sagacity. That was the reason why he was successful. A million other people had guessed wrong. I attended a luncheon, in February 1923, of professional statisticians attached to great industries and banks. Each one of us sitting around the table guessed *when* the peak of wholesale prices

[1] Knut Wicksell, *Geldzins und Guterpreise*, Jena, 1898.

would be reached and *how high* the peak would be. Afterwards I checked up. We did not know what the Federal Reserve Board was going to do to check the inflation. Some of the guesses were completely off in time, or peak. The average was 50 per cent off in one dimension and 40 per cent off in the other dimension. One of the forecasters had saved his bank from bankruptcy at the preceding slump of prices in 1920, by guessing right when his competitors were guessing wrong.

I began to classify businessmen and bankers according to their strategic and routine transactions. The strategic transaction is the one that is controlling; it is "timely." Businessmen call it "timing." The principle is not new—it belongs to the recognized facts of the human will in attempting to control the forces of nature and of human nature.

The principle of timeliness is to be contrasted with the economists' theory of equilibrium. The two are not contradictory. Timeliness is business control of equilibrium at the right time. The nineteenth century economists developed a remarkable theory of natural or automatic equilibrium, provided every individual had perfect liberty to work or not to work as he wished, and provided there were no stoppages, frictions, monopolies, political interferences or wars. This was a theory in which prices and wages adjusted themselves automatically according to supply and demand, determined by the economists' discoveries of margins of production, cost, utility, and other margins. These margins were the points where the equilibrium of forces adjusted wages, prices, interest rates, and rents to the quantities of supply and demand. Thus the early economists assumed a high flexibility of incomes, a high mobility in all the factors of investment, of capital, labor, and land, by which these factors were changed promptly from one occupation of low income to another of higher income. They assumed also a full and continuous employment of all these factors that cooperate in the great complexity of world production.

In course of time this doctrine was improved to distinguish between "limiting and complementary" factors. One of the notable circumstances that compelled this improvement was the stoppage of the cotton mills in England and the serious unemployment, because the Civil War in America made raw cotton the limiting factor. The British government turned its attention to cotton and nearly brought on a war with the northern states in order to get the limiting factor from the south.

These limiting and complementary factors are strategic and routine transactions when viewed as social relations under guidance of the will. When one limiting factor is controlled at the right time, in the right place, and with the right degree of power, then it can be left to routine, while the next limiting factor needing different treatment must be attended to. The farmer, at one time, if he knows agriculture, supplies potash in limited quantities, and then goes on to other activities which are strategic to the production of his crop if done in their proper place, at the proper time, and in proper quantity.

The matter is familiar, universal, and simple enough, when stated theoretically, but the problem of just when, how much, and under what circumstances to act, rises to the degree of genius and can never be reduced to a science. One may point out the general principles of timeliness and strategy, but can go no further. The forces of nature and human nature are so complementary and delicate that a very little human control of what happens to be the one factor that limits the others at the time and place will set the others at work in the direction intended. This may appear simple but it requires managerial genius.

The first change in economic theory which timeliness and strategy involve is from a passive mind to an active participating mind, and second, a change from individual action to collective action—briefly from sensations of pleasure and pain impacted from outside to activities of the will endeavoring to control nature and other human beings by controlling what, at the time, is the limiting factor. Nothing similar is found in the forces with which the physical sciences deal. Economics is a science of the will in action, controlling both physical nature and the routine workers by timely action in advance.

The reason why timeliness cannot be scientific, in the accepted sense of "science," is because it cannot be measured, and it cannot be measured because it always looks to the future for which no facts and statistics are as yet in existence.

A theory of perfect equilibrium in the future can be constructed by assuming that the individual has perfect knowledge in making his choice of alternatives. Failure to realize expectations can then be charged to error or ignorance or even uncertainty. But the individual must suffer the consequences of this failure. Timeliness would have no meaning to either an omniscient or a passive mind. But for an active participating mind, active in the nature of *things*, timeliness is the very essence of the strategy of control.

When industries and banking were on a small scale, a bad guess of the future ruined only the one who guessed wrong. But when the people of a whole community depend for employment on the management of a great corporation, or millions depend upon the guesses of a few bankers in control of the entire banking system, then the *prevention of risk*, that is, the *organization of security*, is the greatest public service that the management or the administration can render to the nation or the world.

In contrast with the timely action of the Federal Reserve Board in 1923 was the disastrous untimely action in the preceding year 1920, and again in 1928 and 1936. In 1920 an inflation of commodity prices had been going at the rate of about 2 per cent increase per month, amounting to about 30 per cent increase from March 1919 to June 1920. If the Reserve Board had advanced the reserve bank rate as early as April 1919, or if it had notified the business world that the rate would be advanced, then the inflation of commodity prices in 1920 would probably have been prevented. Such was the testimony *afterwards* of a member of the Board, before the congressional committee. But no such action was taken. Instead, the Board waited until June 1920, when it became evident that a collapse was imminent, and then the Board suddenly announced a doubling of the discount rate to 7 per cent, which was the immediate cause of the disastrous collapse of commodity prices in the few months following. The Reserve Board was fifteen months too late; and then only an extreme and drastic curb on business was perpetrated.

A similar mistake was made in the years 1925 to 1929. In 1925, a terrifying inflation had begun, this time an inflation of security prices. The Board gave no intimation of using its powers to check the inflation. Stock inflation seemed good for business. Then in 1928 and the first part of 1929 the Board went to an extreme in using all of the powers which it then had, and actually precipitated the worst collapse in the world's history. A gradual use of its powers, and an announcement in advance, during 1925 to 1928 would have checked the inflation and obviated the collapse. It was bad "timing."

Exactly the opposite mistake was made in 1936. The Congress had given to the Reserve Board an entirely new economic power, the power to double the reserve requirements of member banks. In its first use of this power, in 1936, the Board evidently became hysterical and hostile on account of the rapid rise of prices accompanying the recovery which had been started by the new administration in 1933. The recovery had not yet gone far enough to bring back into industry the unemployed workers, but the Board suddenly doubled the reserve requirements of member banks and brought on the second collapse, of 1937. In this case the Board acted too soon and too severely, whereas in 1920 and 1929 it acted too late, but in 1923 it acted just right. Timeliness is the most important principle in all collective economics, especially in the administration of the credit system.

These criticisms of the Federal Reserve Board are confirmed by Mr. Carl Snyder, a long-experienced statistician and economist of the Federal Reserve Bank in New York. He wrote, in 1940, regarding the preceding depression of 1929, compared with the timely policies of prevention in 1921, 1924, and 1927:

A profound misfortune that such a brilliant beginning should come to such an end. In credit control we have a powerful mechanism that might be used to maintain a degree of economic stability such as this country has hitherto never enjoyed.[1]

When I visited factories, and asked the manager what was the most important thing he had to attend to, he said it was "timing."

[1] Carl Snyder, *Capitalism the Creator*, New York, The Macmillan Co., 1940, p. 228. Copyright, 1940, by The Macmillan Co. See also p. 249 of this book.

There were so many things that might stop the whole works. He would ask me to go through the establishment with him. He was proud of the smooth way in which the materials were going through. The cloth came in to the spongers at the top of the building, then came down to workers on the several floors, then out to branch factories, going through several hundred hands, and in seven days the cloth finally came back, a finished suit of clothing to be sent out to the retailers. Formerly to complete a suit required thirty days. The shortening of the process to seven days was magnificent timing.

Since timeliness is not something isolated, but is the timely way in which other factors are controlled, we may name the three factors, degree of power, velocity of transactions, and timeliness of action, as the combination of factors in the strategy of corporate management and public administration.

# Chapter xiii

## CONCILIATION AND LIMITATIONS

---

### 1. MEASURABILITY

When the various sciences, especially astronomy, in our own generation, came to accept the theory of "relativity," then the "pure" sciences had become solely a set of mathematical equations which only a few mathematicians could prove. The other millions of plain people of the world were called upon to accept the proof on the word of the mathematicians, since the proof was beyond the peoples' understanding. Thus the sciences have a field of dogmatism where only the word of a high mathematical authority must be accepted by the unlearned masses of the people—something like the priestcraft of the Middle Ages.

When the science of economics reached this period of mathematical relativity, toward the end of the nineteenth century while emerging from the field of political philosophy, the qualified economists reached a similar attitude of dogmatism toward the masses of people, who could not understand their equations. The popular ignorance and disagreements were counted as illusions or dishonesties, when they disputed the "laws of political economy."

Yet when the science reached the still later stage, when its theories of value were based upon the expected events of the future discounted to a present worth, this field of futurity, for the practical man, had no facts or statistics yet in existence on which measurements could be made to prove their validity for him. The nineteenth century economists, notwithstanding their dogmatisms, had one grand argument for restricting their science to the single field of increasing the production of wealth by liberating the individual from all interferences by governments, political parties, labor unions, or other collective action. It was the argument that if the man-hour efficiency of all industries could be increased so greatly as to bring the world into a period of *abundance* in place of the medieval, feudal, or mercantile policies of *scarcity*, then all the conflicting disagreements and class conflicts, based on contradictory philosophies and religions, would sink to insignificance in the presence of abundance of free opportunities to earn a living and get rich.

This is true enough, as can be imagined for example, of a population of dogs, thrown into a pit and struggling over a limited supply of bones, and the same population liberated in the wide world of abundance. Even the pessimistic theory of Malthus (1798) and its acceptance later by Darwin (1859), of a pressure of increasing population against a slower increase of subsistence, was discounted by the economists' optimistic theory of the expected increase in wealth and subsistence when individuals should be liberated from the restraints upon freedom of trade.

This is indeed the great paradox of the nineteenth and twentieth centuries, that while the productive efficiency of free enterprise has increased the output probably eightfold per man-hour of those employed, yet the increased efficiency has ended in the greatest period of unemployment and world-wide struggle for "bread and work" and for survival, beginning in 1914, that the western world has ever experienced.

The physical sciences had triumphed on the principle of free enterprise and the mathematically accurate measurement of the physical forces to be controlled, but the new economic freedom expected from the increased abundance turned to "grapes of wrath."

We can here consider four of the shortcomings of the narrow science of economics based solely on a theory of increasing productivity but ending in this paradox of abundance and poverty. They are the inadequacy of measurement, the irrelevancy of the discussion, the incomplete analysis, and the personal bias.

What are the factors requiring measurement by economists, distinguished from measurement in the physical sciences? The answer depends upon the purpose of the measurements. Two immediate purposes stand out amidst the diversity of selfish interests. They are the conciliation of conflicting interests, and the limitation on the excesses of individual and collective self-interest.

The quantitative method of accomplishing these purposes is the statistical method of averages. An average is not an entity, like "the average man" or "the average price"—or even the so-called "law of averages." An average in the field of conciliation is a working rule for constructing a "weighted average" for the purpose of rationing to the different self-interests a field of activity according to what is deemed to be their relative importance in accomplishing the purpose intended.

One of the most comprehensive "weighted averages" is that constructed by Mr. Carl Snyder, statistician to the Federal Reserve Bank of New York, in 1928, for the purpose of measuring the quantity of bank credit needed to maintain stability of the general price level in the United States. He named his average an "index" of the demand for credit in the United States, year by year, apportioned to the several industries in proportion to the "weight" of each in composing the total demand, as follows:

### COMPONENTS OF THE GENERAL PRICE LEVEL [1]

|  | WEIGHT % |
|---|---|
| 1. Industrial prices, wholesale (nonagricultural) | 10 |
| 2. Farm prices, at the farm | 10 |
| 3. Retail food—51 cities | 10 |
| 4. Rents—32 cities | 5 |
| 5. Clothing, fuel, furnishings, etc., retail | 10 |
| 6. Freight—transportation costs | 5 |
| 7. Realty values—urban and farm | 10 |
| 8. Securities—bonds and stocks | 10 |
| 9. Equipment and machinery | 10 |
| 10. Hardware prices | 3 |
| 11. Automobile prices | 2 |
| 12. Wages—Fed. Res. Bd and N. Y. composite | 15 |
| TOTAL | 100 |

[1] Published in *Review of Economic Statistics,* Harvard University, Vol. X, No. 1, page 51, February 1928, as part of "The Measure of the General Price Level," by Carl Snyder. Copyright, 1927, by Harvard University, Cambridge, Mass. The index is published currently in the *Monthly Review of Credit and Business,* New York Federal Reserve Bank.

This mental construction of a weighted average is highly important in economics, and is a subject of extensive investigation. A
New York banker-economist advised me that Snyder's "securities"
should be given a weight of 30 instead of 10. Evidently in his
business it seemed to him that the dealings in stocks and bonds
accounted for a frequency of demand for credit much larger than
the proportion allowed by Snyder. Indeed, in the year 1929
stocks and bonds should have the whole weight, 100, judged by
the effect of their collapse on all other prices. On the other hand,
farmers infer, from their own business relations, that the nation
does not have enough money to satisfy the farmers' need for
money. Hence many of them agitate for a large increase in the
total quantity of credit for the nation, although they would require, according to Snyder, only 10 per cent of the total supply.
Other classes are similar. Each of Snyder's twelve classes is
confident that the nation does not have enough money to enable
it to purchase from all others the just equivalent of what it sells
to all the others.

A weighted average, or frequency curve, in this important economic issue, attempts to rid each class of individuals of the self-
illusion that it is the most important of all interest in the need of
money, and asks it to *weigh* itself, that is, to *value* itself, according to its relation to all other classes and to the nation as a whole.
Thus the simple average of wholesale prices, computed seventy-
five years before, becomes finally the highly important but controversial issue of a weighted average of all kinds of prices. In a
democratic country where each group is permitted to organize
and to bring pressure upon the government for more money, this
issue of a mere mental tool of investigation may become the
instrument for inflation of all prices by a few groups, or deflation
of all prices by other groups, or for some "working agreement,"
or rule of action, between all groups.

In such an economic and political conflict something more is
needed than the careful and patient investigations of a statistician,
or even an agreement among statisticians, which others accept
on faith. Also is needed the consensus of the interests affected,
that the averages and proportions arrived at are fair and reason-

able for each within the total limits deemed fitting for the nation as a whole in its need of money.

I have found in such cases, that if the economist is associated as an adviser, or a chairman, or a mediator, with the leaders of the organized economic interests concerned, and having their confidence but not a right to vote, then he is a scientist, not as in the physical sciences where it is necessary for the scientists only to agree among themselves, but in the science of working rules among collective but conflicting economic interests. He is not likely to be successful by himself, but when he investigates and works in a group, he tries to understand their conflicts and to bring them together in the actual laboratory where the conflict takes place. Understanding and concilation, not mere facts, are the goals of economic investigation. Weighted averages help to understand the most important of economic relations—the relative importance of the parts in making up the whole.

A similar, and indeed the same, issue of weighted averages in the effort to avoid extremes and to agree on reasonable value in the use of economic power, was pushed forward by the organized agricultural interests in the legislation on "parity" and "disparity" prices in 1933, but which was declared unconstitutional by the Supreme Court, in 1936.[1]

This was an effort to measure also differences in degrees of economic power, this time exercised by the manufacturing interests in contrast with the agricultural interests of the nation. The average prices of the years 1909–1914 were taken as "parity prices" and given an index value of 100. Then for a succeeding year, at the bottom of the depression, the economic power of the farmers had weakened so greatly, compared with the economic power of the manufacturers, that the index of average farm prices had fallen to 70 per cent of parity, a relative decline of about one-third in comparison with the economic power of manufacturers. This was a measurement of relative changes in degrees of economic power between two classes, quite applicable to and often used for the measurement of relative coercive powers of other classes, such as wage earners, women workers, organized and un-

[1] See "Legislative and Administrative Reasoning," p. 213.

organized economic classes, with a view both to public information and to remedial administration.

Weighted averages are, in all cases, a matter of serious investigation, although the results have not the precision required in the physical sciences. Weighted averages exhibit instead an "order of magnitude" of the statistical quantities, which is all that can be expected in those economic investigations where the purpose is conciliation and restraint against abuse of excessive economic power.

Equally important with giving *weights* to the components of the average is the selection of the components that are *relevant* to the issue.

## 2. RELEVANCY

The selection of similarities and the weighing of their relative importance is a selection of facts that are relevant to the purposes intended, and the rejection of facts that are irrelevant. Economists in times past have sought more solid ground than a mere mental comparison of similarities and differences upon which to rest their science of economics. They have attempted to be too fundamental. The first of these fundamentalist assumptions was derived from the deistic theology of the eighteenth century, as was done by Quesnay, the physiocrat, in France, and by John Locke and Adam Smith, the founders of "classical economics," in England. The assumption was that of a deity of the universe whose purpose was happiness for mankind. When converted into economics this became the assumption of nature's abundance.

This purpose of God was reversed by the theological economist, Thomas Malthus, in his theory of overpopulation and the resulting scarcity. God's purpose, with Malthus, was the evolution of moral character through struggle, which he found in the "middle classes." These divine purposes are, indeed, found in assumptions of national gods intending success for one's nation, or for one's self, or punishment for others who interfere with this divine law. While such beliefs play an important part in the economic life of getting a living or getting rich, they assume the very thing to be investigated and measured, namely, whether a given plan of management or administration is the best plan possible, under the circumstances, for the general welfare of all participants. Fundamentalist assumptions prevent investigation and argument.

There have been other fundamentalist assumptions derived from other sciences. They may be materialistic, physical, chemical, biological, physiological, or psychological. They can be tested by experiments and measurements in their own fields, but not by the kind of experiments known to the economics of getting a living or getting rich, with due regard to the general welfare. It has long since been noted that economic science, in its search for a solid foundation, has taken its ideas and methods from such other sciences as had attained, at the time, a dominant place in the field of research. Various economists wanted to be Newtons, with Newton's harmony of the spheres and his laws of equilibrium. Economists also built on Lavoisier's chemistry, with its affinities and repulsions of atoms. Physics and chemistry appear to be the two main historical sources of materialistic fundamentalism. The science of economics thus became mechanistic, as it had been theological, and this materialistic fundamentalism extends from Ricardo to Marx and to the present day.

Then came biology, reduced to scientific proportions by Darwin, and society became an organism. The analogy to an organism was a fundamentalism descending from earliest times, which asserted some people to be the brains, others the hands, others the feet. Eminent economists adopted this analogy, which we must dismiss as biological irrelevancy, since the analogy cannot be proved or disproved by experiments and measurements in the economics of getting a living or getting rich under existing circumstances and for the general welfare. Instead of organisms, we have institutions. The several fields of the various sciences thus become mechanisms, organisms, and institutions.

More recently psychology, relevant to economics because of the postulate of organism, found for itself an experimental science in physiology, and under the name of "behaviorism," a section of economists found their fundamentals in the intestines, in glands, or in psychoanalysis. But these organs and mental acts are not subject to economic experiment and measurement in man-hours or dollars. Instead of this kind of individualistic "behaviorism," there can be substituted that behaviorism of reaching agreements among conflicting parties on the working rules intending to harmonize their interests and guide their future behavior, which is the economics of negotiations, transactions, management, and administration.

Another type of fundamentalism has arisen from Darwin's distinction between natural selection and artificial selection. Darwin acknowledged that his term "natural selection" was a personification of nature as though it were a human being. It would have been less misleading to have named them purposeless and purposeful selection. His "natural selection," when applied to economics, becomes the tooth-and-claw struggle to earn a living or to get rich at the expense of others, without consideration of rights and duties. This has been, indeed, the assumption in the economics of self-interest combined, however, with "rights of liberty" and "natural rights" as the foundations of self-interest. The violent reaction is found in revolutions avowedly founded on the compulsion of duties, rejecting the fundementalism of liberty and natural rights. But rights and duties do not come from nature, they come from the collective action of human beings. By using the term "nature" with the double meaning of physical nature and human nature, human nature is reduced to the physical nature of a mechanism or an organism.

It has always been uncertain where to draw the line in the theory of evolution between animal and man. But for the economic purposes of getting a living, there is a historical line in the paleolithic age when the animal first began to construct and use tools, and first began to organize communistic institutions for the control of individuals.

Human beings have often been distinguished as "tool-using animals." This means that the animal in question began to look to the future, just as he did in the domestication of animals which were also his tools, and to look to the control of nature and human nature as a present instrument for attaining future ends. Ultimately the physical and biological sciences were constructed, and the evolution of physical nature by purposeful selection takes on an astonishing increase of output which we name "efficiency," or "productivity."

What is true of artificial evolution by mechanization and domestication is true also of that artificial evolution which we name institutionalism. It began as primitive communism. It is the evolution of control of individuals by collective action. Its product in individuals has been named "the institutionalized mind."

The foregoing varieties of fundamentalism have undoubtedly filled gaps during the evolution of economic science. In fact, economic science necessarily uses much of the language of other sciences in order to make clear its own meanings of words, and much of the methodology and mathematics of other sciences in its own theories. But the science of economics uses only parts of what the other sciences have organized as a whole in their own fields, and only in so far as needed to construct its own simplified assumptions and relativities fitted to its own field of investigation and experiment. None of the five assumptions in Part II, as we have simplified them, is found in any of the other sciences. They are constructed out of direct observation of the ways in which human beings act as nations, as corporations, as unions, as individuals, or as political parties in the economic field of making a living or getting rich by acquiring shares of the work done by each other.

Each simplified assumption has previously been made a field of investigation in its own science. But each, in economics, is found to be related to all the others. This mental instrument of relativity has come into economics along with similar developments in other sciences. We can note its incoming during the past fifty years, without resorting to the analogies of fundamentalism, as a method of bringing together physical sciences that formerly were separated. In searching for a similar evolution in economic science we can find the science changing from the fundamentalisms of divine beneficence and punishment, to the mechanisms of physics and chemistry, then to the organisms of biology, finally to the relativities among themselves of the several simplified assumptions, which we have reduced to five. These assumptions are derived, in part, from other sciences whose relevancy to economics is tested by investigations of purposes, experiments, and measurements in the field of making a living or getting rich by reciprocal giving and receiving services.

There is a further distinction between natural selection and artificial selection, or, rather purposeless and purposeful selection. The human will does not override "natural laws," either of physical nature, animal nature, or human nature. It makes use of them in accomplishing its purposes. Custom is a natural law of human beings, but the Court selects *reasonable* customs to be followed in the future as against *obsolescent* customs that now contradict what it deems to be the American public purpose of equal opportunity in earning a living or getting rich. Since customs change, the evolution of custom is the artificial selection by the judiciary of those customs which shall survive. This can readily be tested by investigating historically the decisions of courts for the past three hundred years in selecting between the good and bad customs relevant to the negotiability of debts, with the purpose of making them as nearly equivalent as possible to metallic money.[1]

Philosophers, theologians, and economists have debated much about idealism and materialism, about cause and effect, about determinism and free will. These debates are too fundamental for our purposes. Economics, in comparison, is a rather superficial science. Instead of the fundamentalist opposites of idealism and materialism we make use of the transactional time dimension of future and present. Futurity is the mental field of ideas of a goal to be realized in the immediate or remote future, by means of present activities pressing forward toward that purpose.

We thus have the three stages previously mentioned, of negotiation, transaction, and administration of the rules laid down in the commitments of the transaction. It is only the last, or administrative stage, that is strictly scientific, in that it is the stage of results or consequences that can be measured by man-hours or dollars, although the time measurements tie together

---

[1] See J. R. Commons, *Legal Foundations of Capitalism*, New York, The Macmillan Co., 1924, pp. 246 ff.

the present commitments and the expected performances or payments.

Likewise with the debates on cause and effect, or determinism and free will, economists during the past century have been gradually developing a more transactional and less fundamental theory of cause and effect, or free will and determinism, resting on the relations between future and present, between purpose and experiment. This development is partly in the principle of "limiting and complementary factors," translated into strategic and routine transactions. The strategic factor is the one that limits, for the time being, the operation of all the complementary factors. Yet the two are changing place continously. The limiting factor is continually changing in the moving point of time which we name the present, but is also inseparable from the past and future. By controlling the limiting factor in the present, we expect that our control of it will result in bringing about what we now want but which is, as yet, in the future.

Early economists, copying physical scientists, placed causation in the past and effect in the present. But a science of getting a living or getting rich relative to public purpose places causation in the future and effect in the present. Its questions turn on reasons and consequences. It becomes a science of present worth and future purpose.

This is *why* we act as we do, and this is what we mean by the reasons given for acting. It is purpose in action. Any fact that throws light on this relation, not only of past cause to present effect, or historical development, but of the future to the present, of end to the means employed, of purpose to experiment, is relevant to economic investigation.

All sciences seek understanding, as well as facts. Facts are sought to correct misunderstanding. Facts are the proven experiments. To seek understanding is to ask the question, Why?

But the why in economics differs from the why in other sciences. My electric pump man, after several experiments, gives it up and asks me, "Why do you suppose that pump knocks only on the down stroke?" He investigated to discover a cause that preceded the effect. But if I, as an economist, investigate the pump man himself, I ask, "Why do you leave your family and keep sober, hire an assistant, and work so hard in order to satisfy me by stopping that knock in the pump?" I am investigating a purpose that precedes an effect. His answer I understand when I visit his home, for he has a family to support, and he understands that I intend to pay him 75 cents per hour, in addition to paying his assistant. He was experimenting to find a cause; I was interviewing to find a reason.

This comparison may be objected to because my pump man is an engineer or mechanic, and not a scientist. But I am informed by scientists that nowadays important scientific discoveries are made by engineers. They have previously studied the pure science, and it does not yet answer their practical questions.

The economist's principle of "limiting and complementary factors" applies to man's use of physical sciences as well as to economic science. In either case the practical man is hunting for the limiting factor, which, when once controlled, will by means of what he understands to be the complementary forces of nature bring about the purpose intended far beyond anything he can do as an individual. But in the economics of collective action the limiting factor may be the purposes of participants. By directing the purposes of other people the practical man induces them to do what he wants them to do. The test of his degree of success is in the agreements and understandings reached through transactions. Men do not negotiate with the forces of nature. They put a ring in the bull's nose. For this reason we distinguish strategic and routine transactions. The routine transactions follow, by "laws" of human nature, if the correct strategic transaction is discovered and carried through. What the economic scientist does, as such, compared with the practical man, is to generalize this universal fact of human nature as the mental tool of strategic and routine factors to be used for investigation of particular cases. Any similarity bearing upon this discovery of limiting factors and strategic transactions is relevant to economics, for it is the way purpose acts.

For this reason ethics is relevant to economics. But what kind of ethics? Individualistic and therefore subjective feelings, or institutional and historical ethics and therefore transactions? We find the latter near at hand, in all directions. If we examine ourselves, we find that all of us are participants in this historical ethics. Often this kind of ethics is formulated as codes. It may be business ethics, labor ethics, professional ethics, or even gangster ethics. It is economic idealism, good or bad. It rests on the "foundation" that everybody makes his living or gets rich by getting a share of collective control of services rendered by others. This is accomplished through bargaining, managerial, and rationing transactions.

When I was investigating the constitutionality of acts of legislators or administrative authorities, I looked for the meaning of "legal ethics," which I found defined as "that branch of moral science which treats of the duties which a member of the legal profession owes to the public, to the court, to his professional brethren, and to his client."

When I was acting as arbitrator or mediator in disputes between associated employers and associated employees, and then compared my acts with those of other arbitrators, I found myself in a position comparable to that of a court of justice, with duties to both the employers and the employees as well as to the public, which prevented me from arbitrarily setting myself up as a dictator on my own theories of economics. I was no longer an individual who might act as one pleases—I was an institution. I was selected jointly by both sides of the dispute simply because they could agree upon me, and my freedom was further limited at times by the similar selection of other arbitrators to act jointly with me, under the requirement that our decision should be unanimous.

Bringing together these and similar cases, as is done in other sciences, we may construct a general description of that kind of associated action which is both ethical and economic, and name it, as above, collective action in control of individual action. It is a foundation, if not "fundamentalist." The ethical purpose of that collective action, resting on this foundation fact of economics, is the purpose of creating harmony, or, at least, order, out of conflicts of economic interests instead of presupposing it from divinity or from the harmony of the spheres. Whatever facts enable the investigator to understand this ethical purpose are relevant to economics. The general principle may be named institutional ethics, because it is found by investigating the history of collective action, and the various kinds of transactions, and by testing these findings through interviews or study of experiments. My colleague in the department of philosophy named it "the warfare of moral ideals," taking as a particular case the antislavery movement and the Civil War in America.

I found it difficult to get across to students and to others this economic meaning of ethics. In some cases the difficulty traces back to Jeremy Bentham, who reduced ethics to pleasure, pain, happiness, and repudiated duties as painful. This repudiation is repeated in the diminishing pleasure and increasing pain of Bentham's successors, the hedonistic economists. Later economists, basing their theories on prices instead of on feelings, continue to eliminate ethics as only feelings—under such names as ethical teste, moral sense, emotions, sentiments—all of which are, of course, only individualistic. They have not, as yet, constructed for themselves the mental tool of the history of collective action as a means of investigating such economic facts as business ethics, trade union ethics, professional ethics, legal ethics, banker ethics, and the like. And the prices which they investigate are looked upon as something predetermined or foreordained by natural law, whereas actually they are agreements arrived at through transactions which may be persuasive, coercive, reasonable, extortionate, or confiscatory.

In other cases the difficulty in grasping the transactional meaning of ethics traces back to the great legal authority, Blackstone, who identified the opposites of right and wrong with the opposites of right and duty. I find that students preparing for the practice of law often jump immediately from the opinion of what they think is wrong to the other opinion that whatever is wrong must have a legal remedy. This seems to be a customary way of looking at it. An eminent economist summarized his lifetime of theorizing with the conclusion that all that was needed in economic theorizing was honesty. I asked my communistic friends why they were so vituperative against John D. Rockefeller; only individuals can sin, and their materialistic interpretation of history eliminates individuals. Even on an ethical interpretation of history Rockefeller won out because he practiced the evolutionary ethics of his time better than his competitors, and could not be convicted by the customary procedure of courts. A nation thrashed the Mediterranean Sea in pursuit of Samuel Insull, and a jury of his ordinary fellow citizens acquitted him of criminal intent. He, too, conformed to the business ethics of his time and place.

In my work on the Industrial Commission of Wisconsin I saw the transition made from an individual ethics in business to a corporate business ethics. Previously employers had been prosecuted in a criminal action in case of injury to a workman, or if they violated the law regarding the labor of children or women. Under the Industrial Commission we prosecuted violators on an action for debt. Such an action reaches back to the pocketbooks of stockholders and bankers instead of stopping at the bodies of their subordinate foremen and superintendents.

The earlier criminal prosecutions were based upon an idea of the right and wrong of individual behavior. If the employer had done wrong he should be bodily punished by imprisonment. But under corporations as far as the prosecution could get was to imprison the foremen or the superintendent. This conception of ethics was unable to get at the real problem of conduct in a corporation.

But the action for debt against the stockholders struck home; it was based on an adequate conception of ethical conduct. The corporations are creations of the sovereign power of the state. They are collective action for the specific purpose of making profits. Actions for debt were aimed at this central purpose. Action was brought in the name of the state, the sovereign will of the people of Wisconsin. But they did not treat the violators as criminals. They said in effect that no creation of the state is going to destroy the people who created it. The sanction was the threat of monetary loss.

The Commission early came to work with employers on an administrative rather than a prosecuting basis. The Commission still held the big stick of potential action for debt; the employers understood this fully. But the actual working out of the permissible hours of labor or the various safety measures was achieved through investigation, conference, and negotiation. In this way the employers came to accept the higher standards of employment, and even supported them with enthusiasm. New and higher ethical standards were accepted in industrial relations, but it was an ethics which grew out of and fitted corporate industry.

Thus ethical justification and crimination are relevant to economic investigation. They must be taken into account and given due weight. They animate all collective action. They are the battle cries of political parties, which thereby get control of sovereignty and economic policy. They create enthusiasms and mass movements. They have been named "myths," and sometimes have been named "ideologies." [1] But they are simply "beliefs." They lead to civil wars, revolutions, dictatorships, all with serious economic effects. It is ethical ideals that compel economists to take sides, as Adam Smith justified free trade in the interest of universal humanity, by repudiating the dominant mercantilism; or Henry C. Carey repudiated the dominant free trade by justifying protection in the interest of national unity; or economists condemn communism, and communistic economists condemn capitalism; and so on in innumerable justifications and criminations arising from conflicts of interest. Often when an economic analysis begins to pinch, the economist transfers the dispute to ethics, which is his ideal of right and wrong, honesty and dishonesty. Many so-called "economic" or materialistic interpretations of history, or of the American Constitution, turn out to be criminal interpretations of motives, which are proper matters for investigation to be given their due weight in their own field. Judgments of due weight shift the argument from individualistic opinions of absolute right or wrong to the investigation of institutional relativity among actual rights and duties.

[1] See articles "Sorel, Georges," by Sigmund Neumann, 1934, Vol. 14, pp. 262–263, and "Myth," by Ruth Benedict, 1933, Vol. 11, pp. 178–181, in *Encyclopedia of the Social Sciences,* edited by Edwin R. A. Seligman and Alvin Johnson, New York, The Macmillan Co.

Hence it is not a question of honesty that is implied in asking questions which bear on purpose. It is a question of perspective and human nature. By far the great majority of the people whom I have interviewed in my economic investigations are honest in their answers. But human nature is limited by opportunity and habit. We see vividly the persons and facts nearest to us and dimly those at a distance.

Nor is it a fact of self-interest or selfishness which economists are endeavoring to discover, on which avowedly the traditional science of economics has built since the time of Adam Smith. Self-interest, or even "enlightened self-interest," is one of the facts to be given due weight in all economic investigations. This "due weight" is good judgment, which is necessary because self-interest is always connected with a greater or lesser degree of community of interest which, inversely, is a lesser or greater degree of conflict of interests. This connection between community and conflict we get in answer to questions which evoke ethical justification and crimination. We find the connection always in interviews if the questions are carried far enough into the purposes intended by the witness in proving the particular facts. When we do so, however, we have carried the investigation into the field of ethics by carrying it into the economic fact that self-interest consists in earning one's living or in getting rich by getting legal control of services rendered by others.

### 3. THE PERSONAL EQUATION

Most of us prefer the American economic system over that of any other country. It is founded on liberty and private property, which are freedom to earn a living and get rich by due process of law, which is justice. It is founded also on freedom of the press, on academic freedom, on freedom of assembly. The exercise of these privileges under the sovereign state permits us to organize corporations, labor unions, political parties, strikes, farmers' organizations, or cooperatives. Many of these liberties we get historically from the common law of England.

Economists and other scientists have long since allowed for and have learned how to correct any bias in their observations arising from methods of collecting the statistics, or from twists in their telescopes or other instruments of investigation. They allow for it by some sort of percentage of error repeatedly made in their investigations and experiments. In America the bias in the investigator himself is usually named the personal equation. I always warn students to make corrections for my personal equation, and to devise methods of correcting their own habitual assumptions. Lawyers are especially acute in dealing with the personal equation of judges and juries.

A student of mine from the plains of Dakota thought that labor leaders were criminals. When he heard me interview a militant labor leader who turned out to be a Sunday school superintendent, he became a competent investigator.

Another student came to me with a bubbling love of the working man. When he became a laborer in one of the Standard Oil Company's hot refineries, he investigated the "hunkies." He wrote to me afterwards that he was not suited to that kind of investigation, and had become a wallpaper salesman.

Communist students come with ideas which one can understand from knowledge of their home life in the ghettos or slums. I take them on interviews with aggressive business men of upright dealings, who are leaders of associations of manufacturers, and those students learn to ask questions which are not insulting.

I confess to admiration of fighters for what they think is right. I have seen them change their minds when they are "up against it." I do not expect them to be logical or consistent, like pure mathematicians. I try to frame in my own mind the personal equations of business men, working men, politicians. They and their associates are the subject matter of investigation in the science of economics. I reach an economic explanation of the personal equation, derived from Malthus, as arising from the struggle to make a living, or to get rich, imposed upon them by existing institutions and by abundance or scarcity of opportunities in getting ownership of services rendered by others.

Considering these circumstances, of which the investigator himself is a part, he must construct working rules for himself in the conduct of his investigations and interviews. The first is *skepti-*

*cism*—skepticism of himself and skepticism of others. If he is not skeptical, he will not investigate either his own competency or the competency of others. Inseparable from skepticism is *toleration*. Not toleration of abuses if one is convinced, on investigation, that they are real abuses, but toleration of human beings who must act *now* and not wait for a science which can never tell them anyhow what to do or say in the particular circumstances that compel them to act. The third is *verification* before assertion. It is worth while for the economist, or anybody else, that other people should say of him that, no matter what his opinions, yet, if he merely *says* a thing is a fact, then it is a fact.

Since, in his economic investigations, the investigator is a part of what he investigates, his habitual assumptions incline him to give more weight to some of the facts in preference to other facts. In order to be more accurate he should examine himself for his personal equation. All economists, from Adam Smith to the present day, have advocated or opposed, openly or tacitly, some policy or principle which guides their investigations and theories. The best way to counteract this personal equation is to follow the great leaders who have combined skepticism, toleration, and verification.

# Summary

———◆———

Economics is a science of activity. It is the activity of the human will in conflict and in cooperation, in competition and in regulation. Consequently it is a science of the ideas and methods of investigation by which human beings construct their plans of action and carry on the negotiations that determine their activity. These circumstances make the science more a matter of argument and dialectics than a science proper which goes only as far as experts can agree upon the measurements and equations.

Everything in this dialectic is relative to something else. There is nothing "absolute," standing alone. The simplest quantitative meaning of relativity is a "ratio." It is "pure number." It does not exist in the world about. It is put there by the human mind. But neither does it exist solely in the mind of an individual. It exists in the world of negotiational psychology when two or more minds are reaching the agreement required in a transaction. As such, a ratio is a rule of action agreed upon, voluntarily or by compulsion, as to the relative position each shall occupy in his expected activities toward the other. In a bargaining transaction it is a "ratio of exchange," which we name bargaining power, or value in exchange; in a managerial transaction it is a ratio of input of labor to output of product, per hour, day, or week, which we name efficiency. In a rationing transaction one example is a ratio between the assessed valuation of property and the amount of taxes to be paid per year, which we name the power of sovereignty.

These are simplified samples of relativity. But there are other more complex relations between individuals and groups which seemingly may not be reduced to "pure number," but must be so reduced wherever negotiations have to do with quantities of performance or quantities of money to be paid for performances, or degrees of power and forbearance. To consider them all together in one calculation is impossible. The equation would be so complex that not even the highest mathematical intellect could compile or interpret it. The complexity must be simplified by taking up separately each sample of relativity, as though the others were constant and thereby eliminated.

An exhaustive study of any particular industry, or establishment, or even transaction, as well as a nation, will resolve itself into the five simplified assumptions of Part II, and into the ten or more relativities of Part III. If one desires to be sure that he has covered the ground, he must constantly check up on all of them. This is generally not necessary or advisable. The important thing is to select the few assumptions and relativities needful in order to hear all sides, and, thereby, get agreement on which the parties can work together.

But even these agreements which are needful for working together are not enough. The agreements may be subterfuges, misleading, oppressive, or one-sided. In order that they may be honest, straightforward, and complete, these fifteen or more considerations must be incorporated and weighed as to their relative importance in reaching a practical decision to act. If any one of them is omitted, it must be done knowingly and honestly, and this constitutes a difference between science and propaganda.

The way in which the matter is tested for any particular field, industry, or transaction is by way of arguments pro and con. These arguments are far from the certainties of the physical sciences, for they are the wide uncertainties of the unknown future. The arguments turn on the methods of investigation and the relevancy of the items investigated. Simplified, these methods are comparisons to ascertain similarities and differences which require similar or different methods of inducement, directed to the variety of participants and the variety of concerns through which they conduct their participation. These inducements are focused upon the variable working rules of the particular concern and the historical conditions established in the past and maintained in the present, perhaps by the principle of custom.

These organizations of collective action depend mainly upon the wisdom and sagacity of the small number at the head of the management or administration, especially as to their strategy in bearing down upon the limiting factors at the time and place. These present themselves as timeliness of action under the existing conditions of various degrees of power and the velocity of changes in the repeated transactions.

Inseparable from these factors of strategy are the factors that determine the extent and limitations upon the amount and degree of activity, and the ability to use the arguments that lead to conciliation and agreement among conflicting participants. The speeches of the President of the United States appealing to the managers of corporations, the leaders of unions, and the "bloc" of agriculturists make plain, for example, the complexity and difficulty in a nation of freedom of action compared with the military domination and suppression of corporations, unions, and political parties under a dictatorial system. This leads us to examine some of the arguments used in the critical issues of administration in the fields of credit, agriculture, and the conflicts of capital and labor.

# PART FOUR

---◆---

# Public Administration in Economic Affairs

# Chapter xiv

## *AGRICULTURAL ADMINISTRATION* [1]

———◆———

### 1. From Individual Action to Transactions

The independent American farmer, owning and operating his own farm, is as near the ideal of the classical economists as can be found in practice. This American farmer, too, philosophizes closely along the lines of the classical economists, except when he is in misfortune. Hence the transition from his pioneer independence into political activity and involvement in the problems of administrative economics will illustrate quite precisely the transition from nineteenth century to twentieth century economics. It happens, interestingly enough, that this transition is personified in one family of agricultural editors, the Wallace family, father, son, and grandson. Uncle Henry, the grandfather was preacher, farmer, editor, advocating good living, education, and scientific farming. This is reliance upon individual action. His son Henry C. Wallace was Secretary of Agriculture in the administrations of Presidents Harding and Coolidge. He became an advocate of direct governmental action in the interest of agriculture, through his sponsorship of the McNary-Haugen "two-price" plan of farm relief. The grandson, Henry A. Wallace, became Secretary of Agriculture in the Roosevelt cabinet of 1933 and put into operation all the major "New Deal" farm programs.[2] Their views and policies typify the transition in less than forty years, from individual action to the transactions which make the farmer depend-

[1] Consult especially *Yearbook*, 1940, U. S. Department of Agriculture; and John M. Gaus and Leon O. Wolcott, *Public Administration and the United States Department of Agriculture*, Chicago, Public Administration Service, 1940.

[2] See Henry Wallace, *New Frontiers*, New York, Reynal and Hitchcock, 1934, Chap. XIII; also H. A. Wallace, *Democracy Returns*, New York, Reynal and Hitchcock, 1944, especially the Introduction by Russell Lord.

ent upon the actions of others, typified sometimes as a transition from a stage of production for *use* to production for *sale,* from home agriculture to commercial agriculture, and lately distinguished as a time of direct action by governmental agencies to influence the income and opportunities of farmers.

If we put this general transition, which occurs by stages, in the form of the three kinds of transactions involved in collective action, and relate the same to the individualistic analysis of the classical nineteenth century economists, the three transitions may be stated as follows:

> From proportioning the factors to rationing transactions.
> From self-management to managerial transactions.
> From production for use to bargaining transactions.

This threefold transition is summarized in the Department of Agriculture during the careers of the three Wallaces, from technological investigations in overcoming the forces of physical nature to price and market investigations directed towards equalizing the position of farmers with that of corporations and labor unions through political action instead of economic action. Of course, in an industry as complex and diversified as agriculture with six million farms, the different stages of economy and the three different kinds of transactions are mixed and blended into numberless combinations. We are here discussing only the strategic changes in economic relations.

More specifically but not in detail, the most characteristic of the principles of traditional economics as a guide to successful individual action was that scientific proportioning of the several factors in production, such as land acreage, soil fertility, machinery, livestock, human labor, in such a way as to accomplish an equilibrium at the point of maximum return in the production of wealth.

This proportioning of factors is quite similar to the rationing transactions by the management of corporations on the field of collective action. The distinction between the fields is that the natural factors have no will of their own, so that the proportioning comes under technological self-employment, to be improved by more intelligent control of the natural forces. But the rationing transactions are governmental in character, since they require the legal superiority of a managing board of directors over the legal subordination of the other participants. This is the key to rationing transactions which take the form of apportioning by decree, management or administration the positions which individuals shall occupy in their contributions to the whole activity of the concern, whether the corporation or the nation, at the different levels in the hierarchy of collective action. The acreage allotments and the marketing quotas to individual farms under the Agricultural Adjustment Administration are a rationing of economic opportunities taking the place, in part, of the historical market freedom of bargaining transactions.

The managerial transactions are a similar transition to the legal relation of superior and inferior, and the farmer who makes this transition becomes either a manager or an employee. Managerial transactions have always characterized the plantation economy of the south. They are coming into American agriculture wherever the large scale "industralized" type of farming is developing; this is occurring in the specialized fruit-, vegetable-, and potato-growing areas where the small scale family farms have not been able to meet the competition. The economic relation here, enforced by courts of law, is the relation of command and obedience. Its historical origin is slavery, where the will of the subordinate is wholly suppressed, but with emancipation comes not the elimination of this legal relation of superior and inferior but the liberty of the inferior, protected by sovereignty, to "run away" and "quit," without giving a reason, and therefore to determine, by a bargaining transaction, the terms and conditions under which the one will obey and the other will command.

The bargaining transactions spring from this legal liberty to withhold employment or withhold service, and here the supposition is legal equality instead of legal superiority and inferiority. Hence here are the several bargains wherein the farmers have always asserted, in one way or another, their "disparity" in bargaining power, that is, economic inequality contrasted with the assumed legal equality.

These disparities may be in the credit transactions with bankers, the transportation transactions with railway corporations, the managerial transactions with organized wage earners, and any other class of transactions where inequality of bargaining power is set up against the assumed legal equality of the participants.

## 2. From Economic Action to Political Action

The farmers usually found themselves unable to cope with other classes in this economic organization, even with their own cooperative marketing associations. But temporarily it was found that by influencing the management of political parties, the farmers could be effective. This disparity on the economic field began to show itself in the depression of business following the Civil War, 1867, when the farmers accomplished the organization of the "Grange," or Patrons of Husbandry, as a secret educational and cooperative association. Their first political effectiveness was in the railway legislation of a few western states fixing freight rates, known as the "Granger Laws," in the decade of the 1870's. These laws, eventually taken over by the federal government, resulted in the Interstate Commerce Commission.

Another inequality of economic power was in the farmers' credit transactions, and at different repetitions of business depressions large elements of the farmers were able to get political parties to support the "greenback," or the free silver coinage. In these lines of legislation they had been at a disadvantage compared with the influence of the bankers, the farm organizations demanding price increases, the bankers demanding and obtaining price decreases through retirement of the greenbacks (1867) and demonetization of silver (1879 and 1900).

There is always this weakness in the appeal by the farmers to administrative economics as a remedy for their economic weakness—their appropriations are easily reduced by their opponents in Congress on the plea of economy, and the administration of the law intended to favor the farmers is thereby made ineffective, although remaining nominally in force; whereas, if they could organize like a corporation or like a labor union, they could then finance themselves without imposing themselves wholly on the taxpayers. Farmers' organizational weakness already begins to show itself at the weakest point of the agricultural administration, in the so-called Farm Security Administration engaged in furnishing shelter for agricultural wage earners, both white and colored, in that these do not have the political weight of the farm owners, and consequently are the first to receive a cut in appropriations.

The weakness of political action as a substitute for organized economic action is seen also in the flagrant disadvantage of the farmers in the enactment of protective tariff laws. Here the farmers' representatives have repeatedly been maneuvered by politicians out of their opposition to tariffs favoring the manufacturers; especially when confronted by the arguments for a "home market," which would elevate the profits and wages of consumers of farm products, leaving the farmers themselves exposed to foreign competition, or nominally protected on such farm products as are already produced in surplus quantities at home.

### 3. Legislative and Administrative Reasoning [1]

The promotion of Justice Stone to the position of Chief Justice of the United States, as well as the veto by the President of the Walter-Logan bill requiring judicial interference in administrative investigations, make significant the contrast in opinions of Justice Stone and Justice Roberts in the case, decided January 6, 1936, on the constitutionality of the Agricultural Adjustment Act of 1933.[2]

These two equally competent institutional economists reach opposite conclusions on the same statement of facts in their theories of sovereignty and scarcity. The explanation is not in the facts, nor in the mental capacities, nor in the integrity of the

---

[1] J. R. Commons, in *Journal of Farm Economics*, May, 1942; reprinted by permission.

[2] *U. S. v. Butler*, 297 U. S. 1, 56 S. Ct. 312 (1936).

justices, but in their two methods of reasoning. Justice Roberts, for the majority of the Court, in declaring the act unconstitutional, followed a legislative method of reasoning from extreme cases; Justice Stone, for the minority at that time, followed an administrative method of reasoning from an actual case statistically located somewhere between the extremes.

The distinction, historically in the treatises on logic, is perhaps known as the difference between deductive and experimental reasoning, a distinction, however, not exactly valid for even the physical sciences where it originated.[1] And now, considering the way in which the distinction has come forward in the science of economics, it is the difference between a legislative method of reasoning without the economic distinctions of kind, quantity, degree, time, or place, and an administrative method where the quantities, degrees of economic power, and timeliness of action are the determining points in reaching a practical decision to act.

The economic issue, as it came to the front in this case, was the use of *economic power* by the government in enforcing its commands, in addition to its historical use of *physical power*.[2] The Congress, in adopting the Agricultural Adjustment Act, had assumed, in conformity with traditional economists and the courts, that economics was a field of *voluntary* agreements, contrasted with sovereignty as the field of *compulsory* agreements. But now, with the increased intensity of private use of economic power over individuals in the collective form of corporations, labor unions, cartels, Federal Reserve banking, and with economic power further intensified by the closing of the world's frontiers against economic escape, these arguments of Stone and Roberts become a new constitutional debate whether the American government shall use economic power on behalf of unorgan-

[1] See Morris R. Cohen, *Reason and Nature*, New York, Harcourt, Brace & Co., 1931.

[2] The term "power" as here used relates to the operation of threats and promises in getting obedience in anticipation or avoidance of future alternatives. See Bertrand Russell, *Power*, New York, W. W. Norton and Company, 1938. Russell distinguishes power from energy, the latter being the force in physical science. But he omits economic power by stressing military power and propaganda.

ized farmers and others to counterbalance the organized economic power of other classes. Justice Roberts denied, and Justice Stone affirmed, this governmental use of economic power.

In this debate the meaning of economic power took on the two constitutional forms of "property" and "liberty." Property, whether private ownership or public ownership, is the power of *scarcity*, the power of the owner to command obedience of others by withholding from them what they need but do not own. Liberty, the liberty of an owner, his "economic liberty," took the form of "spending power," equivalent to the economists' "freedom of exchange," or "purchasing power," "buying power," "bargaining power," the liberty to fix or agree on prices or values by control of supply or demand.

In general, it had been assumed by economists and courts that this economic power was limited by free competition between equal individual owners, and this was the reason why economic agreements were deemed to be voluntary rather than coercive. It followed that the only place of government in the economic scheme was in the negative power (*laissez faire*) of preventing conspiracy or monopoly, either of which interfered with free competition and was, therefore, coercive rather than voluntary.

Justice Roberts denied that either a state government or the federal government was permitted, under the Constitution, to use this economic power. He argued that its use by government was coercive against private parties and not voluntary agreement on their part, and was, therefore, prohibited. His leading case was a decision ten years earlier by the same Supreme Court against the use of economic power by a state railroad commission.[1] In that case a state administrative body had attempted to use the public ownership of the highways as its means to compel a private corporation to submit to regulation of rates by the state commission. Justice Roberts showed that the state government and the state commission had then used the same argument of a "voluntary" agreement on the part of the private corporation as the federal government and the Agricultural Department were

[1] 297 U. S. 71, citing *Frost Trucking Co.,* v. *Railroad Commission of California,* 271 U. S. 583 (1926).

now using on the part of the farmers. The Court had then said, as quoted by Roberts:

> Having regard to form alone, the Act here is an offer to the private carrier of a privilege, which the State may grant or deny, upon a condition which the carrier is free to accept or reject. In reality the carrier is given no choice, except a choice between the rock and the whirlpool,—an option to forego a privilege which may be vital to his livelihood or submit to a requirement which may constitute an intolerable burden.[1]

Thus, the economic power, in this case of a state administrative department, consisted in public ownership of the highways. Its use as a fulcrum of bargaining power by the state commission was coercive upon a private corporation by withholding the use of the highways if the corporation would not submit to regulation. The same argument was now advanced by Roberts against the use of the "spending power" by the Department of Agriculture to compel obedience on the part of farmers. He said:[2]

> . . . the Secretary is not required but is permitted, if, in his uncontrolled judgment, the policy of the Act will be so promoted, to make agreements with individual farmers for a reduction of acreage or production, upon such terms as he may think fair and reasonable. . . . The Government asserts that whatever might be said against the validity of the plan, if compulsory, it is constitutionally sound because the end is accomplished by voluntary cooperation. There are two sufficient answers to the contention. The regulation is not, in fact, voluntary. The farmers, of course, may refuse to comply, but the price of such refusal is the loss of benefits. The amount offered is intended to be sufficient to exert pressure on him to agree to the proposed regulation. The power to confer or withhold unlimited benefits is the power to coerce or destroy. If the cotton grower elects not to accept the benefits, he will receive less for his crops; those who receive payment will be able to undersell him. The result may well be financial ruin. The coercive purpose and intent of the statute is not obscured by the fact that it has not been perfectly successful. It is pointed out that, because there still remained a minority whom the rental and benefit

[1] 271 U. S. 593.
[2] 297 U. S., 55, 70, 71.

payments were insufficient to induce to surrender their independence of action, the Congress has gone further and, in the Bankhead Cotton Act, used the taxing power in a more directly minatory fashion to compel submission. This progression only serves more fully to expose the coercive purpose of the so-called tax imposed by the present Act. It is clear that the Department of Agriculture has properly described the plan as one to keep a non-cooperating minority in line. This is coercion by economic pressure. The asserted power of choice is illusory.

This citation to the Department of Agriculture had reference to a leaflet entitled *Agricultural Adjustment,* quoted by Justice Robert as follows:

Experience of cooperative associations and other groups has shown that without such Government support, the efforts of the farmers to band together to control the amount of their product sent to market are nearly always brought to nothing. Almost always, under such circumstances, there has been a non-cooperating minority, which, refusing to go along with the rest, has stayed on the outside and tried to benefit from the sacrifices the majority has made. . . . It is to keep this non-cooperating minority in line, or at least prevent it from doing harm to the majority, that the power of the Government has been marshalled behind the adjustment programs.[1]

Thus the Supreme Court, in these two cases, attacked the two components of economic power. In the state highway case it was the power of ownership to withhold supply from all parties. In the agricultural case it was the power to withhold supply of government funds from a minority of competitors and thus restrain their liberty in order to increase the bargaining power of the class as a whole against all other classes. Justice Stone's arguments, in reply, were concerned with the latter. He said:

That the governmental power of the purse is a great one is not now for the first time announced. Every student of the history of government and economics is aware of its magnitude and of its existence in every civilized government. Both were well understood by the framers of the Constitution when they sanctioned the grant of the spending power to the federal government, and both were recognized by Hamil-

[1] 297 U. S., 71.

ton and Story, whose views of the spending power on a parity with the other powers specifically granted, have hitherto been generally accepted. The suggestion that it must now be curtailed by judicial fiat, because it may be abused by unwise use, hardly rises to the dignity of argument. So may judicial power be abused. "The power to tax is the power to destroy," but we do not, for that reason, doubt its existence, or hold that its efficacy is to be restricted by its incidental or collateral effect upon the States . . . The power to tax and spend is not without constitutional restraints. One restriction is that the purpose must be truly national. Another is that it may not be used to coerce action left to state control. Another is the conscience and patriotism of Congress and the Executive.[1]

Herein Justice Stone agreed with Justice Roberts that the use of economic power by the government was coercive, similar to the power of taxation, and that both were subject to abuse in extreme cases.

The implication, however, that economic power had been equally *coercive* at the time when the Constitution was framed or for a century afterward is doubtful. During that period there was an open frontier for escape, with only a few (or weak) corporations or unions, and no organized administrative banking system. Applicable, however, to its increased coerciveness in recent times, Justice Stone proceeded to show that economic power was not unlimited in its practical administration. His arguments in this field of institutional economics may fittingly be named the foundation for a fourth branch of the American government, an investigational branch implemented with administrative economics.[2]

Justice Stone and Justice Roberts agreed that the Agricultural Adjustment Act was "coercive" instead of "voluntary." They differed on the issue of its administration. The grounds for their respective positions will appear from its provisions. The act started with a preamble of general welfare, defined as the

[1] 297 U. S., pp. 86, 87.

[2] See James M. Landis, *The Administrative Process*, London, H. Milford, 1936. Dean Landis considers mainly the *procedure* in this branch of government compared with the procedure in the legislative and judicial branches, rather than its foundations for a science of administrative economics.

"orderly exchange of commodities" in the "national credit structure," broken down, however, by the "present acute economic emergency," which destroys the value of "agricultural assets." This destruction of value was attributed mainly to the "severe and increasing disparity between the prices of agricultural and other commodities." The stated purpose of the act was to "establish and maintain such balance between the production and consumption of agricultural commodities and such marketing conditions therefor," as will restore the purchasing power of certain designated agricultural commodities to the level of a base period, August 1909 to July 1914. This level was defined as "parity," or "fair exchange value" with manufacturers' prices, to be ascertained by the Secretary of Agriculture from "available statistics" of the department. The termination of the emergency for each commodity was also provided for and was declared to be such date, to be likewise determined by statistics, when "parity" should be re-established for that commodity. The secretary should have the power to provide for the "reduction in acreage," or "reduction in the production for market," or both, by "agreement" with the producers "or by other voluntary methods," including benefit payments to be paid to farmers who agree to the restriction of output, such as "the secretary deems fair or reasonable." The secretary should also have the power to determine an appropriate "processing tax," to be "levied, assessed and collected" upon the first manufacturing of the commodity, for the purpose of paying the ascertained reasonable benefits to the producers.

These were the general features of the legislative act, to be administered for individual cases by the Department of Agriculture. There is no doubt about its novelty in American economics and jurisprudence, although it was modeled, as nearly as practicable, upon the protective tariff, and upon the well-known restrictions of output by manufacturers in laying off employees and shutting down factories in order to maintain prices during emergencies. But in this agricultural case there was something entirely new, the restriction of food supply, symbolized by the extreme case of the slaughter of six million pigs by administrative process, known to the justices, in order to maintain the price of hogs. This shocking fact, although somewhat parallel to the laying off of employees who needed work for the subsistence of themselves and families, was parallel to the case actually before the court which had to do with cotton, the clothing of the people. The slaughter of pigs, or the restriction of cotton acreage, or the limitation of other food production by administrative process, in order to create scarcity and thereby raise prices during a credit emergency, was this constitutional or unconstitutional?

An emotional result of reasoning from extremes is the fear of what an actual case, if once permitted, might lead to. It might lead to communism, fascism, or to anarchism. Short of these last extremities, it might lead to other dangerous extremes. Justice Roberts agrees that this power to spend on behalf of farmers is subject to limitations, but fears what it might lead to. He says:

> We are referred to appropriations in aid of education, and it is said that no one has doubted the power of Congress to stipulate the sort of eduction for which money shall be expended. But an appropriation to an educational institution which by its terms is to become available only if the beneficiary enters into a contract to teach doctrines subversive of the Constitution is clearly bad.

Justice Roberts proceeds with other extremes of what the processing tax and its expenditure might lead to. It might lead to extracting money from one branch of industry for paying it to another branch, throughout the United States. It might lead to transferring money from farmers and miners to manufacturers. It might be used as an "indirect" power to reverse the recent decision of the Court [1] that Congress had no "direct" power to regulate wages and hours of labor in local business. It might lead to an excise tax of two cents per pound on every sale of sugar, to be turned over to the refineries. It might be used to reduce the output of shoes and clothing; and so on, in favor of any business group which thought itself underprivileged. "The supposed cases," said Justice Roberts, "are no more improbable than would the present act have been deemed a few years ago."

[1] *Schechter Poultry Corp.* v. *U. S.*, 295 U. S. 495 (1935).

In order to alleviate these fears of extreme cases of economic coercion, which representative government might lead to, Justice Stone, in reply, referred to other cases not deemed to be absurd or extreme which the Roberts decision would lead to. The government might give seeds to farmers, he said, "but may not condition the gift upon it being planted"; might give money to the unemployed, but not ask them to give labor in return; might give money to sufferers from earthquake or fire, but not impose conditions to prevent the spread of disease; "all that, because it is purchased regulation infringing state powers, must be left to the states who are unable or unwilling to supply the necessary relief." Many other cases are cited, and, in general, Justice Stone asked, regarding the federal government, "Do all its activities collapse because, in order to effect the permissible purpose, in myriad ways the money is paid out upon terms and conditions which influence action of the recipients within the states which Congress might command? . . . If the expenditure is for a national purpose, that purpose will not be thwarted because payment is on condition which will advance that purpose."

The foregoing, again, indicates the difference between the generally understood physical power of sovereignty and economic power. Roberts denies, but Stone affirms the exercise of the latter to both state and federal governments. Economic power has to do with its effect on prices and markets. These are foreign markets and such domestic markets as are beyond the power of the states, acting separately, to control. Both the protective tariff and the immigration restriction laws were designed mainly as economic measures, to enable manufacturers and laborers to maintain domestic prices and wages throughout the states against foreign competition. Justice Roberts' opinion, supported by the majority of the Court, denied the authority of the government to levy a processing tax, analogous to the tariff tax, in aid of those farmers who agreed to restrict output in order to maintain these domestic prices against either foreign or domestic competition. The Congress, in re-enacting the substance of the Agricultural Adjustment Act, omitted the processing tax, but provided for similar payment to farmers out of the general fund of the Treasury, regardless of the taxable sources. Apparently the promotion of Justice Stone, along with similar changes in the Supreme Court, renders the processing tax hereafter constitutional.

Justice Stone, as above quoted, mentioned three limits placed upon the federal government. The third limit, namely, the "conscience and patriotism of the Congress and the Executive," was further enlarged to include "wisdom." Wisdom, in Stone's usage, may be defined as good judgment in deciding upon what is reasonable coercion by government somewhere between the absurd extremes of coercion which were dreaded by Justice Roberts. Justice Stone said:

> A tortured construction of the Constitution is not to be justified by recourse to extreme samples of reckless Congressional spending which might occur if Courts could not prevent expenditures which, even if they could be thought to effect any national purpose, would be possible only by action of a legislature lost to all sense of public responsibility. Such suppositions are addressed to the mind accustomed to believe that it is the business of the courts to sit in judgment on the wisdom of legislative action. Courts are not the only agency of government that must be assumed to have the capacity to govern. Congress and the Courts both unhappily may falter or be mistaken in the performance of their constitutional duty . . .[1]

The other two limits on the taxing and spending powers mentioned by Justice Stone are the two jurisdictional sides of the same physical or economic power, namely, national sovereignty *versus* state sovereignty. The purpose must be truly national, which is the same as saying that it must not interfere with matters left by the Constitution to state control. It was in support of state sovereignty that Justice Roberts, for the majority, finally declared the act unconstitutional, although his arguments, and the former decisions cited, were directed against the use of economic power by those state governments, as well as its use by the federal government.

Besides, the issue of economic power as an instrument of sovereignty was the legal issue of the American attempt to separate the government into legislative, executive, and judicial

[1] 297 U. S. 87.

branches. Justice Roberts would maintain this separation by making out that the Court did not use the physical force of sovereignty. He said:

> It is sometimes said that the Court assumes the power to overrule or control the actions of the people's representatives. This is a misconception. When an Act of Congress is appropriately challenged in the courts as not conforming to the constitutional mandate, the judicial branch of the government has only one duty—to lay the article of the Constitution which is involved beside the statute which is challenged, and decide whether the latter squares with the former. All the Court does, or can do, is to announce its considered judgment on the question. This Court neither approves nor condemns any legislative policy.[1]

Against this disclaimer of judicial power, as a mere logical, or intellectual power of opinion without physical force, Justice Stone set up the argument of a truly sovereign power of the judiciary in that it has the last word in the American system of divided sovereignty. He said:

> The power of the courts to declare a statute unconstitutional is subject to two guiding principles of decision which ought never to be absent from judicial consciousness. One is that the courts are concerned only with the power to enact statutes, not with their wisdom. The other is that while unconstitutional exercise of power by the executive and legislative branches of the government is subject to judicial restraint, the only check upon our own exercise of power is our own sense of self-restraint. For the removal of unwise laws from the statute books, appeal lies not to the courts but to the ballot and the processes of democratic government.[2]

Thus the court, having the last word in affirming or preventing the use of physical force, and having its own executive officers, is really sovereign. Like other sovereigns, it is limited only by its own sense of self-restraint.

We may observe in addition, from the economic standpoint, that this internal sense of self-restraint may find external guidance in the statistical investigations presented by the Department

[1] 297, U. S. 62–63.
[2] 297, U. S. 78, 79.

of Agriculture for the Court's consideration. By reasoning from extremes, these statistical showings of what was to be done between the extremes are ignored. Yet it is their statistical validity, as furnished and critically examined by its own investigational staff, and then subjected to public hearings of all parties, that constitutes, one might say, the whole of administrative economics.

These public hearings include a specialized modern development which would be included under what Justice Stone characterized as "the processes of democratic government." It is not only the indiscriminate and accidental public that is heard, but it is also the more interested public of those directly and economically to be restrained by the regulations to be issued by the department. This was the actual procedure of the Department of Agriculture in its investigations, revising and correcting its own previous rulings and mistakes, and consulting the advisory committees of farmers on its statistics and its proposed economic restraints, as well as submitting the plans to referendum vote of the particular farmers who produced the crop in question. This "democratic process" was prescribed, in part, in the act, and was known to be the process followed by the department. This again enforces the inference that Justice Stone would not, without further congressional mandate, approve the judicial restraints on the Department of Agriculture contained in the Walter-Logan bill, but would refer the investigations back to the department and its process of consulting the farmers.

These considerations emphasize still further the economic character of this alleged fourth branch of American government. Under the American system of attempted separation of powers, neither the legislature nor the administrative agency operating under powers delegated to it by the legislature, has the strictly *executive* power, contemplated in the Constitution, of enforcing by physical force its own commands, or "orders." The only constitutional possessors of this physical power are the President (or state governor), and the judiciary. The former is commander in chief of the army and navy and of such other subordinates as use physical force; the judiciary commands the marshals (or sheriffs) who obey without investigation. Justice Roberts' "power of judgment" is, in fact, a command issued by the Court to the United States marshal (or sheriff), ordering the use of physical force, if necessary, to stop the administrative process.

This command is effective because the administrative department, as just now suggested, is not itself an executive department in command of physical force needed to carry its own decisions into effect. It may not arrest or imprison anybody. It may not resist the marshal or sheriff. It must make application to the Court to issue its own order to use force, and must submit its arguments. Its power is only investigational and advisory in so far as the legislature authorizes and the Court approves. As a so-called "fourth branch" of government, it is more nearly like a standing committee for economic investigations and recommendations to the three recognized branches and to the people generally. If, in addition, it has discretion in issuing orders to individuals, the reason why the latter do not challenge the orders by appeal to the Court for review and reversal is because they and their lawyers expect that the courts will decide as they had formerly decided. In this respect the administrative "orders" are analogous to the force of custom. This is, indeed, the only ground of assurance that the Department of Agriculture will have economic power in each case as it arises, namely, the expectation that the Supreme Court and the inferior courts will follow the reasoning of Justice Stone rather than Justice Roberts, and refuse to interfere with its administrative investigations and decisions.

This assurance is, indeed, also the ground on which corporations and labor unions are able to exercise their collective economic power. They are forbidden to use physical violence, but they have the double assurance, in the American economic system, that the courts will not use their own command of physical force to interfere with the private organizations in their use of economic power, and that the courts will further use this same power to enforce their contracts or "voluntary" agreements. Thus the reason why they also are designated as "voluntary" by their spokesmen is not because their economic power is not economically coercive, but because it is not physically coercive—quite the same meaning of "voluntary" as that which Congress employed in its delegation of economic power to the Department of Agriculture.

These traditional views about noncoerciveness of economic transactions, which are now recognized as coercive by both Justice Stone and Justice Roberts, indicate that the Court has contradicted the arguments of so eminent a jurist as Professor Corwin, who had predicted the "twilight" of the Supreme Court on the assumption that the Court could not, or would not, undertake to control the "spending power" of the government. As soon as this "spending power," which is "economic power," is recognized as coercive through collective action, on account of such evident denial of freedom as suggested by the choice between the "rock and the whirlpool," then the issue falls between extreme cases of abuse and a reasonable use somewhere between the extremes. This reasoning also applies to private collective use of economic power in the hands of corporations, banks, labor unions, and the like, for which the older individualistic meanings of "voluntary" economic agreement continue to be used but are obsolete. The Agricultural Adjustment Act was certainly, as Roberts contended, the use of coercive economic power by the government, not recognized by Corwin as coercive, on behalf of a great economic class who had not themselves learned how to use it collectively in dealing with corporations, banks, and labor unions.[1]

It follows from the foregoing that the reliance on statistics is characteristic not only for the modern science of economics, it is also, more emphatically, characteristic of modern administrative economics in carrying out the legislative policy. But it is not hit-or-miss blind statistics—it is guided by economic theory, which is economic analysis of the several factors. This guidance has both

[1] Cf. E. S. Corwin, *The Twilight of the Supreme Court*, New Haven, Yale University Press, 1934. More recent decisions tending further to overrule Justice Roberts' opinion by tending to enlarge the spending power of the federal government are *Helvering* v. *Davis*, 301 U. S. 319, 57 S. Ct. 904 (1937); *Alabama Power Co.* v. *Ickes, Federal Emergency Administrator of Public Works et al.*, 302 U. S. 464, 58 S. Ct. 300 (1938); *Duke Power Co. et al.* v. *Greenwood County et al.*, 302 U. S. 485, 58 S. Ct. 306 (1938); *California Water Service Co. et al.*, v. *City of Redding et al.*, 22 F. Supp. 641 (1938) decrete affirmed 304 U. S. 252, 58 S. Ct. 865 (1938). These citations furnished by Mr. Philip M. Glick, U. S. Dept. of Agriculture, Aug. 13, 1941.

its legal and its economic side, united in the modern administrative department.

On the legal side the statistical method of reasoning from actual cases had always been, in fact, the historical method in Anglo-American jurisprudence in cases of "fair competition" located somewhere between the extremes of "destructive competition," or "chiseling," and monopolistic competition. As such, it was the point, to be discovered by proper judicial investigation and "due process" of notice and hearing, where each of the conflicting interests at the time and place was given its "due weight" in reaching a judicial decision. The cases turned mainly on valuations of "intangible" property known as "good will," "trade name," "trade reputation," claimed by one or more of the parties to a transaction. In more recent times this method of reasoning from specific cases becomes an administrative method when delegated by the legislature to a governmental department, like the Interstate Commerce Commission or the Department of Agriculture, with its staff of economists and statisticians, instead of the courts without this type of investigators.

But this delegation of authority for economic investigations on which to base decisions was obstructed during about twenty years of hostile decisions by the courts before it was conceded by the Supreme Court in the field of such monopolistic public utilities as railways regulated by the Interstate Commerce Commission. And now, with the public regulation of similar monopolistic competition in other fields, and with changes in the personnel of the Supreme Court, it becomes the recognized method of administrative reasoning, permitted by the Court, not only for the Agricultural Department in the use of economic power, but for other administrative departments, whether headed by an individual like the secretary, by a board or commission, or by a "public corporation," like the Tennessee Valley Authority.[1] All of the administrative departments are in fact standing committees for economic investigations and recommendations to the government and the people, with the power of custom in enforcing what

[1] See David E. Lilienthal, "The Conduct of Business Enterprises by the Federal Government," *Harvard Law Review*, Vol. LIV, No. 4, p. 545, Feb. 1941.

are really provisional orders effective as long as not lawfully contested elsewhere. This is the modern development on the legal side of the American separation of powers.

On the economic side the use of statistics is the starting point of facts and policy. On calculations derived from these statistics the Secretary of Agriculture was directed, in each year in advance of the plantings, to ascertain the amount of rentals or benefit payments to be paid to each farmer the coming year, in consideration of his reduction of crops by such amounts as would be deemed sufficient, with the other farmers during the emergency, to restore the price parities of twenty years before.

These statistical limits, of course, do not of themselves restrict the discretion of the Secretary of Agriculture. In the constitutional government of America the actual limits had been set by the judiciary in its control of administrative officials. In such control, as has happened with the Interstate Commerce Commission, the Court, in actual cases as they arise, eventually learns to respect the investigations and thereby determines whether the final decision of the administrative authority comes within the "rule of reason." Such consideration is superfluous when reasoning from extreme cases. Justice Roberts, on that account, would exclude altogether the use of economic power, but Justice Stone would submit its use to the historical doctrine of the rule of reason.

Thus, on both the legal and economic sides, the transition is made from the dogmatic economics of the nineteenth century to the statistical, investigational, and administrative economics of the twentieth century.

The inconsistency of the proposed reduction of the nation's food supply in order to raise prices at the very time of unemployment was in the background of Justice Roberts' reasoning. The inconsistency was not adequately met in the "Brief of the United States." This brief, using the "infant industry" argument, emphasized the greater possibilities of *reducing prices* of manufactures on account of machine technology, compared with the inability of farmers to use "mass production technics" in order to *reduce* the prices of farm products.

Here the brief did not properly make the analysis of a credit emergency contrasted with the long-time trend of technology. This argument of the government before the Court, on technological grounds, would support the communist conclusion that small-scale production in agriculture must give way in the long-run trend of increasing efficiency to large-scale mass production, so that the independent farmers would be reduced to wage earners employed by agricultural corporations.

But such an outcome was opposite to the purpose of Congress. The statistics purported to show that the inconsistency existed only during the emergency. The emergency was stated definitely to be a matter of the "credit structure" which had broken down, instead of a matter of increased technological efficiency. It is the distinction between "producing power," which increases abundance by machinery, and "bargaining power," which withholds abundance by ownership, and it is the inconsistency of capitalism itself, based on private property. The purpose of the Congress was to preserve, during the emergency, the individual farmer in his bargaining power, as essential to the "national credit structure," instead of permitting him, in the credit emergency, to be reduced to the extreme of a propertyless wage earner. The government's legal argument, at this point, inconsistently supported, in fact, the inference of Justice Roberts that, by government aid, farm prices would be *reduced* by "underselling," whereas the statistics supported the argument of the economists of the Agricultural Department to the effect that, by administrative restrictions of output during the emergency, farm prices would be *raised* relative to industrial prices.

The distinction is basic for economic analysis, and has been brought out by statistical economists under the name of "business cycles," only during the past thirty years. A credit collapse creates an emergency which, in the economic theory of Congress, might be overcome by restoration of the preceding level of purchasing power deemed to be "parity." But a technological trend of increasing efficiency is a long-run trend of centuries, and was, indeed, the kind of gradual change contemplated by the nineteenth century economists when speaking of the temporary displacement of labor by machinery, counteracted in the long run by their optimistic increase of prosperity by increased efficiency over the centuries.

A more fitting emergency analysis of the credit collapse is in the comparison of *methods* of manufacturers in counteracting their falling prices by reducing output through shutting down plants and laying off employees during the emergency, and the *method* of farmers who cannot shut down their farms, nor lay off themselves and families, even for a few days. They must go on producing a surplus at falling prices while the manufacturers are maintaining prices by unemployment.

But the emergency argument recognizes that credit operates in cycles. It, therefore, contemplates that the emergency will disappear by some form of recovery from the disparities of the business depression, either an economic recovery that will increase demand and raise prices, or even a military recovery by war. The latter, we unhappily see, is actually happening, and the restrictions are not only being removed by the department, but the farmers are actually urged to enlarge output instead of reducing output.

This effort of the Department of Agriculture to enlarge output by farmers is claimed by its critics to be a reversal of its policy and an acknowledgment of its former economic fallacies when it was restricting output. But it is not a reversal nor a confession. It is a consistent policy of "adjustment" to the credit cycle, an adjustment by means of an administrative process, the purpose of which is to protect the farmers during the credit depression when needed, and to remove the protection during credit recovery when not needed.

This distinction between credit cycles which are temporary ups and downs, but are the normal workings of the credit system, and technological efficiency, which has steadily increased during the centuries by mechanical inventions, is the most important of all the distinctions revealed recently by statistical analysis. It is a distinction not at all recognized by the traditional economists, by the politicians, by the courts, or by the public generally, as shown by the above criticism directed against the Department of Agriculture. The distinction enforces the need of recognizing administrative economics, as against legislative or judicial economics, especially in the field of agriculture. An administrative department alone can meet promptly the "adjustments" needed to ward off inflations and deflations of prices, or bring relief promptly in time of deflation.

The Adjustment Act of 1933 is almost the first act of American legislation designed specifically to counteract this credit cycle. In the case of tariff legislation, by contrast, there is required a political campaign, spaced at four years, to adjust the tariff to prosperity or depression. This is confirmed by economic history. The high tariff party for more than a hundred years has nearly always won its votes during a depression in business, as an instrument for protection and recovery for the benefit of *producers*. The low tariff party, then, usually gets its votes after prices and wages have risen with prosperity, as an instrument for reducing the high prices of protected industries, for the benefit of the *consumers*. But the Agricultural Adjustment Act, by means of daily investigations and statistics, would increase its protection of agriculture during the depression when needed, and reduce or remove its protection when agriculture recovers prosperity, without waiting for political campaigns, legislation, or court action.

Something similar to legislative delay occurs in the judicial economics of antimonopoly or antitrust prosecutions. A judicial trial requires prolonged preparation and delays, reaching its decisions usually after the emergency has passed; and then there is no effective provision for a rehearing or a readjustment to fit the emergencies of prosperity or depression. But the administrative economics of "agricultural adjustment" was designed to fit itself to the "disparities" of monopolistic inequalities, suffered during the depression by farmers in their dealings with manufacturers or unions, and then to fit itself to the "parities" of restored equality of bargaining power during the ensuing period of prosperity.

This is the emphatic difference between administrative economics and legislative or judicial economics in the American system of attempted separation of powers. The defenders of judicial economics, in their opposition to administrative economics, set up the contrast of a "government by law," meaning a government by courts, against a "government by men," meaning administrative departments. But, with the statistical developments of economics and administration, the contrast is more properly government by delay and exclusion of economics against government by timely economic action based on preparatory statistical investigations.

While the method of extreme cases creates absurdities and is the fruitful field of satire, it leads to no conclusions, of course, regarding the actual rentals and benefits to be paid by the government during the time of emergency, nor the actual restrictions on output or sales made by the farmers. These were not, however, the extremes of "unlimited benefits." The administrative method of reasoning from actual cases, as suggested by Justice Stone's argument, proposes that the Court should consider the statistics of limited benefits during a limited period of emergency, instead of condemning the legislative plan as a whole for all time. It is a change from unconstitutionality of a legislative act as a whole to reasonableness of an administrative act statistically determined in detail for a specific time.

In reviewing the foregoing arguments, we note that there were three points at issue in the case, each with contrary opinions by Justice Stone and Justice Roberts. First, the destruction of pigs, or the restriction of crops, was a *legislative* question according to Justice Stone, but a judicial question according to Justice Roberts. Second, the *spending* power of the government is its economic power, an "indirect" power of withholding instead of a direct physical power of compulsion, and the use of this economic power is a legislative question, according to Stone, but a judicial question according to Roberts. The third issue, how far into the details of control over individuals the administrative authority shall be permitted to go, if not prohibited altogether, was afterwards before the Congress in the Walter-Logan bill, applied to all administrative agencies. The bill was adopted by the Congress, on the theory of government by law instead of by men, but was vetoed by the President. This bill, when reduced to its practical workings from the standpoint of economic investigations, meant the use of the injunction by the courts at any stage of the proceedings, in order to prevent administrative officers from summoning witnesses, taking testimony, or otherwise proceeding toward an administrative investigation or decision. The bill, in effect, authorized the lower courts to rehear and reject any of the testimony or investigations of administrative authority, and to hear any *new* testimony not heard by the administrative body instead of referring it back for consideration by that agency. If such a case should arise, in the absence of further legislation like the Walter-Logan bill, the Supreme Court, if it follows Justice Stone's opinion, would apparently not permit the lower judiciary to interfere *during* the administrative process; but afterwards, in review of the whole case, as provided by the Constitution, would treat the matter as a *legislative* issue to be decided by Congress in its control of the administrative agency.

It is only by the use of statistics that the essential distinctions in economic investigations can be made for guidance of administrative action. The courts, not equipped with a staff of qualified economic statisticians, must depend upon an administrative department, or upon cross-examination by lawyers of the prosecution and defense, for discovering or rejecting the facts. Then they pass only upon the *procedure*, as to whether or not it was a fair fight. They usually exclude the economic facts as irrelevant or indifferent. If, then, they presume to reason without the statistics, they resort to the deductive reasoning in economics which does not discover whether the particular case, under the circumstances, is an extreme use, or a reasonable use, at the time, of economic power. So it is that Justice Roberts did not propose to make the many economic distinctions required in practical affairs, such as differences in kind, differences in quantity, differences in degree of economic power as indicated by different prices, wages, values, or differences in time of depression or prosperity. This is the reason for naming his method the legislative method of reasoning, without use of statistics, and without application of the statistician's "frequency curve" of probability.

But Justice Stone's reliance on administrative reasoning requires many differences to be discovered by analysis and statistics, such as differences in bargaining power, producing power, intellectual power, the "power of judgment," the power of taxation, the regulations of commerce, or the police power, etc.

It also requires distinction in many *degrees* of the same *kind* of power, from the least possible to the highest possible degree, as well as the most vital of all distinctions, that of timeliness in an emergency, or in the slow routine of long-time trends, on which depend the decisions of immediate or deferred action or no action. Deductive reasoning, though it may be perfectly logical and valid as a mental operation at all times, on the assumption of unchanging circumstances, is separated from the realities of actual life where choices are made between different degrees of different kinds of power at each successive moment of living, both in emergencies and in routine. In this process the Court does not abdicate—it always retains the last word in its final review, as provided by the Constitution and asserted by Justice Stone.

The legislature, also, is not equipped with qualified statistical investigators, except as it provides and finances them for the specific administrative departments. Hence the various debaters, pro and con, in the legislature proceed to argue from extremes, and there could usually be no agreement reached were it not for the familiar despotic device of majority vote which suppresses the minority. By such a vote the legislature finally lays down its general policies and gives its instructions to the department to investigate and carry out the policy in detail for the particular cases as they come to the front in the changing circumstances. Here, in the administrative department, there is usually no majority and minority vote—only an economic statistical investigation which finds, for the particular case, the most probable action needed to bring about the results intended by the legislature.

These are the main considerations necessary to build up a practical science of administrative economics, in contrast to the logical deductive science of the nineteenth century based upon the presumption of thousands of isolated individual self-interests. Hitherto it has been impractical to consider the development of such a science, which deals with individuals actually subordinated to collective economic action of corporations, labor unions, and political parties, because it was probable that the courts, without economic investigation, would nevertheless interfere with the administrative investigations and decisions. But with the prospect of the courts' permissive attitude, as formulated by Justice Stone, an administrative science of economics can gradually be built up as an aid to the public administration by state and federal governments, and to the correlated private administration by corporations and labor unions, as well as to the department's advisory agricultural committees, and to the organized banking system. Yet the administration can never do away with wisdom and conscience in its use of statistics.

Such a science of administrative economics depends upon the method of reasoning. In the attempted experiment of agricultural adjustment may be seen a repetition of earlier conflicts between the two methods. The older economists and constitutional lawyers might well have looked with fear, as many of them did at the time, upon what the protective tariff might lead to, since the government thereby departed from the extreme *laissez faire* and individualistic liberty and self-reliance of their free-trade assumptions. But justices, like other people, may change their minds upon further investigation, and new justices may become familiar with what had been fearful when first proposed. In view of such developmental changes, the tariff, in an extreme degree of economic power over prices, later accompanied by extreme immigration restrictions, especially the Act of 1923, has eventually been fixed and accepted in the Constitution. What had been deemed extreme or "improbable a few years ago," as Justice Roberts expressed it, is now taken for granted as customary.

This is because the former majority of the Court, led by Justice Roberts, in the Agricultural Adjustment case, followed an obsolete method of reasoning for an imaginary isolated farmer, whereas the situation called for concerned action in defense against other organizations already in existence. The "call" took the form of a body of farmers sufficient to create a "pressure group in Congress, supported by the economists and statisticians of an administrative department, and reasoned from the historical parallel of the protective tariff, as well as from the immigration laws. The farmers and their advisers proposed that the government should also use both its taxing power and its bargaining power to place the farmers, during an emergency, on a parity with the manufacturers and laborers, who are protected by the tariff restrictions on imports and by the immigration restrictions on labor supply. The older arguments of *laissez faire* and self-reliance, although obsolete regarding manufacturers and laborers, whom the government was abundantly aiding against competition, continued to be repeated by Justice Roberts regarding the farmers. To help the farmers during an emergency, either by use of taxing power or by restrictions of output and increase of bargaining power, might lead to abusive extremes. Justice Stone, in effect, asks Justice Roberts to restrain his fears by examining, economically, statistically, and even historically and comparatively, the actual experiment, along with similar experiments on behalf of others. It is a recurrence of the historical conflict between emotional reasoning from imagined extremes, and "statistical reasoning" from the facts discovered somewhere between the extremes.

Reasoning from actual cases somewhere between the extremes is what is meant in legal science as "reasonable." There had always been, as mentioned above, this other doctrine in the decisions where competition was, in fact, not free and equal, but was more or less "monopolistic" or "unfair," namely the doctrine of "reason" or "reasonable value" and "reasonable practices." The courts thereby created, by imagination, it is true, a situation of freedom and equality applicable to the particular case, to be enforced by their legal control, if need be, of the physical force of sovereignty. It was this doctrine of reasonable value, to be ascertained in each case as it arose, between the polar extremes of coercion by either of the opposed participants in a transaction, that Justice Stone set forth in reply to Justice Roberts. And it is this doctrine, when aided by statistics, that furnishes the foundation for the alleged fourth branch of American government, already including a dozen departments, commissions, and boards, namely the branch for the investigation and regulation of similar collective economic action by private corporations, and by labor unions.

In this administrative reasoning from actual cases found somewhere between extremes we do, or should, conform to Stone's argument, always comparing relatively the gains and losses for conflicting economic interests under actual circumstances in view of their bearing upon the public welfare. In the case of the Agricultural Adjustment Act, if we set up the actual liberty gained by farmers, which is freedom from coercion of prices and wages received or paid by them during the emergency, over against the economic liberties lost by other members of society and by themselves during the emergency, we should have a fair measure of the balanced equilibrium of public welfare intended to be brought about by the statute. This is the economic meaning of Stone's "wisdom" and the legal "rule of reason" when reduced to the economists' statistical "weighted averages," depending also on good judgment of time, place, quantity, kind, and degree of power.

In modern economics the fears are mainly the fear of collective action, whether by governments, by corporations, or by labor unions. All collective action is looked upon with fear as leading straight to some form of dictatorship. But actually, in the cases as they arise, all kinds of collective action can be investigated to see whether, at the time and place, they are conducive to more real and equal freedom for individuals than the type of collective action which they displace. Collectivism and individualism are not incompatible except when reasoning from extremes at either end, which may even lead to revolutions, because the parties cannot agree and will not submit to a majority vote. But between these contradictory extremes of the north and the south poles of reasoning are the actual transactions of individuals governed by the actual collective action of corporations, unions, and governments, at the time and place. This is the field of institutional economics based on good judgment and full investigation of issues between conflicting interests. It is the problem of administrative economics in actual cases rather than unconstitutionality in all cases.

The problem does not simplify the science of economics; it makes the science more complex and difficult, even vital to national existence. But it makes economic science less dogmatic and satirical by making it more investigational and more practicable, perhaps more conciliatory.

This is the broader implication of the Agricultural Adjustment case raised by the urgent issue of totalitarian dictatorship. The question is whether, in the matter of corporations, unions, and other concerted action, the American government shall follow its historical negative policy of preventing conspiracy and monopoly by legal prosecutions in all cases, or follow, in large part, its positive policy of regulating them according to its historic doctrine of reasonable value and reasonable practices during a time of war emergency, as well as during a credit emergency. This is no longer an academic question of theory. It is now a question of survival of the American form of government and its system of economics. Justice Stone's opinion lays the legal foundations for this regulation of private collective action by administrative departments, instead of prosecutions by attorneys or suppression by dictators, while the modern statistical science lays the economic foundations. To suggest a paraphrase of the debate between Justice Roberts and Justice Stone, it is a method of "laying down" the American system of law and economics by the side of the totalitarian system, during the emergency, and passing "judgment" on whether, notwithstanding its monopolistic abuses in extreme cases, it "squares" with a "reasonable" approach, under the circumstances, to a "democratic process."

# Chapter xv

## *CREDIT ADMINISTRATION*

---

### 1. Credit Transactions

When the gold standard was suspended by England in September, 1931, and later by the United States in 1933, there remained the existing method of creating money by private negotiations at the commercial banks, to be used as checking accounts by depositors. This kind of money, "deposits," was not a deposit literally in the old warehouse meaning of a deposit of physical things like gold or silver. Instead, the deposits were banker's debts "past due," and therefore not bearing interest, but created outright in order to purchase the debts of business men "not yet due," and to bear interest until the future date when due.

These debts of bankers not bearing interest became, directly or indirectly, the whole of modern money. The business men, who were the creditors, could draw checks on the bank for payment *directly* on their purchases of commodities, or on stocks and bonds of corporations, from other business men, or for payment *indirectly* on wages by drawing out the small denominations of legal money with which actually to pay wages.

Thus the creation of modern money is a creation outright, for each business transaction, of a new debt by a banker not bearing interest, in exchange for a new debt owed by a business man and bearing interest for a few days or months in the future. The date when the interest is paid to the banker is indicated as a "discount" if the banker deducts the interest in advance from the amount of the deposit debt which the banker creates, or a "note" if the interest is paid at the later date when the principal of the note is paid. In either case this kind of money is strictly a "credit transaction" for a short period of time—an exchange of two debts, a *present* debt not bearing interest for a *future* debt bearing interest.

Deposit money does not "circulate" from hand to hand, as does gold, silver, or legal tender money issued by the government. Deposit money is created anew at each credit transaction and then is canceled, or "liquidated," a few days or months later when the business debt is paid. Hence the total volume outstanding at any period of time depends on whether new debts are being created faster or slower than these short time debts are being liquidated, and thus canceled.

An index of these comparative velocities of creation and cancellation of credit money is the amount of "debits to individual accounts" at the banks relative to the total amount of "deposits" at the banks. This comparison is known as the "annual rate of turnover of deposits," and may be calculated as follows for the peak of prosperity in the year 1929 and during the trough of depression in the year 1932.[1]

In the year 1929 the total quantity of deposits at all commercial banks was approximately 43 billion dollars. This quantity fell in 1933 to 29 billion dollars, a decline of about 33 per cent in the volume of deposit money during 4 years.

The debits to accounts of this larger volume during the year 1929 were 1,276 billion dollars, a rate of turnover 30 times during the year, or a velocity of one in less than 2 weeks. The debits of 437 billion dollars together with the smaller volume of deposits in 1933 gave a velocity of turnover of only 15 times during the year, or about one-half the former velocity.

This comparison would indicate, roughly, that while the quantity of deposits declined about one-third in 4 years, the volume of the credit transactions fell about three-fourths (1,276 to 437 billions), and the total national income, reported by the same authority, fell one-half (83 billion to 42 billion dollars). During the same period of 4 years the average price level of all commodities declined about 40 per cent, and the number of unem-

---

[1] The total quantities are stated in *Banking Studies*, 1941, p. 453, issued by the Federal Reserve Board, Washington, D. C.

ployed wage earners increased from 2 million to 10 million, according to various rough estimates.

This formation and liquidation of credit money and the accompanying changes in national income along with the changes in prices of commodities and in the employment of labor are the problems of credit administration entrusted, since 1913, to the Federal Reserve system of banking. The instruments used by the system are a new "unit of accounts," instead of gold, and several new administrative agencies of control.

## 2. THE UNIT OF ACCOUNTS

The unit of *value* was formerly a unit of *weight*—the weight of gold or weight of silver. With the abandonment of silver and then the abandonment of gold as the unit of business accounting, there still remains the need of a standard *unit of value* for the credit transactions. The clever British economist, D. H. Robertson, described the predicament by way of a supposed dialogue between an "enquiring Socrates from another planet" and an English economist "instructed to explain the nature of the system." [1] The picture fits also an American economist instructed to explain the Federal Reserve system, but substituting the Spanish dollar for the British pound sterling as the unit of a legal accounting system:

SOCRATES: I see that your chief piece of money carries a legend affirming that it is a promise to pay the bearer the sum of one pound. What is this thing, a pound, of which payment is thus promised?

OECONOMIST: A pound is the British unit of account.

SOCRATES: So there is, I suppose, some concrete object which embodies more firmly that abstract unit of account than does this paper promise?

OECONOMIST: There is no such object, O Socrates.

SOCRATES: Indeed? Then what your Bank promises is to give the holder of this promise another promise stamped with a different number in case he regards the number stamped on this promise as in some way ill-omened?

[1] *Lloyd's Bank Monthly Review,* May 1939.

OECONOMIST: It would seem indeed to be promising something of that kind.

SOCRATES: So that in order to be in a position to fulfill its promises all the Bank has to do is to keep a store of such promises stamped with all sorts of different numbers?

OECONOMIST: By no means, Socrates—that would make its balance-sheet a subject for mockery, and in the eyes of our people there resides in a balance-sheet a certain awe and holiness. The Bank has to keep a store of Government securities and a store of gold.

SOCRATES: What are Government securities?

OECONOMIST: Promises by the Government to pay certain sums of money at certain dates.

SOCRATES: What are sums of money? Do you mean Bank of England notes?

OECONOMIST: I suppose I do.

SOCRATES: So these promises to pay promises are thought to be in some way solider and more sacred than the promises themselves?

OECONOMIST: They are so thought, as it appears.

SOCRATES: I see. Now tell me about the gold. It has to be a certain weight, I suppose?

OECONOMIST: Not of a certain weight, but of a certain value in terms of the promises.

SOCRATES: So that the less each of its promises is worth, the more promises the Bank can lawfully make?

OECONOMIST: There are complications, Socrates, but it seems to amount to something of that kind.

SOCRATES: Do you find that your monetary system works well?

OECONOMIST: Pretty well, thank you, Socrates, on the whole.

SOCRATES: That would be, I suppose, not because of the rather strange rules of which you have told me, but because it is administered by men of ability and wisdom?

OECONOMIST: It would seem that that must be the reason, rather than the rules themselves, O Socrates.

This mysterious system, that operates by bookkeeping, by enforcement of contracts, and by units of value accepted by the courts, did not come about on general principles of philosophy or on theories of economics. It came after many failures in a vain scurry to ward off further collapses, and individuals and nations try to adapt themselves to it as best they may. The system is scarcely understood by reasoning from the traditional metallic money or paper money that people handle in their small transactions. Like Socrates, they look for something solid, physical, concrete, imperishable, which they can pass from hand to hand, known as "money in circulation." But this circulating money is only a survival from former times, performing less than one-tenth of all transactions, and can itself be acquired only if the individual or corporation owns a transferable deposit balance at the bank. The system might perhaps be explained to Socrates as the silent enforcement of contracts by law and custom in control of credit transactions, which has changed the "substance" of things while holding on to the ancient names. The "substance" that is actually transferred is not physical things or even corporate securities—it is their *ownership*. The *unit of value* is a *unit of ownership,* instead of a unit of weight, wherever the enforcement of contracts runs in accordance with existing custom and law.

The issue came to a crisis in February 1935 when the Supreme Court approved a change of 41 per cent in the unit of value.[1] The Congress had authorized the President to reduce the *weight* of the gold dollar as much as 50 per cent. The President reduced it 41 per cent. The gold dollar of weight became 59 cents in the legal unit of value, or, inversely, the price of gold in terms of the unit of value was raised from $20.67 per ounce to $35 per ounce.

A unit of *value* was thus substituted for the unit of *weight,* and the unit of value is the unit of accounts. Its "value" is its value as purchasing power, or bargaining power, and it has purchasing power because it has tax-paying power and legal debt-paying power by decision of the courts in enforcing contracts.

In the gold clause cases the Supreme Court was confronted by a choice between the enforcement of contracts and the stability of our whole monetary and economic system. Their decision was to abrogate and nullify the gold clause provisions of existing contracts, *especially bonds.* Furthermore, the Court endorsed the joint resolution of Congress of June 5, 1933, which declared that

[1] See J. R. Commons, "The Gold Clause Decisions," *Economic Forum,* 3: 23 1935.

every obligation, "heretofore and hereafter incurred" should be discharged upon payment "dollar for dollar" in legal tender currency or coin.[1]

How could the Supreme Court, as an ethical proposition, justify this grave impairment of the obligation of contracts? Chief Justice Hughes, for the majority of five, gave two reasons for the decisions. Congress, during the Civil War and by the Gold Act of 1900, had established *two* legal standards of value, gold coin and legal tender paper money, the "greenback." There were then, he said, "two kinds of money essentially different in their nature, but equally lawful." It was, therefore, perfectly legal to insert a gold clause in the contract by which the debtor agreed to pay gold of the legal weight and fineness instead of the legal tender "greenbacks." But, says the Court, the Congress had power, under the Constitution, to establish a *single* measure of value, and, therefore, the gold clause in contracts, while it was legal when there were *two* kinds of money, became illegal when Congress established *one* kind of money. It was a "dollar" just the same, but the *substance* was changed from physical gold by weight to intangible working rules of bookkeeping by value.

The other reason advanced by the Chief Justice was made by enlarging the meaning of what courts and lawyers had previously meant by "unjust enrichment," or the economists meant by "unearned increment." The court held that the plaintiff, who was the creditor, i.e., the owner of the mortgage bonds, "has not shown or attempted to show that in relation to buying power he had sustained any loss whatever. On the contrary," the Justice continued, "in view of the adjustment of the internal economy to the single measure of value as established by the legislation of the Congress, and the universal availability and use throughout the country of the legal tender currency in meeting all engagements, the payment to the plaintiff of the amount which he demands (169 dollars unit of value per 100 dollars weight of gold) would appear to constitute not a recoupment of loss in any proper sense, but an unjustified enrichment."

[1] For both the decisions and the joint resolutions, see *Senate Doc. 21,* 74th Congress, 1st Session, 1935.

The "unjust enrichment" relied upon by the Court was supported by evidence from the official statistics available at the time. The statistics showed that the average of wholesale prices had fallen, in 1934, about 40 per cent below the level of the five or six years preceding 1929, so that, for contracts made prior to 1929, the 40 per cent reduction in weight of the gold dollar placed the creditor and the debtor in respect to "buying power," as the Court said, just about on the level where they had been when the contract was made. The "unit of value" had not changed, though the "unit of weight" was reduced 40 per cent.

On the other hand, of course, if the wholesale price level should later have risen to the level prior to 1929, in terms of the unit of account, as was the intention of the administration at that time, then, at that higher level, the creditor would receive in purchasing power, and the debtor would pay in purchasing power, the value equivalent of what had been loaned and borrowed prior to 1929. Whether this higher level could have been brought about and there stabilized, as the administration intended, was dependent not only on the Socratic ability and wisdom of those administering the credit system, but also on their legal and economic power. We consider this power under the name of "administrative controls."

The abrogation of the gold clause contracts, or any contracts wherein payment might be stipulated in a particular kind of coin, was more than a negative act. The Court affirmed the measurement of monetary obligations in a unit of account. In this they simply adopted the prevailing practice of the business community. The measurement of monetary values by this unit of account had in fact previously become so completely integrated into the financial and monetary system of this country, that the practical consequence of upholding the gold contracts would have been the creation of financial chaos and bankruptcy. Some firms would have been obligated to pay back $1.69 for each dollar of previous debt, while other firms would have been unaffected, since their obligations were measured solely by the dollar unit of account. Henceforth, the unit of money was, in fact, to be an administered unit of account.

### 3. Administrative Controls

At least four major instruments of credit control, unknown heretofore in America, were invented or discovered by experiment or accident, beginning in 1920 after the first world war. They are as follows:

#### (a). *International Equalization Account*

This account was at first an administrative agreement between the treasury departments of England, France, and the United States. Since the conquest of France, in 1940, it has continued as an Anglo-American joint administrative control of the credit system for the stabilization of prices, covering the English-speaking world. The unit of accounts itself and its credit control is only a national control for stabilization of domestic prices. The operation of this international account, at the time when France was a party to it, was explained in 1939 by the chairman of the great Midland Bank to his stockholders at their meeting in London.[1] He said:

The Exchange Equalization Account is an essential part of the machinery for regulating monetary conditions. The new technique of monetary management called into being since 1931 requires for its proper exercise far more knowledge, judgment, and skill than were needed in working on the gold standard. There was no room for doubt then as to the action to be taken. If too much gold was leaving the country the Bank rate was put up and credit restricted until gold flowed back. If gold was coming in beyond what was necessary for reserve requirements, the Bank rate was lowered until foreign borrowing checked the inward flow.

The simplicity, the almost automatism, of currency and credit control under the gold standard has been highly praised. But at what cost to trade and industry did the system operate? The Bank rate might have to be raised when internal conditions required not restriction but expansion of credit—as for example last year, when the outflow of gold would have led to severe credit restrictions at the very time when confidence was already shaken and enterprise languishing.

---

[1] *Midland Bank Monthly Review,* London, Midland Bank Limited, January-February, 1939, p. 3.

Seen in retrospect, the pre-war automatism in monetary affairs meant doing nothing until an acute stage of financial weakness had been reached—a stage at which drastic action was inevitable, however damaging its effects might be on industry and trade. But why should the British industrialist and trader pay more for credit, or find credit more difficult to obtain, because foreign capitalists choose to transfer their bank balances from London to New York? Today human skill and judgment must take the place of automatism.

As the European phase of World War II was drawing to a close in 1944, representatives of the several United Nations met in July in an international monetary and financial conference. One of the major purposes of the conference at Bretton Woods, New Hampshire, was to work out plans for a permanent international monetary fund. To the administration of this fund will be entrusted the stabilization of exchange relations between the several currencies in the world. This is not the place to attempt an exhaustive analysis of the prospective organization and operation of this fund. But it foretells the abandonment of an "automatic" international monetary system and the open and explicit acceptance of international management and control of currencies by a public agency deliberately designed for that purpose.

### (b). The Discount Rate

The "bank rate" referred to above in the British system, as the rate charged by the Bank of England, became the rate of rediscount at the Federal Reserve banks in the United States. The rate has ranged all the way from 2 per cent to 7 per cent charged by the Reserve banks to the member banks for the use of "Reserve bank credit" by the member banks. The importance of this agency of control turns mainly on two circumstances, the substitution of Reserve bank credit for gold as the reserves of member banks, and the narrow margins of profit for business corporations and investment bankers who borrow from the member banks.

By raising the rate to 7 per cent, the member bank, if compelled on account of its low reserves to borrow at the Reserve bank, is prevented from lending to business customers except at very high rates, say 8 or 9 per cent per year. The effect of such a high rate on business customers in preventing them from borrowing at the commercial banks, in order to create deposit accounts, depends upon its effect upon the fear of reducing the narrow margin of profit. This margin of profit was shown in my *Institutional Economics* [1] to range, on the average for all manufacturing corporations, from a maximum of 6 per cent average profit during the prosperous year 1920, to an average *loss* during the depression years 1921 and 1930.

The significance of the discount rate relative to the margin of profit is concealed by three different meanings of the word "profit." The three meanings turn on three different ratios of a given quantity of profit to three different other quantities in the finances of a corporation. The other quantities are the legal *par value*, that is, nominal value of the stock issued; the current *market value* of the stock as quoted on the stock exchange; and the *gross income* of the corporation from sales of product on the commodity markets. The three corresponding ratios are the profit *rate*, the profit *yield*, and the profit *margin*.

For illustration, a given *quantity* of profit, say 20 million dollars declared as dividends at the end of the fiscal year is a *profit rate* of 10 per cent on the *par value* of the stock if the corporation is capitalized at the nominal 200 million dollars. But if these shares of stock are quoted on the stock exchange at a market value of 600 million dollars, then the same dividend of 20 million dollars is a *profit yield*, for the purchaser of the stock, at 3⅓ per cent per year on his investment. Finally, if the gross income from sales of products is one billion dollars, being a fivefold turnover of the nominal capital during the year, then the average *profit margin* on sales income is 2 per cent.

This average margin of profit for the year is composed of thousands of credit transactions during the year, each of which has its own margin of *profit or loss*. Hence a rate of rediscount, say 7 per cent at the Reserve banks, augmented to 8 or 9 per cent at the commercial banks, far in excess of the average margin of profit, is likely to result in a *profit loss* for the manufacturing corporation on that particular credit transaction, and, since the rate extends

[1] Pp. 526 ff.—Statistics from U. S. Treasury.

to all the banks, it is likely to put a stop to industry and to cause a depression.

These comparative ratios indicate that by raising the Reserve bank rate of discount to the high figure of 7 per cent, as was done in 1920 and 1929, the commercial banks, if already in debt to the Reserve banks, are prevented from further borrowing at the Reserve banks, and the business community is prevented from borrowing at the commercial banks, with the resulting depression of business and increase of unemployment that occurred in those two years.

### (c). *Open Market Operations*

An even more mysterious and powerful instrument of control exercised by Reserve banks over commercial banks is the "open market operations." This instrument also was not discovered by the Reserve banks until the year 1923.

Since the reserves of member banks are their reserve bank credits, the Reserve banks can take the initiative in increasing or diminishing those reserves by purchases and sales of stocks or bonds on the "open market" at existing prices. If the Reserve bank *buys* bonds on the open market, it does so by issuing to the sellers its own promises to pay on demand; a seller then "deposits" these debts of the Reserve bank with his own commercial bank; this augments by that much the commercial bank's reserve bank credit; and consequently, by thus augmenting its own reserve, augments on the average tenfold [1] its capacity to lend to business customers. Inversely, if the Reserve banks *sell* securities on the open market, they receive in payment from a buyer his check drawn on his own commercial bank; this augments the debt of that bank to the Reserve bank; this reduces by that much the commercial bank's reserve of credit at the Reserve bank; and this, on the average, reduces tenfold the commercial bank's capacity to lend to business borrowers. Mr. Carl Snyder, statistician to the Reserve bank of New York, illustrates vividly the use of these two instruments, discount rate and open market operations. He says: [2]

---

[1] See "Fractional Reserves," p. 250.

[2] Carl Snyder, *Capitalism the Creator*, New York, The Macmillan Co., 1940, p. 224. Copyright, 1940, by The Macmillan Co.

The procedure is much that of a locomotive engineer. The latter can put on or take off steam as he desires, and in this way increase his speed. Or he may use his brakes, applying or releasing them. When applying his brakes, he will first shut off steam. And when he wishes speed he will simply release the brakes and open the throttle . . . The rediscount rate is a brake that can be used to halt undue expansion; the purchase or sale of securities can be used in either way, to check or expand. Skillfully employed, these two agencies are adequate for any normal emergencies.

These two instruments would have been adequate to prevent the inflation of credit that caused the collapse of 1929, but according to Snyder [1] there was only one person in authority, the Under Secretary of the Treasury, Ogden L. Mills, who understood the impending danger. Mills had said, nearly a year before the collapse, "Of course we are riding for a crash, but nothing can be done about it. If we attempted to apply a check, Congress would be on our back in a moment." As it was, the Board acted too late and then raised the discount rate to the prohibitory 7 per cent, which precipitated the stock market panic of 1929.

The effectiveness of rediscount rate and open market operations depends on whether the member bank is already in debt to the Reserve bank and is compelled to borrow at the Reserve bank in order to replenish its own reserve of credit at the Reserve bank. These controls are indirect. Another more effective instrument of control is the *direct* control over the amount of the member bank's legal reserve, whether the latter is or is not in debt to the Reserve bank. Direct control of reserves was authorized by Congress in 1935.

### (d). Fractional Reserves

The credit system of banker's deposit debts payable on demand depends on the solvency of the commercial banks. If a "run" occurs on a bank, so that it cannot pay on demand, it immediately is declared bankrupt and is closed by the state or federal authorities. If these "runs" are general on all banks, it may be necessary to declare a bank moratorium, a bankers' "holiday," as was done

[1] *Ibid.*, p. 388.

by the President early in 1933 for the entire United States. This means, practically, that all business is stopped for the time being, and only those banks survive which show themselves able to pay depositors on demand. About one-third of the commercial banks in the United States were thus closed permanently after 1933, and the other two-thirds remained solvent.

In order that the solvency of the banks may be protected, they are required by law, in the United States, to maintain reserves of legal money at a certain fraction of their demand debts. On the average this fraction had been about 10 per cent. In 1935 Congress delegated the power to change this ratio to the Federal Reserve Board, to the limited extent of doubling the existing reserve requirements.

In the year 1937 the board of governors used this power and doubled the legal reserve requirements. This was "a drastic step" and "much too effective," bringing on the second depression of 1937.[1]

There are also two grades of security owned by the banks, in addition to the fractional reserve requirements. These may be distinguished as primary security enforced by law and collateral security enforced by sale of the collateral. The primary security is the short-time notes signed by business borrowers whose payment when due is enforced by the courts. The collateral security is the stocks or bonds deposited with the banks by the borrower as additional security, with authorization granted to the bank to sell the collateral on the open market for cash in order to reimburse itself if the borrower fails to pay his note when due.

In enforcing these two grades of security, the banks bring on two kinds of business depression, illustrated by the "commodity depression" of 1920 and the "securities depression" of 1929.

The commodity depression of 1920 was precipitated by business men compelled to sell their inventories of commodities on the various commodity markets in order to obtain the cash with which to pay their short-time notes at the banks. Thus, I was told by the silk hosiery manufacturers of Milwaukee, in 1920, that when the

---

[1] Carl Snyder, *Capitalism the Creator*, New York, The Macmillan Co., 1940, pp. 224, 447n.

sag came in the inflated prices of hosiery, the hidden inventories of raw silk were suddenly unloaded on the silk market and the prices were forced down 75 per cent in a very short time. This started the depression of that year, which soon extended to the forced sale of inventories in other industries and led to the general, but short, depression of 1921.

The more serious and long-time depression of 1929, repeated in 1937, started with the forced sales of the collateral securities which forced down the inflated prices of corporate stocks and bonds, extending to forced sales of commodities whose prices were forced down about 40 per cent in four years from 1929 to 1933.

These forced sales of securities came about, in 1929, by failure of the Reserve authorities to make a timely use of the discount and open market instruments; and failure in 1937 by their excessive use of the new power granted by Congress, the power to double the reserve ratios of commercial banks.

In view of these forced sales of commodities or securities, which bring on the depressions, Irving Fisher has proposed that the legal reserves be raised to 100 per cent instead of the fractional reserves regulated by the Reserve Board.[1] The 100 per cent reserve would be partly in legal tender cash, as at present, but mainly in government bonds. But instead of leaving the banks to the fatal alternative of selling these reserve securities on the open market and thus depressing their prices, as was done in 1929 and 1937, the government would actually redeem its own bonds at par value by issuing *new legal tender* money to purchase them.

In this way, it is proposed that automatically on the initiative of the banks, the volume of *legal paper money* would be augmented at exactly the time when more money was needed to head off the depression. And according to Fisher's reasoning the depression itself would be stopped at its source by relieving the banks of the necessity of forced sale of securities in order to replenish their reserves of legal tender cash. The banks, in effect, would sell interest-bearing bonds for non-interest-bearing legal tender money. Then, when business recovery began, the banks would use their store of non-interest-bearing legal tender, acquired

[1] Irving Fisher, *100% Money*, New York, Adelphi Company, 1935.

from businessmen, to purchase back from the government its interest-bearing bonds, thus automatically retiring the money and preventing an excessive inflation of prices, after the inflation had already begun.

Mr. Benjamin Graham begins with a similar proposal, but his is applied to the commodity markets instead of the securities markets.[1] The government would support storage warehouses for twenty or more of the basic commodities, such as wheat or steel ingots, and business men when in need of legal cash to pay their notes at the banks, could simply sell their warehouse receipts, *not legal tender,* to the government in exchange *for new issues of legal tender money* with which to pay the banks on their notes when due. In effect the business men, instead of being forced to sell their inventories, and thus depress the commodity prices, as in 1920, would actually exchange their inventories for *new issues of paper money* that would help to maintain prices. And again, the depression of commodity prices would be stopped at its source by relieving the banks from the necessity of forcing their business customers to sell their inflated inventories of commodities in order to pay their notes when due at the banks.

Both of these proposals are ingenious and are intended to correct the vicious paradox of credit which augments the supply of money when it should deflate, and deflates when it should augment. Fisher would turn to a literal application of the quantity theory of money, by outlawing credit money, which varies so greatly. Graham proposes the return to the "warehouse" stage of money practiced by the gold merchants before negotiability of debt was made legal. But we think that the clock cannot be turned back. The need is not for the elimination of the credit-transactional system of money but its stabilization through wise and courageous administration.

But there remains the same difficulty of timeliness as that which has been pointed out in the case of administrative control. The blunders of the Reserve Board have been either that it acted too late and then too drastically, or that it acted too soon. In the

[1] Benjamin Graham, *Storage and Stability,* 1st edition, New York and London, McGraw-Hill Book Company, 1937.

commodity depression of 1920 the Board waited fifteen months from the time when commodity prices began to advance in March 1919, and then suddenly, in June 1920, raised the rediscount rate to 7 per cent; again, instead of advancing the rate slightly when stock speculation began in early 1928, the Board hesitated until compelled to advance the rate to the prohibitive 7 per cent, immediately followed by the collapse in 1929. But the Board seems to have acted at the right time in April 1923. This is true also with the proposed automatic action of Fisher or Graham; it is a question whether business men and bankers will act soon enough, or will wait until too late. In either case there must be an administrative control, and the main question is whether this control will be exercised at the right time, with the right degree of power, and with the right quantity of sales or purchases.

### (e). *Political Confidence*

Proposals for a better stabilization of the credit system are based mainly upon a "quantity theory" of money and a "velocity theory" of credit transactions. The quantity theory is a supply and demand theory of money, operating at different velocities at different times. It runs somewhat as follows: if the quantity of money increases, prices of commodities will rise, profits will increase, more labor will be employed, and production of commodities will be increased. These results indicate prosperity. If the collapse occurs, prices fall, labor is unemployed, and this is because consumers of commodities do not have enough money with which to purchase the increasing quantity of commodities.

This quantity theory overlooks the credit system. By means of the credit system the business men and bankers, organized especially as corporations themselves, actually create and reduce the quantity of credit money with which they buy and sell commodities and securities. The credit system might be called a futurity system of confidence and loss of confidence. But this confidence is only secondarily a confidence in whether ultimate consumers, as wage earners and farmers, will have purchasing power; it is primarily in whether a political administration will or will not be favorable to the corporations and bankers in enabling them to obtain payments of money with a margin of profit on their sales to other business men and bankers of new commodities and new issues of securities.

This credit creation actually creates the money with which wage earners and farmers are paid, and with which they, therefore, have the money for consumers' purchasing power by drawing out cash from the banks. The cash is returned by the retail merchants to the banks, thereby replenishing or enlarging the bank reserves and enabling them to renew or enlarge their deposit debts as a means of purchasing the promissory notes of business men.

If we examine the way in which the so-called business cycles of prosperity and depression have actually occurred during American economic history, this political confidence theory is the more fundamental explanation of the cycles, in that it explains both the quantity of money and the velocity of transactions. It is a theory of confidence and lack of confidence on the part of bankers and business men in the political administration of the country. The economic results show themselves in overspeculation, increasing velocity, rising prices of securities and commodities when political adminstration is favorable, but ending in a collapse; on the other hand, when the political administration is deemed to be unfavorable, the lack of confidence results in withholding credit, or reducing its velocity—the so-called "hoarding of money."

The twentieth century has vividly demonstrated this political confidence theory. The election of McKinley in 1900, with its abolition of the fear of a hostile political party, created the great wave of confidence which started off with the holding companies and the expansion of bank credit. The election of Harding, in 1920, restored for ten years the confidence in new issues of stocks and bonds. This confidence was suspended by the collapse of overspeculation in 1929, and the suspense was continued by the election of a party favorable to the unemployed laborers and to the farmers, but deemed unfavorable to the corporations and banks.[1]

In view of this lack of confidence in the political administration, the Board of Governors of the Federal Reserve System, the presi-

[1] Mr. Carl Snyder, in his *Capitalism the Creator*, has expressed views strongly favorable to this political confidence theory.

dents of the Federal Reserve banks and the Federal Advisory Council, representing, as they do, banker control of the system, addressed the Congress of the United States in December 1940, recommending the abdication by Congress and the President of control of the credit system and favoring delegation of that control to this centralized organization of the Reserve banks of the country.[1]

Such recommendations would not have been made if the election of 1940 had returned a President and Congress thought favorable to the corporations and banks. The recommendations are equivalent to what would be the situation in the administration of railway regulation if the administration were turned over to the presidents of the railway corporations instead of the Interstate Commerce Commission appointed by the President and the Senate.

In view of this aggressive attitude of centralized bankers and corporations, and their policy of coming into the open with their presidential candidate and monetary program, there is evident a recurrence of the proposal that governmental ownership and operation shall be substituted for banker control. But even with this remedy there would remain, and might be intensified, the defect of ignorance and lack of managerial ability. The issue of public or private ownership of Reserve banks is subordinate to representation of organized economic interests in the administrative management by the original Federal Reserve Board of Governors. Evidently the only effective economic interests are those already organized. These might be organized into a powerful advisory committee, instead of the present bankers' Open Market Committee, each organization electing its representatives to the advisory committee, as is now done by the bankers in control of the Reserve banks. The existing national economic organizations are the National Industrial Conference Board and the National Association of Manufacturers, representing manufacturers; the Association of Railway Management; the three farmers' organizations —Farm Bureau Federation, Grange, and Farmers' Union; the American Federation of Labor and the Congress of Industrial Organizations, representing organized labor; and the American

[1] See *Federal Reserve Bulletin*, January 1941.

Bankers' Association. These are the most representative self-governing organizations, whose members are affected by the monetary and credit policies of the Congress and the administrative authority.

The idea of such an "advisory committee" is usually misunderstood as something that has been tried and "would not work." This is because advisory committees were usually appointed by the political administration itself and did not represent the actual corporations and unions, but represented the dominant political interests. The self-governing advisory committee, electing its own representatives, is similar to the advisory committee of organized manufacturers and organized labor, which drafts the safety rules and unemployment compensation rules for the Wisconsin Industrial Commission since its organization in 1911.[1] It constitutes a kind of occupational legislature, instead of the territorial legislatures, and its recommendations are adopted by the legislature and the commission, regardless of political changes in the administration itself.

The advantage of this advisory method of administration is that each organized interest is compelled to bring forward its proposals in the open and in face of the similar elected representatives of other interests. The advisory method thereby practically eliminates the partisan politics of the American system of government. It is a substitute for the special interest lobbyists who operate by maneuvering legislative and administrative bodies back of the scenes and in secret.

### (f). *Instruments of Value Control*

Monetary arguments, for more than a hundred years in America, have waged pro and con over the so-called "quantity" theory of money. But the incoming of administrative controls, exercised by the Federal Reserve Board and banks, throws a new light on this discussion. It clears up a distinction between a so-called static theory and a so-called dynamic theory, which should rather be named a distinction between a mechanistic theory and a managerial theory, or between an equilibrium theory and a volitional

[1] See "Capital-Labor Administration," p. 261.

theory. The analogous distinction in the physical sciences is something similar to the distinction between a groceryman's scale of weights in measuring out sugar by pounds and ounces by a sales clerk behind the counter and an instrument board on an airplane operated by a pilot or navigator with a dozen different levers and meters, the whole moving at a velocity of two or three hundred miles per hour towards an "objective" unseen but mapped in a preceding plan of campaign. It is, in effect, a change from quantities to transactions.

All of the different instruments are, indeed, quantitative measures and controls, but there are dozens of different kinds of quantities, all the way from measures of weather, wind, clouds, velocity, gasoline flow, temperature, to measures of height, with the over-all complication of timing and timeliness. So with the Federal Reserve Board and banks operated by "governors" whom Robertson and Socrates above indicated must be men of "wisdom" and "ability," but whom the physical scientists would indicate as "pilots," navigators, engineers of training, skill, and quick judgment. To indicate the similar institutional arrangement of bankers as a "quantitative theory of money" is as obsolete as to attempt the solution of a problem of airplanes by an "equilibrium" theory of balancing weights on a grocery counter.

This is also the problem of all modern administrative agencies, distinguished from legislative and judicial departments of government, which we designate as the volitional theory of value distinguished from equilibrium theories of the physical sciences.

The guide to such a theory, which makes it workable, is always the purpose or aim which is set up for the pilot, the navigator, the Board of Governors of the Federal Reserve board and banks. The former vague purpose was so-called "sound money," meaning "gold," regardless of price level. But the transactional goal or purpose has come to be named sometimes "stabilization of the wholesale average price level," which, more concretely, was stated by President Roosevelt, in 1933, as follows: [1]

[1] Quoted by Clark Warburton, principal economist, Division of Research and Statistics, Federal Deposit Insurance Corporation, in *Amer. Econ. Review,* June 1944, under title "Monetary Expansion and the Inflationary Gap." Warburton

The Administration has the definite objective of raising commodity prices to such an extent that those who have borrowed money will, on the average, be able to repay that money in the same kind of dollar which they borrowed. We do not seek to let them get such a cheap dollar that they will be able to pay back a great deal less than they borrowed. In other words, we seek to correct a wrong, and not to create another wrong in the opposite direction . . . Let me be frank in saying that the United States seeks the kind of dollar which a generation hence will have the same purchasing and debt-paying power as the dollar value we hope to attain in the near future.

To which we add that the preventive of inflation and deflation as proposed by the President is the preventive also of overspeculation alternating with unemployment such as the nation suffered during the years preceding and following 1929.

The main administrative instruments, or "techniques," available for the Federal Reserve System, with their possible range of operation under legislation by the Congress, may be summarized as follows, referring to preceding discussion:

1. Rediscount rate, 2 per cent to 7 per cent.

2. Bank reserves for commercial banks, 5 per cent to 100 per cent, similar to preceding proposals by Fisher and Graham.

3. Open market operations, indefinite but extensive.

4. International equalization accounts.

5. Control of the gold billions of dollars hoarded underground in Kentucky.

6. To these are added all the possible aids towards timeliness, such as the existing hourly reports to the New York Reserve bank from member banks of incoming and outgoing deposit accounts—indicating the velocity of credit turnover—and the changing quantity of paper and metal "money in circulation."

The exposition and use of these and other instruments of credit control of checking accounts and money in circulation remain to be worked out by such administrative economists as Warburton in America and Keynes in England, who must be backed up by

---

endorses the President's objective as "reasonable and practical," saying also "the development of suitable techniques for its accomplishment is neither impossible nor difficult."

popular understanding, by practical politics, and by "wisdom and ability" of the administrative department of government— the Federal Reserve Board and banks.

Regarding this matter of wisdom and ability there should be added the ethical attribute of public purpose superior to private purpose. The Federal Reserve Board was originally created by legislation during the administration of President Wilson to regulate the twelve reserve banks and the thousands of private commercial banks. But after the discovery by Governor Benjamin Strong, of the New York Reserve bank, of the powerful regulative influence of open market operations, the Congress was induced by the bankers to amend the law by placing the controlling power over these instruments in the hands of an "open market committee" appointed by the twelve private reserve banks instead of by the President and Senate of the United States—a substitution of private purpose for public purpose—as though the Congress should amend the Interstate Commerce Law by substituting a committee of the American Association of Railways for the existing Interstate Commerce Commission.

Just the opposite, but negative action in favor of private control was taken by the congressional committee under the influence of the bankers in the year 1928 when they rejected the bill introduced by Congressman Strong of Kansas instructing the Federal Reserve Board to use its instruments of control for the public purpose of stabilizing the general price level, on which the present writer made arguments as a witness before the congressional committee in charge of money and banking.[1]

[1] This argument was published in the *Stabilization Hearings,* House Committee on Banking and Currency, 69th Congress, 1st Session on H. R. 7895 (1927), pp. 1074–1121, and 70th Congress, 1st Session on H. R. 11806 (1928), pp. 56–104, and pp. 423–444.

# Chapter xvi

## *CAPITAL-LABOR ADMINISTRATION*

———◆———

### 1. From Territorial to Economic Government

It was the organization of railway corporations and railway labor unions, covering the entire area of the United States, that began to convert the sectional, local, and other territorial organizations of representative government into national economic organizations of corporations and unions, overriding state boundaries. National administrative boards and commissions for regulation of railway corporations and railway unions began as early as the 1880's and 1890's after the business depression and railway competitive wars of the 1870's.

At that time, it began to be discovered that the traditional antimonopoly legislation and the judicial prosecutions of conspiracies did not fit this organized expansion of a basic industry.

The antimonopoly and territorial self-government policies continued for other industries until reversed temporarily by the National Industrial Recovery legislation of 1933. This reversal was an attempt, under the New Deal theory of administrative economics, to recover from the deep depression affecting all industries which began in the collapse of 1929. This collapse followed the excessive speculative expansion of bank credit in aid of issues of corporate stocks and bonds. In brief, it was the expansion of transportation and banking that initiated the national economic organizations of capital and labor, and the resulting national legislation and administration counteracting and regulating these organizations.

The railway brotherhoods of operating trainmen on a national scale had acquired a reputation of conservatism, from the time, in 1894, when they resisted the revolutionary unionism led by

Eugene Debs in the national railway strike of that year against the Pullman Sleeping Car Company. Twenty years after that economic revolt, as a member of President Wilson's Industrial Relations Commission of 1913, I was trying to convince one of the employer representatives, president of a transcontinental railway company, that he and his fellow employers should support me and Mrs. Harrimah in our report favoring collective bargaining between labor unions and their employers, but without governmental or political interference. The trade union representatives on the commission, led by the lawyer chairman, were favoring and giving publicity to political action and political campaigns, but I used what, to me, as a lifelong member of the typographical union, was a convincing argument against government interference and against party politics. I then argued: "What we want to do is to strengthen the conservative unions in this country against the radical and communistic organizations which want to switch the unions into politics and to overthrow the corporations and the government by revolution." "Hell," he retorted, "you don't call these railway brotherhoods conservative, do you? They'll take the last cent we've got, or else stop the whole railway system of the country."

Now I go further than I did twenty-five years ago and contend that the preservation of the American economic system against a totalitarian world, and against its own internal disruption, consists mainly in the collective bargaining between organized capital and organized labor, as against government by the traditional political parties. Other economic organizations, whether of farmers, merchants, bankers, or the professions, must conform their policies and methods to this major economic issue of "capital and labor." In other words, as will appear, both political science and economic science are beginning to recognize a transition from territorial governments to economic governments.

This was demonstrated a few months after the report of the same Industrial Relations Commission in 1915, when these "conservative" railway brotherhoods actually compelled the President and the Congress, by threat of a national strike in face of a world war, to enact the Adamson Law, reducing the hours of labor without reduction of wages, and then compelled the government to take over the entire railway system of the United States, as a war measure, from the private owners.

The representatives of the employers on the Industrial Relations Commission finally supported Mrs. Harriman and myself, in opposition to the trade union representatives led by the political chairman. The twenty-five years that have elapsed since that time have convinced me that one of the active mistakes that precipitated the second world war was the confusion of communism with trade unionism by enemies of the unions, made plausible by the switch of a few unions, or their leaders, into politics. Unions have at times fallen under control of gangsters and political actionists even though the rank and file are opposed to gangsters who exploit them and to communists who undermine them by demanding political action. If self-governing unions are destroyed, or switched to political parties, the alternative for this country, as it has been the alternative under dictatorships, is suppression or even elimination of self-governing corporations and unions, or at least suppression of their leaders, by military governments. If American democracy is "saved," it will be saved by collective economic organization of corporations and labor unions. Instead of the traditional equilibrium between equal individuals of economic theory, the alternatives today are between an economic government based on balance of power between self-governing corporations and unions, and a suppression of both organizations, or their leaders, by military power.

What happened in the totalitarian countries, and, at times, has become a potential menace in this country, is the suppression of the most directly antagonistic enemy of communism, the labor unions, or their own selected leaders. Then by their destruction of self-governing concerns the corporations or their leaders are also suppressed by the military power that suppressed the leaders of the unions. The attacks on unions that label them communists are a part of a political pretense. The real decision to be made is the choice of alternatives between self-governing labor unions and militaristic governments. The unions may not be "conservative" from the standpoint of bargaining power, but they are conservative from the standpoint of representative democracy.

Yet the whole system of political economy, as theoretically developed in the nineteenth century by professional economists and approved by the public generally, has been so built upon the ideal of a perfect society of liberty, equality, and fraternity among individuals, under the ideal name of "democracy," that people have not learned to think and act in terms of the actual "collective democracy" of economic organizations of capitalists and wage earners in the form of existing corporations and unions. Even a new world war, after these twenty-five years of military revolutions, does not clear up the desperate issue that it is not a matter of idealistic individual democracy in a world of abundance, but is a choice between militarism and the increasingly organized economic governments in a world of closing frontiers with good and bad leaders on both sides.

These economic organizations, in their existing form and activities, arose out of the extension of political suffrage from the limited property suffrage at the time when the Constitution was framed in 1787 to the universal manhood suffrage of the northern states prior to the Civil War, physically imposed upon the southern states by the victors in that war. "Democracy" had meant only universal political suffrage for individuals, and not collective bargaining between organizations. The consequences showed themselves first in the great cities where the labor element was influential in voting. Tammany Hall in the 1830's was the pioneer, and it became a political labor organization whose main purpose and success consisted of finding jobs or relief for laborers menaced by unemployment and of financing themselves as politicians in exchange for favors granted to the corporations. After the Civil War this economic foundation of employment and unemployment, financed by privileges for influential corporate capitalists, became the basis of the American national political "machines." These machines were simply the disciplined organizations of political parties dependent for their funds on the economic interests of contributors. So that the three basic economic institutions in

America became the corporations, the labor unions, and the political parties.

The American Constitution had provided an independent Supreme Court, with the last word of the three branches of government in deciding upon the constitutionality of the acts of the legislative and executive branches. After the Civil War in which the territorial conflicts had culminated, the farmers, followed by the wage earners, began to organize politically in order to impose economic legislation and administration in control of corporations and employers generally, whom they began to distinguish as "capitalist" classes. Now a new theory of the place of the Supreme Court in the constitutional scheme began to be accepted by the Court, in interpreting, not the original Constitution, but the amendments forbidding the "taking of property or liberty without due process of law." Former interpretations turned on the "obligations of contracts." The new interpretation turned on "due process of law." This new interpretation supported substantially the extension of its jurisdiction by the federal courts, followed by state courts, from control over territorial or political conflicts to control over collective economic conflicts arising from these corporations, labor unions, and political parties. The economic conflicts became intensified and outstanding, in contrast to the former territorial conflicts, with the closing of the western frontiers to migration and investment in the last decade of the nineteenth century. The Supreme Court of the United States extended its protection of property and liberty by personification of corporations as individuals; from protection of corporeal property belonging to individuals to the protection of corporate property; and the liberty of individuals to the corporate liberty of management in buying and selling commodities and "hiring and firing" employees.

The Supreme Court henceforth had two major activities in the constitutional scheme: the territorial preservation of national unity by balancing state governments with a national government, and the economic preservation of the property and liberty of capitalistic organizations by holding in check the political and economic collective action of farmers and wage earners. This collective action had taken two forms: administrative departments of government, like the Interstate Commerce Commission, and the collective bargaining of organized employers with the trade unions of wage earners.

## 2. FROM CLASS WAR TO CONSTITUTIONAL GOVERNMENT

The foregoing recital indicates that not only does the complete recognition of collective bargaining create a constitutional government for industry, but collective bargaining also subordinates the territorially organized legislatures to the moral control of this economic government. It also indicates that every disputed economic issue between organized capital and organized labor can be settled by administrative agreements except the fundamental issue of *economic power*. The discovery was made in Wisconsin, as also in other states and the federal government, that the effort to include this creation and supervision of collective power within the same administrative agency as other labor laws was impracticable and actually defeated the procedure of agreements on the administrative issues.

The reasons for this discovery are plain. The question of *power* is the fundamental question of class war, or class struggle, breaking out in strikes, lockouts, and even in military revolutions. As such it requires a branch of government entirely different from an administrative agency, namely a constitutional convention or a Supreme Court, with power to substitute for class war the constitutional legislative system of collective agreements between opposing organizations of power.

This judicial function in the economic field was loosely organized, its beginnings known as boards or commissions of "conciliation, mediation, arbitration," culminating in the federal field as the National Labor Relations Board of 1935. These supreme judicial boards in regulation of collective bargaining, in the states and nation, as against the older ideas of individual bargaining, were endowed with power to negotiate or decide upon methods of voting, upon jurisdictional disputes, or upon other details necessary to create the independent, authoritative bargaining agencies themselves, which then entered upon the collective legislative agreements and the administrative decisions above described. In these respects there came about the development of constitutional government in the field of economic power, repeating substantially the original constitutional government in the territorial field of local self-government, also with its three branches of government, the judicial, the legislative, and the executive or administrative. The judicial branch is the board of conciliation, or mediation, culminating in the National Labor Relations Board. The legislative branch is in the equal bargaining power of organized capital and organized labor, making their administrative rules governing individuals. And the executive department is a bifurcated arrangement of the managers and foremen of the corporations acting within the business agents and executive boards of the unions.

Temporarily, while the American Supreme Court, under its historical doctrine of conspiracy and "due process," was outlawing the labor union side of this economic government, these analyses and distinctions could not clearly be made, but with the revised Supreme Court, and its decisions supporting equality of collective bargaining power, the way is prepared for ultimate preponderance of the above roughly outlined scheme of economic government over the former scheme of territorial government before there were corporations, labor unions, or political parties.

The remaining but deadly opponent of this constitutional development of economic government, after the Supreme Court has acquiesced, is the dictatorship type of government proposed nearly a hundred years ago by Karl Marx in his "Communist Manifesto" of 1848. It is not surprising that Marx and his associates could not imagine anything different from military revolutions and dictatorship, for there had been, at that time, practically no joint stock corporations, no trade unions of the modern type, and no political parties based upon universal suffrage. This extension of suffrage now includes the propertyless class of wage earners, along with the development of large-scale corporations, permitted to participate with propertied classes through political parties in the control of government. The communists, therefore, had for many decades after Marx no practical appeal to the unpropertied except military revolution.

But in every case when they and their liberal associates attempted these revolutions, beginning with the revolutions of 1848 and with the exception of the Russian Revolution during World War I, they were easily overthrown by dictatorships organized in the interest of the propertied classes. But a constitutional government of balanced equilibrium of propertied and unpropertied classes, capable of holding its own against military despotisms, may be foreseen on the American field. This economic government, although feared by economists and lawyers trained under the individual system, is to be looked for in the organized corporations and unions that are able to build upon the decay of territorial representation and the distortion of political parties. The system of economic government is not idealistic nor even voluntary because it is not built upon an ideal of a perfect society of socially minded individuals, but, on the contrary, these economic governments are dictated by the closing of the world's frontiers of natural resources, predicted by the economists' doctrine of diminishing returns, and by the resulting intensified conflicts of the organized economic power of corporations, unions, and political parties.

The constitution of a balanced economic government is confused by various doctrines of the jurisdiction of such a government over the transactions between individuals. The longest history of this problem of jurisdiction is in the railway corporations and railway unions. The decisions of the Supreme Court, in a number of cases,[1] treated the negotiations between a foreman and a laborer as though they were an individual bargaining transaction between equal merchants on a commodity market, where rules of equality were carried over to a labor market; whereas they were in fact the orders of a subordinate executive officer of a huge economic government in control of the means of livelihood of an individual laborer and his family. When the laborer and his family could escape to other employers, before the incoming of these corporations, the doctrine of equality had some leeway; but when whole economic governments controlled the opportunities for employment of specialized workmen fitted mainly for that kind of

[1] *Coppage* v. *Kansas,* 296 U. S. (1915), and other cases. See also J. R. Commons, *Legal Foundations of Capitalism,* New York, The Macmillan Co., 1924, p. 48.

employment, then the nation by these decisions of the courts was confronted with a conflict of inequality of power between great corporations and unorganized individuals.

The doctrine of equality was violated by these legal decisions. Twenty years ago, I wrote that if a corporation with 10,000 employees loses one employee, it loses only one ten-thousandth part of its labor force, but the employee loses 100 per cent of his job.[1] No wonder the laborers should reason that if the 10,000 should quit or were discharged as a unit, then the corporation also would lose 100 per cent of its working force, while each laborer was losing 100 per cent of his job. It is not surprising that in its recent revised reasoning the Supreme Court squarely declared the former line of reasoning was no longer constitutional in the United States.

The issue of the "closed union shop" is now, therefore, transferred from the courts to the field of administrative economics. What proportion of all the workers in an establishment shall be members of the union? Outside the union the workers are competitors for jobs with the members of the union. Inside the union they are subject to the working rules which follow lines of seniority or other procedure in employment and unemployment of individuals, determined by collective bargaining. But whether inside or outside the union they are under the jurisdiction of the corporate management. Consequently collective bargaining means, if it is really effective as the legislative branch of economic government, that *all* the employees of the corporation shall be subject to the jurisdiction of the joint agreements of the corporate management and the labor unions. This signifies that the shop is, in effect, a union shop or a closed union shop. There is to be no individual bargaining contrary to the joint legislative working rules which treat all individuals alike, whether nominally members of the unions or not.

Many intricate questions and formalities arise, difficult for administrative adjustment. The late Justice Brandeis, before he became a member of the Supreme Court, proposed an ingenious and

[1] J. R. Commons, *Legal Foundations of Capitalism,* New York, The Macmillan Co., 924, pp. 71 ff.

apparently effective solution for the clothing trades of New York, under the name of the "preferential union shop." This scheme was both constitutional, under former decisions of the courts, and comprehensive under the need of complete jurisdiction over all individuals employed by the corporation. Other devices economically equivalent to the union shop have been worked out, under seniority or other rules, for the railway and other unions.

These are questions of economic power, the jurisdictional questions which always are coming to the front before the administrative questions can be entertained, and in the present status of the issue they are questions entrusted to the economic supreme court, the National Labor Relations Board.

### 3. Administrative Procedure

The so-called collective bargaining is, more accurately, economic legislation by representatives of organized capitalists and organized laborers, with executive and judicial departments. The system repeats, on the field of strikes and lockouts, the origins of parliamentary government in England after the fourteenth century on the field of battle.

Bargaining, on the other hand, from the historical standpoint, was something entirely different. It was negotiations and contracts between individual merchants enforced by their own voluntary associations, the guilds, without the use of physical force. This so-called "custom of merchants," which was really economic government by guilds of merchants, was eventually taken over by the king's courts much the same as recently the "custom" of stockbrokers enforced by their own voluntary "guild," the stock exchange, has been taken over by the Securities and Exchange Commission.

The stockbrokers are a modern section of merchants, originating out of transactions in the stocks and bonds of joint-stock corporations. The corporations themselves became, eventually, great economic governments using economic coercion, beginning with railway corporations and extending to every field of production, manufacturing, banking, and investment, and controlling today nine-tenths of the industry of the country outside agriculture.

The corporations have developed their administrative department, under the name of "management," out of their legislative, executive, and judicial departments, which were provided in their charters of incorporation. "Management" has several subordinate divisions, delegated to high salaried specialists, according to the class of people with whom the corporation has transactions. A legal department deals with courts, legislatures, and politicians. A credit department, with a sales department, deals with bankers, investors, merchants. A production department deals with the employment, discharge, and discipline of wage earners. A self-governing department of "management" controls its own board of directors, through restrictions on voting and on proxies of its stockholders, as well as cartel agreements on policy with competitors. A "public relations," or propaganda, department deals with newspapers, radio, and voters generally. The unification of these various activities under the name of "management" we name *private administrative economics*.

When various classes of the so-called "public" with whom the management dealt began to organize and to use their political power to create boards, commissions, or other public administrative agencies in self-protection against, or in aggression upon, the management of corporations, the purpose was to obtain, by participation in the power of government, a greater influence than they were able to obtain through the regularly constituted courts whose members were well known to be predominantly appointed or elected through the political influence of the corporations. The high-grade lawyers appointed to positions on the federal courts, and the equally high-grade and highly paid lawyers representing corporations before the courts, were recognized as so far superior in ability and in maneuvering to the lawyers representing labor and agricultural interests that the resort to administrative agencies in the various economic fields appears to have been a consequence of the attempt to obtain a more favorable administration by laymen in place of the technically trained lawyers.

This was especially the case in the field of capital-labor administration. In this field there have developed labor organizations equally powerful in their bargaining power—the power to withhold labor supply in the form of strikes—with the capitalist organizations in their power to withhold employment. It was these equally powerful organizations on the opposing sides that entered upon the collective bargaining agreements that repeated on the economic field the system of parliamentary government previously developed on the field of physical force under the technical name of "sovereignty." Here the two "houses," the Senate and the House of Representatives, obtained an equilibrium of economic power, as parliamentary government in England six centuries earlier had obtained an economic equilibrium in Parliament of the House of Lords as landlords and in the House of Commons as tenants and merchant guilds of the towns.[1]

The traditional opposition of the courts to this balancing organization of labor, descending from their doctrines of conspiracy and antimonopoly, was finally displaced by the Supreme Court of the United States in sustaining the act of Congress in 1935, which gave to labor unions as complete and independent powers of economic legislation and treaty making with employers as the preceding legislation had given to corporations. This act of Congress created the National Labor Relations Board as an economic supreme court to decide disputes concerned with organization of labor as a bargaining agency entitled to make the working-rule treaties of collective bargaining with similar organizations of capitalists. Since these decisions of disputes came at the time of creation of similar agencies in other fields, the lawyers of the United States, organized as the American Bar Association, began their systematic investigation towards weakening the administrative agencies and succeeded in obtaining from the Congress the Walter-Logan enactment, vetoed however by the President as not sufficiently considered when it was prepared.

In line with this veto, the Attorney General of the United States, instructed by the President, appointed a Committee on Administrative Procedure, which submitted investigations of the principal administrative agencies of the federal and state governments, said to be "the most thorough and comprehensive study of

[1] Cf. my article in *American Review of Reviews,* March 1901, on the two-house system as developed at that time in the field of bituminous coal mining.

federal administrative procedure that has ever been made." This committee submitted two bills for adoption by Congress, a majority bill favorable to independence of the administrative agencies and a minority bill calling for restoration of restraints upon these agencies by the courts, similar to the restraints contained in the Walter-Logan bill.

These majority and minority bills were supported and criticized at a meeting of the American Bar Association, and reported in the *Journal* of that Association, November, 1941. The review and criticism by Dean Roscoe Pound, supporting and going further than the minority committee, constitutes a well-balanced argument from the accepted legal standpoint against the tendencies of these administrative agencies. These tendencies, according to Dean Pound, turn on the incapacity and lack of training of the laymen members of these agencies as to the procedure developed in the Anglo-American history of the courts for the protection of individual rights and liberties against the overwhelming and arbitrary power of government. The fear of Dean Pound is expressed by him as the tendency toward "absolutism" the world over, and his recommendations propose a restoration of the power of the legal profession, abdicated by the revised Supreme Court, in restraint of administrative agencies.

These tendencies of laymen agencies, as condensed by Dean Pound, are:

1. Failure to hear both sides.
2. Private consultations and undivulged reports.
3. Determinations without basis in substantial evidence.
4. Policies outside the statute.
5. Policy determining the facts, instead of facts investigated independent of policy.
6. Undifferentiated finding of facts and law.
7. Delegation of decisions to subordinates.

Dean Pound's recommendations to correct these tendencies run exactly contrary to the administration by laymen, and he proposes the restoration of legal review by the courts with power of revocation of the administrative rule making and adjudication, on all of these seven grounds of failure to protect individual rights. His arguments are moderately yet forcibly presented, and they must be met by advocates of administrative economics.

From my experience in administrative bill drafting of public utility and industrial commission statutes, and participation in the administration of the latter, I make the following observations in general.

Dean Pound attributes these seven defects to the "zeal" of administrative officials. This criticism, in fact, applies only to new commissions, the "new broom" that sweeps clean, and not to long-standing commissions like the Interstate Commerce Commission whose procedure has finally been standardized on the basis of fifty years' experience.

More serious is the observation that these commissions come to be controlled by party politics and the powerful corporations which they were designed to hold in check. The corporations cannot be held in check because their own legal attorneys are appointed or elected to the judiciary and their own high-salaried legal staff is employed in drafting the laws and appearing in cases before the courts.

A third observation relates to the poor qualifications of the "subordinates" to whom decisions are said to be delegated. These subordinates, however, are not the secretarial clerks as asserted or implied by Dean Pound. They are the technically trained statisticians, economists, lawyers, engineers, and physicians employed as needed by the particular agency, whose abilities are limited relatively by the much higher salaries paid to experts by the corporations, and by the political control of their appointments.

More fundamental is the fourth observation, that the "rights and liberties" which are jeopardized by this administration through laymen instead of protected by the courts are not the rights and liberties of equal individuals, as contemplated in the Constitution and by Dean Pound, but are the rights and liberties of the modern economic governments by which the "management" of those corporations in transactions with individual laborers, investors, and farmers, has gained control of nine-tenths of all production of wealth and a corresponding proportion of all wage earners.

Since the real issue, as emphasized by Dean Pound and also by those who advocate relative independence of the administrative agencies, is the issue of control by simple laymen, such as business men and laboring men, as against the alternative control by the technically trained lawyers; however, the solution from the standpoint of administrative independence is the method of selection of these laymen. Many attempts have been made by legislation to designate, either as members or as "advisors" of these commissions, representatives of the opposing economic interests affected by the investigations and orders of the commission. But all these efforts failed, basically because the spirit of American institutions seemed to insist on *individuals*, in place of *organizations*, as embodying the interests to be represented. Consequently the appointing power selects individuals, either eminent or nondescript, who are favorable to its own economic or political point of view. This is a complete indifference to the actual historical development which has taken place over the past hundred years. That development has been the organization of economic interests in self-governing corporations, or similar associations of economic government, which elect their own officers and representatives.

The independence of labor organizations, for example, has centered on the prevention of "company unions" and "yellow-dog contracts," which had indicated control by employers over the selection of union representatives. This control was counteracted by legislation enforcing the power of the unions to select their own representatives—an assertion of representative democracy for the economic organizations of wage earners paralleling the corporations. A similar rule is needed for the selection of representatives by both organized employers and organized employees in the administration of laws regulating the transactions between employees and employers. These transactions have to do mainly with accidents, health, unemployment compensation, old age pensions, and with hours and minimum wages of unorganized employees, of women, and of children.

Beginning in 1911, in the state of Wisconsin, advisory committees were authorized in the law creating the industrial commission of that state, and the actual administration, of which I was a member, adopted the policy of calling upon the State Manufacturers' Association and the State Federation of Labor to name the members of these advisory committees. Such committees were created in formulating the rules for accident prevention, minimum wages, child labor, regulation of employment offices and extended finally to unemployment compensation after the enactment of that legislation in 1932. In order to show the operation of this system of representation since the year 1911, I have selected extracts from a letter written to me by Mr. Paul Raushenbush, August, 1941, salaried employee of the commission and chairman of the advisory committee on unemployment compensation, and included them as Appendix II.

As will be seen from this communication, the advisory committees, if actually appointed by the organized employers and organized employees, accomplish practically a complete administration by laymen without interference from courts or politicians. Yet the committees have available the experts, physicians, lawyers, and engineers, as needed. A large feature is the complete elimination of both the labor lobby and the employers' lobby before the legislature, the reduction of legislative committee hearings to a minimum, and the unanimous adoption by successive legislatures, notwithstanding all changes in political elections, of the jointly recommended amendments to the legislation as shown to be needed. From my own experience in the development of this system in Wisconsin since 1911, I infer that these representative committees overcome the objections raised by Dean Pound in the matter of protecting the rights of individuals in the conduct of administrative agencies, at least in the agency which administers the usual labor laws.

The other branch of labor legislation, equality of collective bargaining power, has been found in Wisconsin and elsewhere impracticable when administered by the same agency. It involves questions of *power* of conflicting organizations, rather than questions of *administration,* and these are questions of constitutional government in the modern economic field emerging out of the territorial government established by the Constitution of 1787.

It is not convincing that this device of advisory representation of organized capital and organized labor would be practicable if applied to the other administrative agencies. Those agencies are not created on account of strikes and lockouts, a kind of economic war that stops production. Indeed, the device is not equally important in those fields, because the capital-labor conflict is evidently the one that dominates all other economic relations, and is the one that, in Europe, ended in the military revolutions. All other administrative agencies must conform to this fundamental agency which negotiates these capital-labor agreements, whose major issue turns on the prevention of unemployment, either the voluntary unemployment of strikes and lockouts, or the involuntary unemployment during credit depressions. In so far, indeed, as the administrative banking and securities boards or commissions control the inflationary and deflationary causes of involuntary unemployment, they also are administrative agencies for the prevention of strikes and lockouts.

### 4. Cooperation of Public and Private Administration [1]

I can speak to you only of my own experience twenty-five to thirty years ago in promoting the safety of employees by means of mutual insurance by employers. It was forty years ago that I got my first ideas of how wonderfully effective mutual insurance can be made in preventing casualties, by my acquaintance with the fire prevention work of the mutual organization of textile corporations in Massachusetts. I learned this principle of human nature: if you think somebody else, say a stock corporation or the state government, is going to pay for your losses on account of fire or accident, then what is the use of taking extra precautions to prevent fire and accident? But if you know that you yourself must pay your own losses, then you will take extra precautions to prevent fire or accident.

This is human nature. We hear it often said that you cannot bring about social reform because you cannot change human nature. But I have seen human nature actually change in the state of Wisconsin in less than twenty-five years by mutual insurance

[1] Address by J. R. Commons at Wisconsin State Conference of Mutual Casualty and Fire Insurance Companies, February 6, 1935.

and a change in the laws and administration of the state. Employers were formerly negligent about the health and safety of their employees. Indeed, their negligence was so notorious that it was by far the strongest and most bitter argument brought forth by communists against the whole capitalistic system which they proposed to abolish. They had a battle cry: "Capitalists make their profit out of the blood of their employees." And their battle cry was true to the facts at that time.

But we hear that battle cry no longer in this state. The employers themselves have changed their human nature. They have built up in their industries the strongest safety movement in the United States, and the watchword of employers in this state has become, not how to defeat their employees in a suit for damages at law, but what they call the "safety spirit," that prevents accidents or restores to health their employees just as soon as the best medical and hospital care can do it.

This change in human nature has not abolished the profit motive. It has changed the motive from making profit out of injuries to their employees to making profit out of the prevention of those injuries. This change in the profit motive I attribute, more than anything else, to mutual insurance and the cooperation of the state government with employers instead of antagonism and criminal prosecutions. Human nature, in this case, has been changed by changing the direction in which capitalistic profit can be made. I have an idea that it can be changed in many other fields, such as unemployment prevention, by mutual insurance and state cooperation.

My similar experience was in 1907 in the factories of the United States Steel Corporation at Pittsburgh. I was there supervising an investigation of accidents in the steel industry. That industry was reputed to be the most ruthless and dangerous of all in the United States. The steel corporation was like a huge mutual insurance company operating plants in many parts of the country. They were then just beginning to employ safety engineers to prevent accidents. I made the acquaintance of these engineers. At that time employers throughout the country were resisting all efforts to bring about changes in employers' liability laws by making employers responsible for *all* accidents to their own employees whether caused by the negligence of the employee, the hazards of the industry, or by the fault of the employer himself. It was contended that these new proposals of universal workmen's compensation would greatly increase the costs of production, and these increased costs would have to be shifted in higher prices of their products to be paid by customers and consumers.

There were at that time no mutual insurance companies to which we could point as examples of actually reducing the costs of insurance by preventing accidents. We had to point only to what individual corporations had been able to do. The then existing liability insurance companies also took the same ground as the employers, and actually, in Wisconsin, they doubled or trebled the insurance premiums on all employers who came under the new compensation law after it was enacted in 1911. So strong was their opposition that the law was made voluntary and only about 10 per cent of the employers in the state volunteered to come under the law. Not until several years afterward was the law made compulsory.

But I had been shown by the safety engineers of the steel corporation that if they were permitted and employed to go into the factories with their plans to prevent accidents, there would be no increase of costs whatever, and therefore no decrease of profits, no raising of prices to customers, and no need of raising the premiums charged by the private insurance companies. Universal workmen's compensation would cost nobody anything above the older laws of liability, if accompanied by the reduction of accidents by qualified safety engineers.

I puzzled several years as to how this idea, coming to me from the safety engineers of the steel corporation, of not increasing but actually reducing the costs of workmen's insurance could be gotten across to the people and the legislature of Wisconsin. Then, in 1910, I made the acquaintance of Dr. Fricke, formerly State Superintendent of Insurance in this state. He showed me that this would be a very simple matter. Merely let the legislature authorize the creation of employers' mutual insurance companies with power to employ safety engineers. Let these companies compete freely, without discrimination, with the old line companies. He was himself at that time drafting the articles of incorporation of such a mutual company. I proceeded to draft an industrial commission law for the state, whereby accident prevention and workmen's accident insurance should be brought together under the same state commission, and the state would cooperate with employers, instead of antagonizing them, in reducing accidents and thereby reducing the costs of accident insurance compensation.

When the new law was enacted in 1911, I was made one of the three state commissioners, and at about the same time, Dr. Fricke organized and became president of the first employers' mutual liability insurance company, a privately owned company, with headquarters at Wausau, Wisconsin. We called it the Wausau Mutual. Fricke proceeded to organize his safety department, and I proceeded to organize safety committees of employers, employees, factory inspectors, and safety engineers throughout the state. These safety committees were to draw up rules and regulations for the various industries, to be then issued by the Wisconsin Industrial Commission, as orders having the effect of law. I had an idea, with which Dr. Fricke agreed, that the Wausau Mutual would be able to prevent accidents far better than the state's factory inspectors. Our Industrial Commission soon found that this was distressingly true. We found that Fricke's organization, the mutual, was pulling away from us at higher salaries some of the very best of our factory inspectors. I see that one of them, A. E. Kaems, now over 75 years of age, is still on their list of safety engineers as head of their punch press work. Indeed, I find among the copies of letters furnished me by the Wausau Mutual a letter from a policyholder containing this statement: "Several weeks ago A. L. Kaems appeared at our plant as safety engineer for your company. I was particularly pleased . . . Mr. Kaems understood the problems of the factory and could talk shop with the superintendents . . . We had two problems . . . The writer discussed these with the idea that Mr. Kaems could probably from his vast experience find a clue to solve them. The same afternoon, Mr. Kaems returned and offered suggestions . . . One of the jobs is finished, the other is developed . . . You may be sure that we appreciate this and that any suggestions from Mr. Kaems will not go unheeded."

I had to laugh when I read that letter. It came from a company with which our Industrial Commission had had the greatest of difficulties and abusive opposition 25 years ago, when the same Mr. Kaems was one of our factory inspectors. This letter in 1934 certainly showed a change in the human nature of that manufacturing corporation.

But it was not a change in them alone. We found that all our factory inspectors hated their job of snooping around to find violations of law by employers and then acting as prosecuting witnesses. All of them were glad when we changed them to safety engineers to cooperate with employers in preventing accidents. Mr. Kaems became probably the best man in this country on the prevention of punch press accidents. I wonder if the state of Wisconsin, under the old law, would ever have discovered his abilities or kept him as long on the state payroll. But the Wausau Mutual took him from us and keeps him in old age, because he makes more profits for their employer policyholders than could any other man by reducing accidents on this most dangerous class of machines. Human nature had changed all around when mutual insurance and state cooperation took the place of prosecutions, district attorneys, jury trials, and litigation.

Other able men were also pulled away from the Industrial Commission by the Wausau Mutual. Their secretary, Mr. W. H. Burhop, was the head of our statistical department. It is he who furnishes me with statistics and information which keep me up to date regarding the operations of this mutual. He has furnished me, through their safety department, the bound volume of *Special Safety Engineering Reports and Insurance Recommendations*. He has sent me similar reports in previous years.

I am amazed at what is revealed through the wide activities of this mutual at the end of 25 years. This compilation should be in the hands of every mutual insurance company in the state. This privately owned Wausau Mutual spends 25 to 30 per cent of its operating costs on accident prevention. I find the names of 30 safety engineers operating in the field force of its safety engineering department. Would the state of Wisconsin ever spend that much money or employ that many factory inspectors and safety engineers, or pay the necessary salaries, on behalf of the safety and health of workingmen employed in this state? No. The taxpayers would immediately cut it down to probably less than one-fifth the amount. Safety work would be condemned as a fad created to make more jobs for politicians, or for university graduates who could pass a civil service examination. But a mutual insurance company is not handicapped by these objections.

I find, also, in this compilation of the Wausau Mutual, that the change in human nature from negligence to the safety spirit is not anything automatic that comes about by merely changing the laws of the state. The change requires in addition a most expensive education and propaganda, conducted by the most expert advice of policyholders, as I have just now noted in the case of Mr. Kaems. It is only necessary that I should read the index of this employers' mutual to get an idea of the great ingenuity and widespread activities that a mutual insurance company can eventually put on in the work of prevention. Here I find no-accident contests, canners' contest, fleet service for automobile drivers, an industrial hygiene laboratory, punch press service, logging, construction, safety bulletins, even an "Eddie Cantor circular," payroll inserts, seasonal hazards, circulars addressed to foremen, school service, organization for safety in the shop.

I might go on with many other details and comparisons regarding the Wausau Mutual. I am not playing up this company invidiously against any other companies. It is only because I know personally from its very beginning so many members of its staff and can almost consider myself, with Dr. Fricke, as one of its originators. After 25 years I can look back with pride to those days when a place was being made for mutual insurance companies in this state, not merely for insurance but most of all for the prevention of accidents which they were insuring.

I can see how this idea can be extended to many other fields besides employers' liability. The state of Wisconsin has extended it even to unemployment insurance. I have, however, found the greatest difficulty in extending this idea of combining prevention with insurance in these other fields and in other states: no more difficult, however, I think, when I look back, than the same difficulty 25 years ago in combining prevention and insurance in the field of employers' liability for accidents. The opposition then was just as impregnable as it is today in extending the idea to other fields. It is partly due to inertia that is afraid to venture into anything new. To overcome this inertia requires many years of propaganda, experience, and especially the help of experts, like the safety experts of the Wausau Mutual and farseeing experts like Dr. Fricke, 25 years ago.

Most of all it requires putting over the idea of a new kind of government. Lawyers, judges, and politicians are instinctively opposed to it. It takes much business out of their hands. They have the traditional idea of government as a coercive power from above imposing laws and inflicting punishments on those subject to their authority. But if we look at government as it actually operates, what is government? What is the state of Wisconsin? What is the United States of America? It is the political parties that elect the legislators and judges and appoint the hundreds of deputies, inspectors, statisticians, and clerks who administer the laws. It was exactly for this reason of party politics that Mussolini in Italy abolished the legislature, and himself appointed the judges and appointed all the deputies and inspectors to administer all the laws.

We may take it for granted that political parties can never be eliminated, and, indeed, should not be eliminated if we propose to maintain a democratic system of government. It is only because we have popular elections and legislatures that we can preserve the liberty of mutual associations to participate in drawing up their own rules and regulations.

But we must learn to keep party politics within the field where needed so that voluntary associations can operate in the field where they can be effective. This has been fairly well done in the state of Wisconsin in so far as applied to the field of workmen's accident prevention. As I have said, the factory inspectors have largely become safety experts helping employers and employees actually to make the laws for safety, to be issued as orders and given legality by the Industrial Commission. Then we find that mutual insurance companies, and even self-insurers if they are large enough, go much further in prevention of accidents than the state can possibly do with its politics. I look with hope on this present movement to extend all mutual insurance companies, with the cooperation of the state, into the field of prevention formerly occupied only by the state, just as I looked with hope twenty-five years ago when, with Dr. Fricke, I looked forward to a new kind of government cooperating mainly with mutual insurance companies in the prevention of accidents to workingmen.

# Summary

## PART FOUR

——◆——

We have closed this part of the book with a rather small episode in a small state, out of the world-wide tragedies of the science of political economy. Yet it shows how the cooperation of plain, ordinary people in the prevention of accidents raises all of them to a high level of promoting the public welfare, and starts them devising remedies for the former weakest spot of the capitalistic civilization. This weakest spot was then accidents to employees. The weakest spot remaining is unemployment and insecurity.

In less than 150 years this civilization of western Europe and America has multiplied probably tenfold per man-hour the volume of production of wealth, and thus has far more than realized the great expectations of the founders of economic science. Yet this very increase in efficiency turned to wrath in the greatest catastrophe of unemployment, followed by the greatest world-wide war and destruction of life by scientific inventions that could possibly have been imagined by the most pessimistic and most extreme economists of 150 years ago, at the time of Adam Smith, the optimist.

Why this culminating tragedy of unemployment and war? I have watched economic action as a participant and investigator for sixty years, fully one-third of the history of the capitalistic system since Adam Smith. I pick out three economic features which seem to me to have been strategic and decisive. They are the credit system, which is the debt system; the agricultural system, which is the food system and which still remains a primitive system as it was before corporations and labor unions took possession; and the capital-labor system, which is the field of revolutions in the form of strikes and lockouts since the beginning of the nineteenth century. On the continent of Europe, the culmination has been the military suppression of self-governing corporations, labor unions, and political parties, under the banner of "bread and work" in their armament to conquer the so-called "plutocratic democracies."

The science of political economy which began in England as the wealth of nations, with the purpose of liberating the inventive genius of individuals from the restraints of feudalism, mercantilism, and militarism, has become, by the very triumph of that inventive genius, an investigation of how to prevent the former military restraints from suppressing again the freedom of individuals.

# Chapter xvii

## CONCLUDING REMARKS

———◆———

The main criticism to be directed against the economists and technicians is their mechanistic imitation of the physical sciences after the examples set by Newton and Darwin, in attributing all progressive evolution to inventions in the strictly mechanical forces of nature, whereas not one of such forces can be cited by any person having acquaintance with the ethical principles of mediation, conciliation, or religion that for 6,000 years have more or less brought together opposing self-interests of mankind in the attempted practical measures of harmony and cooperation. However astonishing these mechanical discoveries, their avoidance of ethical principles has been leading to the final misuse of science for the ruthless destruction of mankind, where their triumph should have been the saving of mankind.

The foregoing (Parts I to IV) is an attempted critical abstract of the development of the mechanistic science of political economy during the past forty to fifty years. The practical change noted is from a physical exchange of commodities to the negotiational transactions of a credit economy. The rationing transactions, instead of apportioning shares of physical objects, become legislative enactments by political and economic governments, laying down rules for subordinate bargaining and managerial transactions. A large corporation, for example, buying physical goods or making wage bargains, is in fact an extension in two directions of the former transactions, the difference being that the former bargaining transactions become a distinct inequality of bargaining power between a corporation and an individual instead of the traditional equality pictured by the early economists and lawyers if freed from governmental or feudal power. But now these corporations themselves lay down governmental rules—the rationing transactions—to be obeyed by their own employees, agents, and foremen in their wage bargaining and price bargaining with outside subordinate individuals or merchants, through the instrumentality of another capitalist class—the banking corporations, centralized under a national administration.

When, however, these wage earners and small producers finally reach a point, by the aid of government and the courts—only within the past few years, especially after the utter breakdown of the big capitalist system in 1929—when they can also organize collective unions or political parties, then the old bargaining exchanges as supreme in economics become obsolete. Now there are three collective organizations, in two alignments—the corporations and unions on one side, and the farmers and administrative political commissions on the other. These are powerful enough to negotiate the bargaining end or general working rules of the rationing transactions. The whole nation burst forth, during the past thirty years of the twentieth century with the three types of apportioning transactions, namely, the rationing by labor unions, corporations, and nationalized bankers leaving the unorganized classes helpless. All are alike in that they get their franchises from government and courts where formerly only the political government, that is, the military government, was strong enough as a sovereign to control the entire field of rationing, instead of dividing up the rationing process among banking corporations, manufacturing and other corporations, and labor unions.

The fallacy in economic and legal reasoning is that the old formula of individual exchanges of physical commodities continues to be used, where now it is more fitting to recognize joint political and economic governments, each with coercive powers over the subordinate bargaining and managerial transactions. The traditional reasoning, in law and economics, of free individuals trafficking with their neighbors, nevertheless, continues even when the individuals have become subordinates or participants in governments, with legislative, executive, and judicial departments.

This traditional reasoning is side-stepped, without clear understanding, by the resort to administrative commissions or boards, as branches of government, such that the extension of commissions to all fields of economics could easily become a large step toward complete fascism, socialism, or communism, instead of retaining the primitive capitalistic system of private property and private initiative.

The economic fallacies are twofold—failure to distinguish monopolies from other forms of collective action, and failure to distinguish the margin of profits from other forms of income, such as interest, rent, and wages. These latter categories are all incomes, but they differ immensely in their effects on an administrative national economy.

Rationing transactions are monopolistic, but they are not monopolies, like patents. Their clear distinction requires a corporate organization into legislative, executive, and judicial departments of an organized establishment. There is the board of directors setting up its legislative budget for the future; the executive department with its managerial transactions and its bargaining transactions; the judicial department with its treaty-making departments for disputes between participants or classes of disputes, finally known as conciliation, mediation, or arbitration, thus performing much the same functions as the judicial department of political government. This is the ethical culmination of economics.

A board of directors, like a legislature, apportions its appropriations to different departments or purposes, the amounts to be paid as wages and salaries, the purchase of materials, the construction of extensions and improvements, and dealings with bondholders and stockholders and these decisions to be obeyed by its subordinate officials. This is not a fanciful analogy—it is the actual government of nations, corporations, and company towns.

The task is too huge for a legislature in a political government or a board of directors in an industrial government, and the latter finally falls into the hands of the political "machine." The "management," by the legalized proxy or similar system, actually elects and dominates the board of directors, so that, with the growth in size, the corporations begin to speak of "the management" and not of the board of directors. They thus indicate how quietly they have slipped into dictatorships instead of representative legislatures. The legislative department remains a shell of camouflage, covering the real economic power of "management." And management controls, by the power of employment and unemployment, all the subordinates who execute its will. These are the different departments, so called, meaning the dictatorial managerial departments.

Consequently, when reformers of the fifty years since 1890 have become sufficiently alarmed at these natural results to beware of economic dictatorships, they have experimented with different attempts to restore the democratic powers of the primitive individualistic ownership, especially the following attempts: first, "smashing the trusts" by dissolution, which turns out to be impossible; second, public regulation, which is usually captured by the corporations; third, public competition, like the T. V. A.; fourth, public monopolistic ownership; fifth, counter-organization by unions and cooperatives; and lastly, subordination in totalitarian governments by military dictatorships. A seventh attempt, postponed by the world military revolution, is the attempt to use existing departments of government to trim off the most destructive edges of these dictatorships, especially their use of holding companies and monopolistic patent rights. If we follow the same path as other countries, these attempts are largely utopian, and will turn into military dictatorships, like those of Asia, South America, and Europe, and for the similar reason, inability and lack of intelligence to organize universal suffrage except by crude physical force.

These observations are not intended to excite discouragement, however true they are to the facts and the probabilities. They are intended toward reorganizing the ethical or democratic forces along the new lines to be discovered by investigation of the actual facts, instead of the former or prevailing legal injunctions against organizations which may have been practicable when there was yet a remaining western frontier for escape, if the operations did not succeed.

It is not in opposition to any of these attempts to restore the primitive democracy that these remarks are made. It is only to emphasize the seriousness of the existing economic and political issues, and to point out the futility of entering upon their solution in the jovial movie-picture attitude that, like dramatic poetry, blinds the people to the economic changes until too late. More promising is a complete change in attitude toward the corporations, cartels, and unions which are now becoming economic governments, with the closing of economic frontiers.

The most serious blindness is the illusion that it is possible to return to any of the individualistic devices of our founding fathers which they had simply borrowed from individualistic English and French philosophers of the eighteenth century. Something more far reaching and fundamental is needed. The former attitude was primitive, derived from the criminal law. The future attitude needs to be cooperative, derived from principles of prevention instead of punishment.

The contest between technological utopians and institutional organizations, following the wars for individual liberty and property of the American and French Revolutions, a century ago, became the underlying ideas of fraternity and association which came uppermost for the theorists and philosophers and reached the peak in the decades of the 1830's and 1840's. The exponents of associationism were numerous, extending from Saint Simon, Fourier, Brisbane, and the Christian socialists, to the communists, Marx and Engels.

These associationists were all utopian, because, while they set up ideals of mechanically increasing efficiency that were proper enough, they did not work out any practical institutional details, by which, under the then existing circumstances, the ideals could permanently be worked in a form of continuous succession by entering upon contracts that could be enforced by the courts. Finally, it was only the American economist, Henry C. Carey, contemporary with the associationists, who then seized upon the workable practice of associations, the joint stock associations with bonds and limited stock liability. The East India Company had demonstrated the workability of such private corporations by conquering India for the British Empire, in competition with similar private corporations under government franchises of the Portuguese, Spanish, Italian, and French nations. Carey would and did propose to bring these into the United States, under state charters, but strengthened by a federal protective tariff against England, in order enormously to increase the wealth of the American nation far beyond what even the British economists could conceive for the pioneer England in the midst of a world of agricultural nations. His proposition fitted the incoming of the American railway system with its investments of huge fixed capital for railway tracks, steam engines, and trains of cars never before conceived as possible by the hand workers of the mercantile economists and petty partnerships with their unlimited liability of partners in individual enterprises. Eventually forty-eight states competed with each other in offering liberal unregulated franchises of economic joint stock governments to these hitherto unknown corporations of limited liability, which soon demonstrated their sovereignty by controlling the state and federal legislatures and by robbing the confiding farmers and local speculators who purchased these stocks issued with a maneuvered limited liability. An era of corruption, legislative exposure, and popular attack followed, culminating in the federal attempt at governmental regulation under the new Interstate Commerce Commission of 1886, which, under the hostile decisions of the courts, did not become even partly effective until the beginning of the twentieth century. This was followed in the twentieth century by the Federal Trade Commission and the Securities and Exchange Commission, among others.

Meanwhile came the new holding companies of the twentieth century, which united, merged, and combined, contrary to the childlike antitrust laws of 1890, the manufacturing and mercantile corporations, as well as the railway and public utility corporations of the nineteenth century. These corporations and pyramided corporations of limited liability were the realistic and workable associations of capital bound to survive and dominate in face of the visionary and utopian associations of labor and capital experimented upon by the idealists of the third and fourth decades of the nineteenth century. The Supreme Court legalized them in 1920. The big difference between the two was the unity of ownership and the limited liability of the owners in the joint stock corporations, treated as such by the courts, in place of the friendly cooperation and unlimited liability of the owners in the utopian associations. The joint stock corporations survived, multiplied, grew, and pyramided while the cooperatives fell apart by bankruptcy after futile trials, again and again. In European countries, with an oppressed peasantry of propertyless wage earners, both the utopians and the trade unions worked together until the incoming of the huge military dictatorships of the twentieth century forcibly suppressed both the cooperatives and the trade unions.

At the beginning of the twentieth century, especially in America, the former associational utopias of the nineteenth century gave way to the technological utopias of the present century. The wonderful technological engineering of electricity, gas, and chemistry, by creating a new technology far beyond the hand workers of the associationists in the nineteenth century, seemed actually to bring in the very utopias of increasing productivity which the associationists had predicted by their fourierisms and socialisms of voluntary cooperation in place of individualistic competition. It is amazing what these technologists have predicted and are predicting for a future when this world war is happily terminated with the assumed victory of the "democracies."

These utopias remind the skeptical investigator of what was proposed in the early nineteenth century, or in the Greek mythology of Hercules or the Roman Romulus and Remus rescued by the she-wolf. They lack the two practical essentials of providing the finances and organization, even of organizing the military forces that actually could have been found in the history of Genghis Khan or his modern imitators, or even in the American pioneers who wiped out the Six Nations and the Sioux Indians.

The transition from the ideal economics of individual equality to the twentieth century differential economics is a transition from *laissez-faire* economics to *control* economics. The same economic factors are present, but the economic analysis does not permit the former indifference to the results and the variety of instruments of control. Instead of the classical division of labor between equal individuals, we have administrative specification of controls with regard to results.

The methods of investigation have been changing and expanding, along with this enlargement of the field of economics. The methods, now, are predominantly a comparison of alternatives, and the measurements are the statistics of probability and frequency, instead of the former theories of equal individuals animated all alike by a simplified self-interest.

In this book we outline the centuries of legal and economic foundations of our capitalistic system and these future problems. The system has amply demonstrated, in America, its capacity to make huge increases of wealth per capita, but has strangely collapsed at periods, far more disastrously than more backward nations. It is the problem of the sciences of politics and economics not to create an imaginary utopia, but to reconstruct by investigation and experiment a reasonably successful world of fairly equal opportunities for everybody, beginning with the United States.

# Appendices

# Appendix i

## ECONOMIC GOVERNMENT BY CORPORATE MANAGEMENT *

A Research Proposal Based upon a Comparison of *The Modern Corporation and Private Property* with *Legal Foundations of Capitalism* by the Author

Some of the central problems for economic investigation in the coming decades can be set in clear relief by an analysis and appraisal of *The Modern Corporation and Private Property*, by Berle and Means. I was invited to appraise this work [1] and to link it up with my *Legal Foundations of Capitalism* and to place myself in a suggested position as follows: "I was trying to do thus and so in my work, and as I see it Berle and Means were orienting problems and developing methods in such and such ways. The two seem to me to be related, and as I look at them in the perspective of the evolving problem, it seems to me that this shows itself to be better workmanship, or that seems to present certain weaknesses or limitations." My instructions go on regarding details: "The more intimate and searching you make your remarks, the better we shall be pleased."

The book by Berle and Means is the outcome of a joint investigation made by a lawyer and an economist. My *Legal Foundations*, published in 1924, was the outcome of collaboration with lawyers and committees of a state legislature, beginning seventeen years earlier in drafting an administrative public utility law for the state of Wisconsin; afterwards in drafting an industrial commission law and serving for two years in its

* Written in 1938 for the Social Science Research Council, and reprinted here by permission.

[1] A. A. Berle and G. C. Means, *Modern Corporation and Private Property*, New York, The Macmillan Co., 1932. Copyright, 1932, by The Macmillan Company. Numbers in parentheses refer to pages in the Berle and Means book.

administration with a lawyer, chairman of the commission; meanwhile drafting a state market commission law; and finally in drafting an unemployment-prevention law in 1921, substantially enacted ten years later.

Hence my experience in collaboration with lawyers covered the subjects of labor, public utilities, and market prices of commodities. I had no experience of similar collaboration in drafting legislation or administering laws in the field of corporate stocks and bonds or their marketing on the stock exchanges. I can see how this book by Berle and Means must have laid the foundations for the culminating and most important of these administrative bodies, the Securities and Exchange Commission, created by Congress some two or three years after the first publication of their book. The investigations which they made are evidently carried forward by this administrative commission, and I can thus see, what was true in my case, the outcome of joint legal and economic investigations in a peculiar fourth branch of American state and national governments. I have distinguished it as neither the traditional legislative, executive, nor judicial branch of government, but an investigational branch called forth by the stalemate of the three branches in dealing with the new economic issues of organized and maneuvered collective action in control of individual action.

Nowadays I see vividly what I only envisaged dimly fifteen years ago, that the preservation of so-called "American democracy" from the extremes which occur in other parts of the world will turn mainly upon the success or failure of these administrative investigational bodies. If the SEC breaks down through incompetency or lack of appropriations, then this work of Berle and Means will remain a studious academic venture which furnished arguments for revolutionary extremes. I can already see that their work is used elsewhere to confirm the conclusions of Marx and Lenin as to the "self-destruction" of capitalism, and equally to confirm the conclusions of Pareto and Mussolini as to the incapacity of legislative governments elected by universal suffrage to protect the savings of the millions of middle-class investors upon whose thrift the capitalistic system since the time of Adam Smith has been known to be founded.

This is a line of investigation which I would propose, in conformity with my instructions to suggest what the Social Science Research Council could do by "considering the working techniques which have been employed" by social scientists, and thereby to "improve the quality of future product and promote a somewhat systematically developing succession of contributions to be called 'knowledge' and susceptible of being 'built brick by brick into a structure of social science.' "

I suggest promoting investigations of this fourth branch of American government as to its competency in filling the gaps of our constitutional system. I suggest that these investigations should focus on their competency as investigational bodies toward assisting the legislative, executive, and judicial branches of government in dealing with the collective conflicts on economic issues that press upon those departments for solution.

These commissions, as I see the matter, have sprung into existence to meet the most urgent of collective conflicts brought about by new economic conditions and organized pressure, which the classic theories of government and economics could contemplate only with horror. All of these conflicts are separate aspects of the central problem dealt with by Berle and Means—the emergence of corporations out of individual enterprises and their domination over American life.

Berle and Means give the clue to this central problem in their detailed account of the emergence of "management" or "control" in its dealings with millions of unorganized investors. They distinguish between that "entity" the corporation, an artificial person created by legal theory, and the millions of stockholders and bondholders who are marshaled by the controlling management towards collective action in perpetuating the existence and supremacy of the entity. It is a special case of what I call "maneuvered collective action," somewhere between organized collective action and the unorganized collective action of custom. This manuevered collective action is to be found elsewhere also, in politics, in labor movements, and in farmer movements. The SEC is created and administered to deal with this conflict between controlled management and the unorganized investing "public," estimated by Berle and Means at somewhere between 4,000,000 and 7,000,000 persons (pp. 60, 374).

Other conflicts arising from this same concentration of control are dealt with by other state or federal commissions. The conflict between "big" and "little" taxpayers has brought administrative tax commissions into existence. The conflict between corporations and labor unions has called for industrial commissions and boards of mediation. The conflict between corporate public utilities and the shippers, users, or consumers is entrusted to "public service commissions" and to interstate commerce and communication commissions. The conflict between "big" and "little" competitors has its state market commissions and its federal trade commission. All of them deal with organized, unorganized, and maneuvered pressure groups, a mass conflict not contemplated by the older economic or legal science except as something obnoxious which had to be opposed.

The difficulty with these commissions is in the misunderstanding as to whether their functions are legislative, executive, or judicial, or all three combined, whereas their function is primarily investigational in the newly emerged varieties of collective conflict. If they are legislative, then the regular legislative bodies, through control of appointments and appropriations, seize upon them as legislative agents in opposition to the executive or the judiciary. If they are executive, then the executive branch of government seeks to control them by appointments and removals. If they are judicial, then the judiciary, whose historical function is that of investigating and deciding disputes between individuals, when now called upon to decide disputes between collections of individuals, sets these commissions aside as not conforming to their historic due process of law, and proceeds to settle the matter by a trial in court. A court trial, with its weapon of injunctions, is not fitted to settle these conflicts between collective organizations and pressure groups. That is primarily a legislative problem. But if the function of these administrative commissions is primarily investigational of just that type of conflict, then they should be so organized with competent investigators and a procedure of investigation and decision fitted to the issue.

Such a method of organization of administrative commissions is already indicated by our courts, and I endeavored to conform to those indications in cooperation with the lawyers in drafting the public utility and industrial commission laws of Wisconsin. A legislative act may be made to take effect at some future date, upon the future findings of fact directed by the legislature to be investigated and found by the commission. Consequently, in drafting these commission laws the legislature provided that the commission should "investigate, ascertain, and determine" what were the "reasonable" regulations or "orders" required to carry out the legislative intent. "Reasonable" was the word derived from the judiciary, and is peculiar to collective action. When such determination should be made and published, then the legislation would go into effect. There are many details, which themselves should be investigated. I only mention the important position already recognized, in the American constitutional system, of organized investigation as a fourth branch of our constitutional development.

The commissions are not delegations of legislative power if they are investigational. They are not judicial bodies, since they must go to the independent judiciary to prosecute violations of their orders. They are not executive organs because they must call upon the executive for the policemen to enforce their orders. They are the investigative bodies, created to aid the original three branches of government in their dealings with different angles of the emerging group conflicts, and to issue their own orders in conformity with the final determination made by the other branches, especially the judiciary under the American system.

Thus two lines of joint investigation for the social sciences are suggested. Each of them relates to the delegation of legislative power; one is the delegation of legislative power to private corporations, the other the delegation of legislative power to administrative commissions. In the first line of investigation the outlines are sketched by Berle and Means. It would be a series of investigations of particular private corporations, which they designate "quasi-public" corporations, meaning thereby corporations that appeal to the public in general for investments. But there should also be included banking and finance corporations and partnerships, such as the J. P. Morgan partnership mentioned by them. It is these financial organizations, as shown by the investigations of Berle and Means, through which the "control management" of their 200 "nonfinancial" corporations is effected.

Each of these corporations or partnerships, financial and nonfinancial, operates as a delegation of legislative power under the state laws of incorporation or partnership. This is the main significance of the problem selected for investigation by Berle and Means. Their statement of the problem in their closing paragraph repeats substantially what they had said five years before about the rise of the modern corporation on equal terms with the state in the use of economic power.[1]

The "modern state," or "political power," there referred to, is increasingly focused upon the delegation of power to administrative commissions whose members are officials of government, while the "new economic state," or "economic power," is the corresponding delegation of power to private corporations whose officials are the boards of directors.

Thus an appraisal of the work of Berle and Means turns upon the purpose of their investigation and upon the materials available or discoverable in view of that purpose. They have in fact two purposes which dominate their work, an ultimate purpose and a provisional purpose. The ultimate purpose is that just now quoted, which they set forth as what they call "speculations" or "observations," but which, they say, "must be set aside from the data" contained in the body of their work. I have above suggested how this ultimate purpose might be made specific by focusing investigations upon administrative commissions as the point

[1] See Chapter IV, p. 58.

of contact where their "economic power versus political power" occurs.

Their provisional purpose is a showing of the way in which American corporations have been approaching a position, not contemplated in traditional economic science, where a super-management is separated out from investors and stockholders with the specialized function of controlling industry and government for the purpose of obtaining and distributing the largest practicable net profit for the concern as a whole. The materials selected for this purpose are the grants of power delegated by American state legislatures, and also the decisions of federal and state courts interpreting the grants. These materials lead to a comparative statistical showing of the extent to which the managements of their 200 corporations have made use of these grants of power, stimulated by the profit motive, in their efforts to control American industry.

These two purposes, or "objectives," must be understood, else criticism of their work will miss the point. They are not endeavoring to show that in all industries there is an equal tendency toward concentration of economic power as against the public in general. And they are not endeavoring to show a tendency toward monopoly. Hence, they do not distinguish between public utilities, such as railways and electric companies, and the manufacturing and merchandising corporations, such as chemical companies and chain store companies. They are endeavoring to show that, as corporations increasingly appeal to thousands of investors, where formerly, on a small scale, they appealed to only a few wealthy capitalists or a few interested neighbors, there has emerged a new function of management, or supermanagement, separate from the stockholders who were supposed to be the active "entrepreneurs" of economic theory assuming the risks of business, but who now are becoming mere passive participants, like wage earners, for example, depending upon this supermanagement for their opportunities of investment, as the wage earners depend upon them for opportunities of employment. It is a further evolution of Adam Smith's "division of labor," where not only the "entrepreneur," seeking profits, came afterwards to be distinguished from the investor, the landlord, and the wage earner seeking interest, rent, and wages, but comes now to be separated further as "management," organizing industry for pure profit, distinguished from stockholders seeking "dividends."

The bondholders, also, traditionally assumed to be the "pure investors" seeking interest without assuming the risks that constituted the justification of profits, now become, at the hands of Berle and Means, affiliated to the stockholders in a hierarchy of risk-taking investors arranged according to degrees of risk from the least risky to the most risky investments. High-grade bonds are the least risky; then low-grade bonds, each of which may be reduced in value by receiverships and reorganizations; then preferred stocks, cumulative dividends, debentures, stock-purchase warrants, par and nonpar stock, senior and junior securities, voting and nonvoting stock, down to the most risky of common stocks (278 ff.).

The "management," however, does not take these risks. The risks are apportioned to the hierarchy of risk-taking investors. This hierarchy of passive risk-taking investments is classified by Berle and Means according to two kinds of security and insecurity of investments, legal security and economic security. The degrees of *legal* security and insecurity are in the legal rights and legal machinery for enforcing these rights. Their discussion of the weakening of these rights constitutes their contribution to the changed meanings of private property brought about by the rise of the modern corporation (pp. 1-287). The degrees of *economic* security and insecurity are determined upon the stock exchanges and other securities markets, where this hierarchy of legal rights is convertible into cash—the "liquidity" of the financiers (pp. 289-331).

It is the combination of these different degrees of legal and economic security that constitutes the joint problem of the legal and economic investigator, which they summarize as "Re-orientation of Enterprise" and the "Effects of the Corporate System on Fundamental Economic Concepts" (pp. 331-357). This is what I name the "provisional purpose" of the authors, whereas their "ultimate purpose" is not fully disclosed until the last two paragraphs of the book (pp. 356, 357), and then only in suggestions as to what might further be investigated as a topic in "economic power versus political power, each strong in its own field." Their work and workmanship must be judged not by this ultimate purpose, but by the way in which they direct their investigation toward the intermediate purpose of the changed meanings of private property brought about by new legal adjustments to new economic conditions.

My own idea of the fundamental significance of their studies is in the closing of the frontier, within the past fifty years, through private ownership, whereby neither labor, enterprise, nor investment can "move west" but must "move up" within the corporate structure. Out of this upward movement there emerges "management" as the topmost "control" over other participants, and the stock market is the controlling market.

Under these legal and economic circumstances the provisional or immediate purpose of the authors reaches its conclusion in their own statement relative to stockholders and bondholders as follows:

The stockholder, "conceived originally as a quasi-partner, manager and entrepreneur, with definite rights in and to the property used in the enterprise and to the profits of that enterprise as they accrued, has now reached an entirely different status. He has, it is true, a series of legal rights, but they are weakened in varying degree by the text of the contract to which the stockholder is bound. . . . He becomes simply a supplier of capital on terms less definite than those customarily given or demanded by bondholders . . . Though the law still maintains the conception of a sharp dividing line recognizing the bondholder as a lender of capital and the stockholder as a quasi-partner in the enterprise, economically the positions of the two have drawn together. Consequently, security-holders may be regarded as a hierarchy of individuals, all of whom have supplied capital to the enterprise, and all of whom expect a return from it . . . In practice, the bondholder, for all his legal rights, has not a legal machinery enabling him in fact to collect his interest or his principal" (pp. 278, 279).

It is, as the authors show, on account of the lack of this "legal machinery" that the stock market becomes the economic "machinery" to which both stockholders and bondholders must resort in order to "collect," by the sale of their stocks and bonds, the capitalized market values, not only of interest and principal, but also the discounted present values of expected profits.

From the standpoint of economic analysis this situation enables the economist to distinguish what I had named "pure profit" and "profit yield."[1] The aim of "management" is to obtain "pure profit," which I had named the "profit margin," on the enterprise as a whole, but the aim of stockholders is to obtain a "profit yield" on the market value of their stocks. Economists, almost universally, direct their attention to "profit yield," on the traditional analogy of the comparative earning power of their "capital," when invested in various enterprises. This reasoning, while valid enough for the investor or stockholder, when comparing the "yields" from different investments, goes in a circle when carried over to a given enterprise as a whole, which is the concern of "management." If the "profit rate" declared by management to stockholders, is, say 6 per cent of the "par value," that is, nominal value of the stock, then if, through speculation or manipulation, the market value of the stock goes up to 200, or double the par value, the "profit yield" is only 3 per cent. Inversely, if the market value of the stock falls to 50, then the same "rate" of profit on par value rises to a "yield" of 12 per cent on the market value.

This market valuation is familiar enough. It takes place on the stock exchange. But when we come to the operation of an enterprise as a whole under the control of management, the familiar reasoning does not apply. Here it is the "margin for profit," the pure net profit, determined by the spread between gross sales income on the one side and gross operating and overhead expenses on the other side, that determines whether the concern as a whole shall survive or go bankrupt. This "profit

[1] J. R. Commons, *Institutional Economics*, New York, The Macmillan Co., 1934, pp. 526–589.

margin," with the emergence of large-scale corporate industry, becomes, on the average, a surprisingly narrow and sensitive margin, and accounts, more than all else, for the emergence of "management" as the specialized function described by Berle and Means. If I were to carry out the economic analysis for which they lay the legal foundations, I would exhaustively investigate for as many corporations as possible not only the "profit yield" for investors, as determined on the stock exchange, but also the "profit margin" for the concern as a whole, determined by gross sales and gross expenses. Here is where operating management necessarily becomes supermanagement and all other participants become necessarily subordinate.

Taking, therefore, the limited objectives which Berle and Means set up for their investigations, their methods and workmanship must be judged within that new but limited field. The working technique of their joint investigations is described by Mr. Berle in his preface to the book. He cites Professor William Z. Ripley, of Harvard University, as the pioneeer in this area of investigation. I observe that he was a pioneer on account of his method of interviewing. He represented a minority interest of stockholders on an important railway board of directors, placed there by one of the "revolts" which Berle and Means describe (p. 81 and elsewhere) in order to protect the minority against the management. Through his interviews with all parties concerned, Ripley was able to discover the extremely subtle connection between investment, banking, management, boards of directors, et al., which could not have been discovered otherwise than by his participation and interviewing. I have known of some of his interviews, and they were gems of cross-examination. The documents, court decisions, statistics, which furnish the materials for Berle and Means could not have been handled and selected, or their relative importance appraised, except for the clue traced out by Ripley that here was a line of inquiry unknown to previous economists but known in a very practical way by the lawyers who advised the management and drafted the legislation which fitted the modern emergence of corporate management into the American scheme of economic and political government.

Consequently I place participation and interviewing as the most important "working technique" to be cared for in the organization and conduct of investigations of this character. Mr. Berle's acquaintance with legal practice is evident in his handling of the many diverse technicalities by which management has achieved its outstanding supremacy. There still remains the question, just exactly how it is in any particular corporation that such insignificant minority holdings of shares of stock can achieve such dominance in the control of management. I see no way of discovering it except by being on the "inside" and persistently interviewing all of the wide variety of parties who lead and follow.

My own experience and friendship with James B. Dill, when he was drafting the New Jersey holding company law for the purpose of incorporating the United States Steel Corporation under that law, suggests to me how much I might have learned from him if I had only known this clue, afterwards run down by Ripley and now by Berle and Means. I was there at the very beginning of these holding companies and did not know it, like a friend of mine in the physical sciences about the same time, who was puzzled by the darkening of his photographic plates hidden from the light in the drawer at the bottom of his desk and did not know that it was the X ray afterwards discovered by Roentgen.

As to the organization of a joint investigation of this character, the acknowledgment is made by Berle and Means that it was "prepared under the auspices of the Columbia University Council of Research in the Social Sciences acting on behalf of the Social Science Research Council of America." Dean Smith of the Columbia Law School made it possible by "his willingness to embark that institution on the uncharted field of legal-economic work." Professor Bonbright, of the Columbia University School of Business, is given "particular thanks" for his work of revision and constant help. Professor Gay, economist of Harvard, "molded into concrete form the suggestion that work should be done in this field." Mr. George May, accountant, contributed his "wide experience" and "shrewd comment." Thus lawyers, economists, and accountants were joined in a large undertaking, with adequate financial resources, and it would have been impossible to carry through such a comprehensive and detailed investigation without this extensive collaboration. The book itself is in fact only a summary by the authors, with tentative conclusions. References are made to other publications where the two authors, a lawyer and an economist, presented the more technical details which they worked upon in their joint investigations. The contrast with former investigations by individual economists, from Adam Smith to Ripley, who did the pioneer work, is vivid indeed. The modern great corporations have their purely research laboratories where modern physical scientists work together. The federal government has made notable beginnings. The social sciences of the future must be large-scale university research bureaus, as well as training laboratories for beginners, and this present piece of work indicates how they may successfully be organized.

Mr. Berle speaks of the main difficulty in the joint investigations by lawyers and economists—the difficulty in agreeing upon a "common language." This I have also found to be the main difficulty. The practice of law and the study of economics have been so widely separated in this country that the lawyer and the economist scarcely know what the other is talking about. Both are really talking about the same thing, though the lawyer speaks of it as "property" and the economist speaks of it as "scarcity." I devoted several years trying to formulate this common language of law and economics, leading to my book, *Legal Foundations,* and endeavored to show that the separation of economics from law, since the time of Jeremy Bentham, had been a disastrous division of labor in English-speaking countries, not so evident in Continental countries where the faculties of law are also faculties of economics. Economists have criticized courts on the ground that they had no consistent theory of value, and courts have excluded economic investigations from their deliberations on the ground of irrelevancy to the constitutional and legal issues which lawyers alone were trained to adjudicate.

This matter of a "common language" suggests what I have long been advocating: that the elementary course of instruction in departments of economics should begin with corporation finance, in order to train future economists for present day investigations. If some 90 per cent of the output of all American industry, excluding agriculture and distribution, is already in the hands of corporations, big and little, as appears to be the fact, then the training of future economic investigators should apparently begin with corporations instead of with primitive communism, or the wants and satisfactions of consumers. Corporation finance evidently brings together the legal student and the economic student, and the accountant also. The subject matter is assets and liabilities rather than wealth; its procedure is by way of double-entry bookkeeping; its working tools are commercial law, constitutional law, and accounting, as well as statistics and logic. Corporation finance deals with balance sheets, margins for profit, equities, the stock markets, and so on. Its materials are corporate balance sheets and income accounts, running over into the organization of a plant, its modern technology, and the field of scientific management. With such a course, elementary for both legal and economic students, each would be trained in a common language, and it would also be the language of accountants, such that they would learn to carry on the joint investigations required in modern economics.

There is no doubt that lawyers and economists speak different languages. One of the reasons is that law schools have been mainly vocational schools, and when colleges of commerce were separated from departments of economics the purpose was that the science of economics should also be made vocational. If the two are united on corporation finance, then prior to their vocational training would come the scientific training which should deal with general principles and the logic of correct interpretation.

The issue of a common language runs everywhere through this book, and crops out in a double meaning of "assets" and of the "dilution of stockholders' assets" by the management, known popularly in some of its phases as "stockwatering." The particular occasion of a double language is in the dilution of assets by the issue of "stock-purchase warrants" by the management, a dilution which, like other "dilutions," reached its high point of permissibility in the Delaware statute for holding companies. That statute "was shocking to most students at the time" (1929), but, by the competition of other states, "within a few months perpetual warrants became so common as to excite little comment" (p. 181n).

The debate between the economist and the lawyer turned on the *date* at which the "dilution of assets" occurred. Was it the date at which the management *issued the stock warrant,* or the later date when the purchaser of the warrant *exercised his option* to purchase the stock? That is, was it the date of issue of the *stock warrant* or the later date of issue of the *stock itself,* authorized by the articles of incorporation but not yet issued by the management?

Berle took the position that the dilution did not occur until the *stock was issued* and the owner of the warrant thereby exercised his option to purchase at the issue price. Means asserted that the dilution occurred at the time when the *warrants were issued* and not at the later time when the stock was issued at the option of the warrant holder.

The debate turned on the economist's theory of value contrasted with the lawyer's mechanism of procedure, including legal convertibility and divisibility, which the economist would not recognize as a concept of economic value. Says Means in a footnote:

If "assets" are to be defined as book value and if a pro-rata share amounts to the book value divided by the number of shares outstanding, Professor Berle's position is unassailable. On the other hand, if "pro-rata share in assets" means the stockholder's share in a property which is valuable primarily because it is expected to earn an income in the future then the free gift to any other person of a right to share in any part of these prospective earnings lessens the original stockholder's share in the property and thus dilutes the assets represented by his share of stock. Such a definition would indicate that a stock purchase warrant—an option to share in the future earnings of a company—tended to dilute the assets represented by a share of stock at the time of issue unless an appreciable sum were paid into the corporation treasury as a result of its issue . . . If the market values fairly represent the share in assets represented respectively by the stock and warrants before the latter were exercised, there would be no change in the amount of assets represented by each share before and after the transaction.[1]

In other words, the economist has in mind *market value* based on future net income, which is the value of "intangible property," but the lawyer, and with him the accountant, has his mind on *book value*. The latter, for the economist, is *nominal* value, or *par* value. It is set up on the liability side of the corporation's accounts with reference to the stockholders as claimants, and must be balanced on the asset side by a more or less nominal value, as distinguished from market value, of the corporation assets. The economist cannot see in either the lawyer's legal mechanism of transferability of titles of ownership, or in the acountant's balancing of accounts having only nominal or perhaps arbitrary values at the dictation of the management, a truly economic valuation. He must go to the stock exchange for his concept of value.

The issue of par value and market value of stock is of practical importance, and, indeed, is the greatest difficulty assigned to the SEC in breaking up these huge holding companies. For upon this issue may turn a court decision as to whether a stockholder may obtain an injunction preventing the issue of purchase warrants on the ground of confiscation of the *value* of his stocks, or must wait until the management proceeds to issue the additional shares of stock called for by the owner of the warrant. According to Berle, he must wait until the stock issue is imminent, but according to Means his remedy is fruitless at that later time because, economically, the stock issue itself does not reduce the value of his shares of stock. Their *value had already been reduced* on the markets by approximately the amount of the value which the market had given to the purchase warrants. The dispute will doubtless have to be decided by the courts, and the

---

[1] A. A. Berle, Jr. and G. C. Means, *Modern Corporation and Private Property*, New York, The Macmillan Co., 1932, pp. 181–182 n. Copyright, 1932, by The Macmillan Company.

economists would presumably side with Means, whereas the courts might side with Berle, unless they would take another angle suggested by Berle. They might decide that the purchase warrants were gambling contracts, and rule them out on that account, in which case the plaintiff investors would have to shift their action against the issue of stock instead of the issue of stock warrants.

On the legal theory of Berle, he notes that the market speculators are puzzled as to why these purchase warrants should have a value, or how that value can possibly be calculated, owing to the many mathematical variables. But on the economic theory of Means there is no mystery about it. The value of the purchase warrants is simply a market value abstracted from the market value of the original shares, and depends, like the latter, upon the expected share of the future earnings not yet known but nevertheless capitalized as a *present worth.* Just how much is the destruction of stockholders' asset values is not known except as the market actually appraises the two values. It is the familiar problem in economics as to just where is the point at which illegitimate gambling passes into legitimate speculation. According to Means, the court should decide that both contracts are speculative contracts and not gambling contracts, but they are illegitimate speculations based on an abuse of managerial power permitted by the loose legislation of the states, but not permissible on the equitable grounds of protecting the original stockholder's reasonable expectations. Perhaps the solution of the disagreement is in the saving clause injected by Means, "unless an appreciable sum were paid into the corporation treasury as a result of its issue" (that is, the issue of stock-purchase warrants).

The two kinds of investigation are necessary in the social sciences, the "legalistic" and the "valuistic." Society is an organization, a mechanism, characteristic of the subject matter of all sciences. Its causes are in the past. But the subject matter of the social sciences, human beings, also have purposes which look to the future, unlike the subject matter of other sciences, and it is in the expectations of future consequences that the values, valuations, and reasons are found for present activities, the economists' theory of "present worth." Properly speaking, legal science investigates the rules of conduct laid down by superior authority for the future transactions among subordinate individuals. And economic science, which started with mechanistic principles in imitation of the physical sciences, has become "futuristic" since the time when the credit system, based on rules of action for future behavior, became a recognized part of the science. In their study of corporations Berle and Means are dealing directly with working rules of collective action which guide the expectations of investors and stockholders as to whether they will or will not invest and thereby assume the risks of the future. These expectations of the future are values and valuations.

I mention the foregoing instance of stock-purchase warrants because there is the only spot where the authors felt called upon to debate in public their legal and economic theories. But these purchase warrants are only one item in a long list of legal devices which have been made permissible, by state legislation and judicial decision, to the controlling management in depriving investors of what were, in simpler days, the unquestioned legal rights of stockholders to participation in the assets and earnings of the corporation. As the authors say, the part played by the purchase warrants can be understood only when the warrants are interpreted with reference to the other devices. The authors proceed with what, I think, is one of the best pieces of historical research to be found in economic literature. It deserves to be set alongside the conventional economic sketches of the "industrial revolution" made understandable first by Karl Marx, and now a part of all economic textbooks. It is a chapter in the evolution of "institutional economics" paralleling the customary chapters on the evolution of what is more properly named "engineering economics," or "technological economics." Indeed, the ingenuity of lawyers, as shown by Berle and Means, in the invention of new legal devices is not excelled by the ingenuity of physical scientists in inventing dynamos and gas engines.

The account by Berle and Means of the "evolution of the modern corporate structure" begins with the general incorporation laws which took the place of special acts of the legislatures granting charters to specifically named incorporators. I had previously placed that date as the year 1850 in both the United States and Great Britain, gathering my information from the *New York Tribune* of that period in its reports and editorials on bills then before the legislature of New York. At that time the arguments in favor of the new policy turned mainly on prevention of the lobbying for special charters in the legislature, such that only Democrats could get charters in one legislature and only Whigs could get charters in another legislature. The date conformed also to the change in the policies of labor unions, in England and America, from utopian unionism, in which labor organizations had attempted to displace capitalists as cooperative business managers, to modern "business unionism," where the laborers accept their position of permanent wage earners and content themselves with organizations for bargaining with employers for higher wages, shorter hours, reduced speed of work, and security of employment. It also conformed to the period when Henry C. Carey, the first independent American economist and a contemporary of Karl Marx in Europe, set forth his new arguments for a protective tariff in order that American capitalists might organize manufacturing corporations freed from the competition of the established manufacturers of England.

I made that date, 1850, the beginning of modern capitalism, which has become corporate capitalism confronted by labor unionism. But the researches of Berle and Means place the beginning of general incorporation laws at the year 1837, and continue through to the end of the nineteenth century (pp. 136 ff.).

In the period of special charters where I had noticed in my *Legal Foundations* the flagrance of corrupt lobbying and the creation of political "machines" financed by capitalists seeking corporate franchises, Berle and Means find an offsetting advantage in the public debate before the legislature over the details of the charter, with special reference to the protection of three groups, "the general public, the corporate creditors, and (to a less extent) the corporate shareholders." On this issue the authors say, "there seems to have been no thought that shareholding might become so common as to make shareholders' interests a consideration in protection of the public. . . . Shareholders were supposed to be capitalists reasonably able to protect themselves" (pp. 130, 131).

After the enactment of general incorporation laws this public debate in the legislature ceased, and the attorneys of the incorporators drafted privately their articles of incorporation and filed them with an administrative official, usually the Secretary of State (p. 136). The general incorporation laws were continuously being "liberalized," according as it was found that the older laws hindered the granting of desired powers to the management, finally reaching the enlarged scope described by Berle and Means.

While the shareholders, during the period of special charters, were less protected than the creditors and the general public, yet there were three "typical protections" set up in the special acts (pp. 130 ff.).

1. The enterprise was carefully limited in scope, usually limited to one specific purpose which the public and the shareholders could readily know about.

2. The contributions of capital were usually required to be "paid up" in cash before business started, as a protection to creditors and incidentally to shareholders against "dilution" of their interest by issues of stock not fully "paid up."

3. While there might be permitted a classification of preferred stock intermediate between common stock and bonds, the classification was scrutinized by the legislature and supposedly by the state administrative authorities, with the purpose of holding the management rigidly to the limitations prescribed by the legislature.

These were the legislative and administrative precautions during the period of special charters. To these were added certain precautions set up by the courts and derived from the common law as it stood at the time.

1. While the management was necessarily delegated to the board of directors, any fundamental change in the capital structure could be made only by a unanimous vote of the shareholders, thus preserving to the individual shareholder a protection of his interests.

2. Shareholders had the sole right to invest new monies in new issues of capital stock, known as the "law of pre-emptive rights."

3. In general, dividends were permitted to be paid only out of

surplus profits and not out of the capital assets of the corporation. While this was primarily designed as a protection for creditors, it also incidentally protected the future interests of shareholders against dilution through frittering away the assets of the corporation.

With the incoming of general incorporation laws, however, beginning apparently with Connecticut in 1837 (p. 136) and developing with the increase in numbers of shareholders, these rigid requirements were relaxed, nearly always in the direction of greater power for the management and less protection for the individual shareholder, though apparently justified in the interest of the shareholders. First was the right to vote by proxy, designed for the convenience of absent shareholders. But proxies eventually became "one of the principal instruments, not by which a stockholder exercises power over the management of the enterprise, but by which his power is separated from him" (p. 139).

Next is the disappearance of the shareholder's right to remove directors at will, and the emergence of the principle that the directors, while in office, have almost complete discretion in management (pp. 139, 140). With this came the permission, first, for a majority vote of shareholders to amend the charter, and then the avoidance of even such an amendment by provisions inserted by draftsmen in the original charter, to which stockholders gave their consent in advance (by merely purchasing), permitting the management "to do substantially anything and everything" in any kind of business which could be suggested by "the imagination of its organizing attorneys, and by their ability to embrace the world within the limits of the English language" (p. 140). Along with this came the device of "voting trusts," authorized by statute, by means of which *all* controlling powers of shareholders "might be more or less permanently delegated" (p. 140). Concomitantly came the privilege of directors to create certain classes of stock without the right of shareholders to vote. Most drastic of all came "the grant of power to a majority to authorize the sale or lease of the entire property of the corporation without unanimous vote, thereby handing over the enterprise to a different management altogether beyond the control of the former participants in it. At common law any dissenter could prevent this" (p. 141). This situation, the authors remark, was "presently rectified by many statutory provisions." But it is still the basis of holding companies.

The stockholders' position was further weakened (pp. 141 ff.) by permitting the issue of stock at par value but not fully paid up, presumably in cash. Up to the year 1886 (p. 142) it had been considered a violation of the equitable rights of stockholders, who had paid up, to allow any person to have the benefits of membership who had not contributed the amount of his shares to the company's capital. If he had not paid up, he was personally liable to the creditors up to the par value of his stock, if the corporation was unable to pay its debts. This rule was weakened by provisions that stock could be issued for property as well as cash, and that a valuation of property made by the board of directors was valid, and finally broken down by the advent of nonpar stock after the year 1912.

Other weakenings of the stockholders' rights are described. The pre-emptive right to subscribe to new issues of capital stock was diminished. Dividends were permitted to be paid even though the corporate capital had been reduced by losses. Corporate managements inserted in their charters a power, by vote of the majority, to amend the charter in respect to contract rights, preferences, participations, and voting power.

It must, however, be remembered as further pointed out below, that these weakenings of stockholders' rights were legally permissible, but not necessarily and economically acted upon to the extent thus legally permitted.

I shall not attempt to enumerate all of the other headings under which Berle and Means describe this evolution of corporation law in America by permitting the management to become supreme through reducing the rights of stockholders. The enumeration should be summarized in any elementary textbook in economics. It is even more important than the usual subjects in elementary textbooks. I call attention to certain efforts—which I often found in my newspaper investigation of the history of labor movements —to introduce protection of stockholders by minority representation and similar devices. These efforts should also be investigated. The efforts were futile, because corporations which were created under such laws could not have that unity of central management required to meet the competition of those which had centered authority in the management. American economic history is full of efforts to organize "cooperatives," especially in the history of labor movements and farmers' movements, on the "democratic" principle of "one-man-one-vote," instead of the "capitalistic" principle of "one-share-one-vote." Nearly always this democratic principle made the cooperatives incompetent, bankrupt, or converted them into corporations. Consumers' cooperatives gave way to chain stores. Producers' cooperatives would not elect and re-elect competent managers. They would not pay the salaries which capitalistic corporations paid. And yet those huge salaries should be compared, not with other salaries, but with the responsibilities. A salary of $100,000 is only one-tenth of one per cent of an annual sales income of one billion dollars, which is a cheap price for a good manager.

Historical investigations in these related fields might show an almost inevitable tendency—call it "economic determinism"—toward centralized management and "dictatorship," away from "democracy." The alleged futility of antitrust laws would be a chapter in this history. The "cooperatives" succeeded, somehow, in Europe but were outright abolished in fascist countries by taking over the appointment of their "management." In America they simply wither away in competition with private management. Always there have been waves of agitation in support of these cooperative movements. I have had most enthusiastic friends pushing these efforts. I should like to see cold-blooded comparative investigations, adequately financed, of corporations and cooperatives in this and other countries.

A further question arises. Have our authors exaggerated this separation of management from ownership and this concentration of control in the hands of a few great capitalists?

I should perhaps go further than they go. The actual numbers of those in control is unimportant, whether 2,000 or 20,000. The trend is important. This is the clue which they offer for further investigations. I would say that they have shown how America is becoming the truly capitalistic nation of the world, while others, like England and France, are weak followers. The United States are, in fact, 48 sovereignties competing with each other as to which can give the most liberal grants of power to capitalistic management, and then this nation is also a national sovereignty protecting, by the courts, these grants of the most liberal states in the other less liberal states, and in foreign lands. Other nations may become communistic, fascistic, nazistic, or totalitarian, but ours becomes more capitalistic.

I see in this work of Berle and Means the elaboration in detail of what the Swiss-Italian economist Pareto meant when he repudiated his earlier magnificent work in mathematical and individualistic economics and laid the foundations for fascism by his characterization of the democracies of Italy, France, and America as "demagogic plutocracy." The capitalistic system depends on investments. America, with the highest incomes and highest standards of living in the world, has been the nation where the largest amount of savings could easily be set aside for investment instead of consumption. These savings increasingly go, as our authors show, into the stocks and bonds of corporations, and into the land values of real estate. These investments are increasingly tied up in family corporations or trusts and in other corporations.

If these investments are jeopardized by insecurity, then the capitalistic system stops for the time being. The security of these investments, no matter how lawfully or unlawfully the properties may have been acquired, is more important than the efficiency of labor or the inventions of scientists and engineers. We may expect, as has now happened since 1929, deeper and more prolonged business depressions and doubtful recoveries than those of the nineteenth century. We have seen a nation aroused to extreme national measures of control over these concentrated capitalistic controls which had destroyed their savings and their jobs, and then the very remedial and relief measures add their insecurity of investments to that which management had brought upon itself. The remedial measures go first in the direction of actually strengthening the capitalistic control by a national industrial recovery act and then, when this is declared unconstitutional, in the opposite direction of "smashing the trusts."

It is the resulting impasse between corporation management and political management which makes me go further into the ultimate purposes not directly investigated by Berle and Means. I base much on scientific investigation, but it may be too late and too slow. People must act before scientists can show them how, even if the scientists can agree on showing how. If it turns out, as the authors indicate, that investors turn to those corporations in whose management they have confidence; if the administrative commissions fail on account of political incompetence and judicial interference; and if the alternative public ownership on a large scale also fails; then what they call "classic corporations" would tend to absorb the business of other corporations, and the mere selective confidence of investors would go further than even the authors indicate toward making corporate management the dominant economic state.

I have suggested two lines of historical investigation—the history of individual corporations, and the history of individual regulatory commissions. These lines of investigation have a practical bearing. In reading the book I seem to discover why it was that I instinctively had been advising my small-monied friends nevermore to put their savings into stocks or bonds of corporations, but to put everything into a bank with government-insured deposits, or into government bonds, even if they should get no interest on their savings. I had seen too many life savings of the teaching profession destroyed, along with the investments of good country banks in Wisconsin, because they had trusted the word of their bankers, or of eminent financiers, or of well-known investment advisers.

Yet these conclusions of mine may have been based upon inadequate investigation of the facts, and I am still uncertain whether Berle and Means have given a balanced view of the situation. Their book is, in fact, only an investigation of the extent to which corporations can legally go, and not an investigation of the extent to which they economically and actually go. They mention only two corporations which have not taken advantage of the legal delegations of power which they describe. These two corporations, the American Telephone and Telegraph Company and the Pennsylvania Railroad Company, are mentioned as "classic" exceptions (p. 204). I should like to see historical investigations of these companies and the other classic exceptions, as well as investigations of those which have gone to the legally permissible limit.

And yet I may have been right in my conclusions. While at work on the examination on this book I found a statement by the leading investment adviser, Roger Babson, almost wholly committing himself to my own apprehension regarding the insecurity of investments and to a confirmation of those apprehensions by Berle and Means. What Babson says emphasizes the need of the two lines of investigation. He says:

> The average small stockholder is too often misled. He puts his money into the securities of companies about which he knows little or nothing. The information he receives is too often vague, incomplete and meaningless. Decisions are concentrated in the hands of an inside group of officials, bankers and lawyers . . . One of the major faults of the railroads today is absentee ownership. Banker and lawyer managements have run many roads into the ash heap. Stupid handling of labor problems has raised havoc with the carriers. Few of these directors would handle their own money as they have handled their stockholders' funds. The same is true of certain directors of utility, motor, movie, food, and other mammoth concerns. We growl about graft in public places; but do the net results exceed the huge salaries which have been paid in private places? . . . Corporation executives have done things that public officials could never get away with and vice versa . . . President Roosevelt, on his part, has also unfortunately hurt business and increased unemployment by his relentless, intemperate antagonism.

Babson goes on:

> Small stockholders need a union which would take its place beside the managements' "luncheon club" and Labor Local No. 102 . . . To watch over their own interests, therefore, investors need a protective organization just as workers need unions and political parties need machines.[1]

[1] From a speech given by Mr. Roger Babson in Florida in 1938. By permission of the author.

It is exactly these administrative commissions which have been created to become Babson's "protective organizations for investors and other small-monied people." They are created, however, as bodies of investigation and mediation between his "protective organizations," his "unions," and his "political machines" on the one hand, and the "management of corporations," which Babson criticizes, and Berle and Means investigate.

Taking their "nonfinancial" corporations, their estimates show that, out of the 300,000 such corporations in the country for the year 1929, "200 of these, or less than seven-hundredths of one per cent, control nearly half the corporate wealth," and they control nearly one-fourth of the entire national wealth (p. 32). This corporate and national wealth is necessarily, however, investigated by them in terms of "assets" rather than in the ambiguous term of "wealth." As such, our authors assert that "the influence of one of these huge companies extends far beyond the assets under its direct control." It extends to prices of commodities (p. 32). The smaller companies "sell to or buy from" the larger companies, and the influence of the latter on prices "is often greatly increased by its mere size, even though it does not begin to approach a monopoly." Consequently they conclude that "much more than half of industry is dominated by these great units," the other less-than-half being in the hands of the remaining 300,000 small companies. To this they add that "approximately 2,000 individuals out of a population of one hundred and twenty-five million are in a position to control and direct *half* of industry" (p. 33).

I wonder if they mean 2,000 families out of say twenty-five million families, and whether, when prices are included as well as assets, they might go further and say that these 2,000 individuals "control and direct" the *whole* of American industry. The United States Steel Corporation, for example, apparently "controls and directs" the prices of rolled steel products for itself and for its competitors which, in turn, modify costs and prices through to the farmers and every family. Or when the Standard Oil Company raises or lowers prices at the filling stations, the other companies, big and little, simultaneously must do the same. When these and the 200 other companies which they itemize (pp. 95 ff.) are included, then practically everything which the American people purchase and sell, including stocks and bonds, is "controlled and directed" by these "2,000 individuals."

If banking and similar financial corporations are included, and if these "2,000 individuals" also control the largest of them, and if prices of commodities or services are included in the investigations as well as in capitalized assets, then this investigation by Berle and Means may well be the starting point for their suggestion of a "potential constitutional law for the new economic state."

These hypothetical conclusions of theirs are based on their preceding investigations which show statistical estimates of the "relative importance" of their 200 "nonfinancial" corporations. The banking corporations are not included in their estimates, and evidently the picture is incomplete until these financial corporations and partnerships, which furnish the funds and credits, are somehow tied up with the nonbanking corporations dependent upon them.

From these considerations I suggest, as above, that the measure of the power of control by the management of the 200 leading corporations should be found, not in their "assets" nor in their "wealth" but in the "gross-sales-income," or "sales turnover," of these and other corporations, and upon the "margins for profit" derived from those sales. A study of these margins for corporate profit may greatly reduce the foregoing inferences of the wide influence of "management" upon the whole of American economic life. For "management," however powerful, is itself subject to extreme uncertainties of these narrow margins of profit which, in turn, depend on national and international conditions. The profit margins are usually wider in periods of prosperity and narrower, or converted into loss, during periods of depression. Consequently the economic power of management over investors and the public generally differs greatly at different times. Its function is to take advantage of a rising tide of prosperity and to escape the falling tide of depression. However, this widely changeable position of management is not a part of the Berle-Means investigation.

Yet it is upon the expected changeable magnitudes of these margins for profit that the values of corporate "assets" depend, so that "assets" are secondary, and "gross sales" are primary. This principle I developed as a sequel to the discussion of assets and profits in my *Legal Foundations*,[1] and I think, as will appear presently, that it serves both to reconcile certain discrepancies between Berle's legal and Means' economic points of view, and ties up their discussion with the concept of "national income," meaning monetary income, which nowadays takes the place of Adam Smith's "wealth of nations." Modern economics is primarily concerned with the *income of nations*, not the *wealth of nations*. The "assets" of corporations and individuals are the "capitalization" of their expected shares out of those national incomes into a "present worth." And the national incomes themselves are national shares of a world income trickled down through the hierarchy of "economic governments" into the shares acquired by individuals. The incomes are measured by money which measured assets, not wealth.

This suggestion conforms to a report made some time ago by the National Industrial Conference Board to the effect that 90 per cent of the physical output of manufacturing industries is in the hands of corporations. If to manufactures are added public utilities, merchandising, and finance, and if "output" is made to include "services," then it possibly is true that 90 per cent of the "value output" of all American industry is in the hands of corporations. It is this highly changeable value output of commodities and services that constitutes the changeable income of the American people. It is also this value output that is the field of investigation for the other administrative commissions mentioned above, such as public service commissions, industrial commissions, trade commissions, and tax commissions.

I have mentioned above two aspects of investigation suggested by this book: first, the subject matter of joint investigations; second, the materials, technique, and methods of investigation.

[1] J. R. Commons, *Legal Foundations of Capitalism*, New York, The Macmillan Co., 1924, pp. 28–36; see also J. R. Commons, *Institutional Economics*, New York, The Macmillan Co., 1934, pp. 526 ff.

As to the subject matter, two lines of investigation are indicated: a study of particular corporations under powers delegated by the state governments, and a parallel investigation of the delegated legislative powers to be found in the administrative commissions of the state and federal governments in the fields of taxation, public utilities, labor, commodity markets, and security markets. The subject matter of the latter is control of the former, or, inversely, the subject matter of the former is control of the latter.

First would be investigation of the legislative charters of incorporation of the private organizations and of the state and federal commissions. These grants of power are evidently to be found not only in the "written law" of the statutes, but mainly in the "unwritten law" of court decisions and in the business customs and practices which are changing, yet dominant at the time. This feature marks the value of the work by Berle and Means. Each angle of investigation is carried through to the decisions of state and federal courts, as well as through the business practices prevailing or modified by those decisions.

The peculiarity of American charters of incorporation is that they are granted by state governments, instead of by the national government, as in other countries. These state charters, on the principle of comity among the states enforced by decisions of the federal courts, become, in effect, national charters of incorporation, although there is no federal incorporation law covering the field. Consequently the "management" or the "control" has a choice among the states as to which state offers the largest grant of control to these 2,000 individuals. Our authors point out a decided "trend" toward the state of Delaware (p. 206 n), which within a few years preceding their investigation, had adopted what they call the "loosest," or "most liberal," of all incorporation statutes. By this the authors mean the loosest in protecting investors against the management, and the most liberal in strengthening the management against investors. The lawyers who draft the charters under the Delaware statutes and decisions can give to the "management" the largest scope of immunities and privileges in their defenses against suits brought by investors. Prior to Delaware's emergence as the fountain of this economic power, first was New Jersey, in the years 1898–1910, when the great movement of mergers, mainly through holding companies, first took place as a refuge from the federal and state antitrust laws. Then Maryland seems to have competed with New Jersey for the profitable business, but Delaware won out as the most liberal and "loose" of all.

I wish that in their statistical summaries, Berle and Means would have designated the states in which their 200 dominant companies were incorporated, and that in any future investigations or summaries the state of incorporation should always be attached to the name of the company owning or controlling the stock of subsidiary companies. I know that in the state of Wisconsin the public utility law of 1907, which I then thought was a sensible and fair law to both investors and the public, has been nullified in some of its provisions by holding companies coming into the state with special grants of power from other states. Any investigation of the subject must inquire into the corporate statutes of the particular state from which these grants of authority are derived, as well as into the decisions of the federal courts and the courts of that state.

Since it is the state legislatures that grant these articles of incorporation, the extent to which the managers of corporations exercise their powers throughout the nation is in the hands of the federal courts. The Supreme Court of the United States, therefore, takes the place of a congressional act of incorporation. To counteract this situation, and to make economic as well as legal investigations, Congress creates federal administrative commissions. These commissions make their investigations and issue their orders, but there is a final review by the federal courts upon the constitutionality of these delegations of power and upon the reasonableness of these administrative investigations, and upon the hearings and the orders sought to be enforced through the agency of the federal courts. There is grave ambiguity and misunderstanding in this field, revealing itself in the faulty bill drafting of the administrative laws enacted by the Congress, faulty because not conforming to the rules laid down by the Supreme Court. The interstate commerce law of 1886 governing railways went through at least 20 years of unconstitutionality and experimenting before it reached a form finally sustained by the Supreme Court. The history of this commission throws light on the other commissions. When the art of bill-drafting was improved, and the Court sustained the jurisdiction of the Commission, then the decisions by the Court turned on the reasonableness of the administrative rules and on the procedure of investigation and hearings, instead of on the constitutionality of the delegation of power to make rules. Similar periods of unconstitutionality are evident in other federal administrative laws relative to marketing, agriculture, or labor, though the long period seems to have been somewhat shortened in the case of the Securities and Exchange Commission.

It was exactly these questions of constitutionality and reasonableness which I was compelled to investigate jointly with the lawyers in drafting the public utility law of Wisconsin in 1907, and which began to furnish the materials for my *Legal Foundations of Capitalism* in 1924. Berle and Means have investigated the present status of the delegation of legislative authority to private corporations, and a similar joint investigation is called for in the matter of the present status of delegation of power to commissions designed to regulate that other delegation of sovereign power to private administration by what our authors call "business practice."

Besides a history of the Interstate Commerce Commission, an investigation of similar administrative bodies in European countries would give information as to the workable procedure of investigation and administrative orders. I made such an investigation with my students when drafting the industrial commission law of Wisconsin in 1911. We had only documents and reports. But joint field investigation by lawyers and economists, familiar with American commissions, is needed. At that time it was found that the countries offering the best suggestions for American commissions were England, Belgium, and France. These investigations of administrative commissions would have a practical bearing upon the issue of "smashing the trusts" or in regulating them.

When the matter of constitutionality is finally settled by the

Supreme Court, then the Court review is concerned with the procedure, the rules of investigation and testimony, as practiced by these commissions. Here the issue turns on the difference between an economic investigation and a legal investigation. The legal investigation takes place in a trial at court, with rigid rules of inclusion and exclusion of evidence and procedural technicalities. The economic investigation takes place with a staff of statisticians, accountants, and economists not bound by technical rules. A comparison of these two methods of investigation is called for. Such a comparison has been started by the legal investigator, Thurman W. Arnold, of the Yale School of Law, in his book on the *Folklore of Capitalism*, wherein he contrasts a trial at court with the investigations by an administrative commission. The need of carrying on such an investigation of contrasted methods of investigation is more recently indicated in a protest by the Secretary of Agriculture, in 1938, against the decision of the Supreme Court setting aside an order by the Secretary regarding the Kansas City Stockyards, and by the answers made to that protest by the Chief Justice and the lawyer on the other side.[1] The Court's decision in that case bore directly on the ultimate purpose of Berle and Means as to the probable domination of private corporations over the political government, for the Secretary makes the issue turn on the enlarged opportunity for corporation lawyers to delay and obstruct the work of an administrative commission, which in that case was a delay of apparently four or five years. The Secretary's protest turned solely on the methods of investigation pursued by his department, which he contends were exactly the methods prescribed by the Court. In meeting the issue raised by Berle and Means, there is evidently needed a series of joint investigations by the social scientists of the contrasted methods of investigation followed by economists, by courts, and by administrative bodies.

Next should be a thorough investigation of methods of selection of the boards of directors of the corporations, and of the boards of commissioners of the administrative bodies. These officers are the policy-making superiors within the limits of the legislative delegation of powers. The selection of these policy-making officials

[1] *New York Times*, May 8, 12, 15, 1938.

is the focus point of management control, as it is the focus of administrative commissions. Berle and Means reveal that, in course of time, through the system of proxies, these directors of corporations are selected, not by the legalized stockholders but by a mysterious "control" over the so-called "management." The directors become "dummies." The similar evolution occurs in administrative commissions. In a newly organized commission enthusiastic individuals undergo material sacrifices of their private business in their eagerness to make the thing a success. But they usually get tired of the exposure; they go back to their private affairs, and figureheads take their places acting under orders that come mysteriously from somewhere. There are exceptions to this development, and the reasons for these exceptions also require investigation.

Berle and Means have picked upon the proxy system as the instrument through which management selects its own board of directors. It is doubtful whether the proxy system is an adequate explanation. The stockholders send in their proxies to be voted by the management. There are thousands and hundreds of thousands of them. The astonishing thing is the small fraction of the shares of stock held by even the wealthiest of stockholders as shown by our authors—scarcely as much, in some cases, as one per cent of the total number of shares. We were brought up on the assumption that a wealthy man must own 51 per cent of the shares in order to maintain control. Berle and Means mention the famous fight of the Rockefellers, owning only 14 per cent of the shares, in their successful ousting of a manager, on grounds other than his efficiency in making profits for the stockholders. This was very unusual. It went against the almost universal interest of stockholders merely to get dividends on their shares of stock.

The Rockefellers got enough proxies to oust a manager who delivered the dividends, and without depressing the values of the stocks on the stock exchanges. It is confidence in the "control" rather than confidence in the "management" that gets the proxies from stockholders. In the case of administrative commissions the voters give their proxies to governors, presidents, and senators, and they have a hundred conflicting interests other than stocks, bonds, and dividends. Their confidence is not in the commissioners personally, but in the political organization—call it "machine" or "propaganda"—which has enlisted their votes by the variety of promises that appeal to them. I noticed, recently, in the meeting of stockholders of the General Motors Company, that it was the argument of Mr. Du Pont, whose family held about 30 per cent of the stock, that carried the day in favor of the high salary of the chairman of the board. Likewise it is reputed to have been the high reputation of the J. P. Morgan Company that made Judge Gary the chairman of the board of directors of the United States Steel Corporation, although the combined holdings of the 20 largest stockholders was only 8.8 per cent of all the common shares of that corporation, and 1.7 per cent of the preferred shares (p. 382). Berle and Means mention the two "classic corporations" above referred to, the American Telephone and Telegraph Company and the Pennsylvania Company, two holding companies that are "classic" because they have been "scrupulous not to take advantage of their powers" (p. 204). The authors point, as evidence of this confidence in the management, to the nearly half million stockholders of the A. T. & T. Co., and yet the 20 largest stockholders, taken together, hold only 4.6 per cent of the shares (pp. 108, 381). They speak of "a few other classic corporations," not itemized. If there are only "a few" of such corporations, the need of historical investigations of particular corporations becomes apparent. What were their changing policies towards investors? Who were the individuals or institutions in the "control" that dominated the selection of the "management?"

The precariousness of the situation is evident when, owing to the collapse following 1929, an amazing number of the estimated seven million shareholders lost their life's savings which presumably were gathered in by others at depressed prices. Only in relatively few cases has there been evidence of any malfeasance in the management. Yet those few cases, added to the universal losses suffered by investors, seem to terrify investors in all other corporations and to throw what ought to be investments into the hands of speculators. Those who are in the "control" naturally complain of their difficulties arising from the attempts of the political organization of the state to prevent similar losses to future investors, rather than in the precariousness of the whole situation that has transferred the control from investors to their own management. The administrative commissions are thus attacked and weakened, not directly but by reducing their appropriations and through substituting political figureheads. We may expect this fate to fall upon the Securities and Exchange Commission, and thus may expect the prediction of Berle and Means as to the future economic government by private corporations to be further realized. These apprehensions re-enforce again the suggestion for further joint investigations by social scientists of both particular corporations and administrative commissions.

Berle and Means have compiled significant statistics on the sources of growth in assets of their 200 corporations (p. 43). The net growth during the years 1922–1927 was about $20 billion. More than one-half of this increase in assets (55 per cent) was acquired by the sale of new issues of securities. About one-fifth (18.5 per cent) was accomplished by mergers, including holding companies. About one-fourth (26.5 per cent) consisted in plowing back into the industry corporate savings withheld from stockholders. Thus about four-fifths of the growth in assets, during these six years of apparent prosperity, was accomplished through savings—the voluntary savings derived from other sources and the compulsory savings imposed on their own stockholders. The significance of carrying forward investigations of the interrelations and duplications of these three sources of assets is apparent.

Here we reach the focus of the transformation of private property, brought about, or in process, by the emergence of corporate management. Berle and Means work it out by bringing into the picture the part played by a public market, the New York Stock Exchange (pp. 289 ff.). On this market the values of the investors' rights of participation in the earnings, or expected earnings, of a corporation are appraised. I had come across it, in 1907, in the decisions of courts relative to the values of public utility corporations for rate-fixing purposes, and had traced it back to a decision of the Supreme Court in a Minnesota rate case of 1890. The Court, at that time, reversed its former holdings in the slaughter house cases (1872), and the case of *Munn* v. *Illinois* (1876). The concept which the Court now introduced became known as "intangible property," distinguished from the two older forms of "corporeal" property and "incorporeal" property. Incorporeal property had long been recognized as ownership of contractual debts, which, by the legal device of negotiability, could be bought and sold like metallic money. The ownership of physical things, like land, materials, slaves, had been the primitive form, known as "corporeal property." This had been the only form of property recognized in the constitutional interpretation of the slaughter house and Munn cases, though a minority dissented. The court, in the latter case, decided that the power to fix rates and prices for the sale of services or output was a "privilege" granted by the state legislatures and not a property right protected by the federal Constitution. Consequently the railroad and warehouse owners were advised to look for their remedy, not in the federal courts, but in the legislature and the voters of Illinois. But, in 1890, when the legislature of Minnesota, through a railroad commission, reduced the rates charged by railroads in that state, the federal court took jurisdiction on the ground that the "reasonableness" of the rates was a judicial question, and thereupon annulled the rates fixed by the Minnesota commission.

This left the railway corporations in their original position, claimed by them, of power to determine their own rates for the transportation services rendered by them.

It was this power to fix prices that came to be known as "intangible property." This transition to earning power was simple enough and logical enough. The corporeal property of tracks and locomotives was valueless if the corporations were not permitted to charge adequate rates to sustain the values of their stocks and bonds representing investments in those physical properties. Their titles of ownership were "empty" and must have a "content." The content was earning power. This idea of "intangible property" as expected earning power, whose present value is assets, was afterwards extended to many special cases. It became, in labor cases, the "right to do business," the right of "access to markets." It was extended to include the "good will" of a business, to "going concern value," to patent rights, to trade marks, and to trade secrets, none of which were "corporeal" property and none of which were the "incorporeal" property of debts. They were, however, similar in that they also could be bought and sold, their ownerships could be alienated and acquired on the markets, either separately or united with the corporeal property. Their conjunction in a going concern with the corporeal property became the ownership of the shares of stock of the corporation, distinguished from the incorporeal property of bonds which were deductions from the corporate assets.

This matter of a change in the Constitution by merely enlarging the meaning of the word "property" I look upon as fundamental for an interpretation of this book by Berle and Means. This change was accomplished during the years 1872 to 1897. During that period the meaning also of "liberty," "person," and "due process of law" were changed to fit the change in the meaning of property. These several changes in the Constitution laid the foundations for the further changes in private corporations, as portrayed by our authors, from investors to management.

For Berle and Means now discover that even corporation bonds, the "incorporeal property" of the common law, become the "intangible property" of modern law. They are "intangible" in that the supposedly fixed contractual rights may be infringed by the "management," and in the fact that their values are not in the empty contract but in their market valuations upon the stock exchanges. Hence the authors build up a "hierarchy" of security holders "all of whom have supplied capital to the enterprise, and all of whom expect a return from it. These expectations," they say, "are based, *prima facie* upon their legal rights, that is to say upon the words of the contract" (pp. 279 ff.). This hierarchy, as above mentioned, of what now becomes "intangible property" because not based on contracts is the bondholder, the preferred stockholder, the common stockholder, the owner of purchase warrants, and so on, all of whom depend, not on their legal rights, but upon their ability, through bondholders' committees, stockholders' committees, or other influences, to bring pressure to bear upon the management. Ultimately, all of the hierarchy comes to depend, not on legal rights, but upon the stock market, the place where investors find "liquidity" of their investments (pp. 299 ff.) and the market value of their assets.

This is the meaning of "intangible property." In my *Legal Foundations* I was concerned with "going concern value," an "intangible property" belonging to the enterprise as a corporate unity, and based upon the power of the corporation, as a unit, to fix the prices of services and commodities sold to the public. Now, for Berle and Means, "the corporation as a unit" is the management, and they break down the constituents of the corporation into a series of privileged, semiprivileged, and unprivileged investors. The primitive "corporeal property" disappears, the "incorporeal property" rights are with difficulty enforceable in the courts, and private property becomes a hierarchy of investors looking to the stock markets for the value and liquidity of their savings.

There is one "general protection," however, as Berle and Means indicate (pp. 280 ff.), "beside the power of active revolt," which remains "to guarantee a measure of equitable treatment to the several classes of security holders. The enterprise may need new capital." A little more than one-half of their growth (55 per cent as shown above), comes from new issues of stock or other securities. "This need for new capital sets a very definite limit on the extent to which those in control can abuse the suppliers of capital." But, they go on, whether this protection is adequate "depends on factors that are wholly beyond the investors' control: —the state of the industry, the position of the particular corporation; and the attitude of the management." The "net result is to throw him upon an agency lying outside the corporation itself— the public market" (p. 281). This, again, is the meaning of the modern "intangible property."

# Appendix ii

You are certainly right as to the *representative character and importance* of the Wisconsin Industrial Commission's advisory committees.

First, as to the *Advisory Committee on Unemployment Compensation,* I should be able to speak with some degree of authority, —since I have served as presiding chairman of this Advisory Committee for the past seven years.

The Committee was created early in 1932, pursuant to a specific provision of the newly enacted statute,—and has functioned actively ever since.

As the law now stands, Section 108.14 provides (in part) as follows:

> (5) The commission shall appoint a state advisory committee on this chapter, and may appoint additional committees for industries or local districts. Each such committee shall consist of a salaried commission employee, who shall serve as chairman, and of one or more representatives of employers and an equal number of representatives of employees, who shall receive for each day of active service such reasonable compensation as the commission may determine and reimbursement of necessary expenses, and shall assist the commission in administering and carrying out the purposes of this chapter.
>
> (5m) The state advisory committee appointed by the commission under subsection (5) of this section shall submit its

recommendations with respect to *amendments of this chapter* to each regular session of the *legislature,* and shall report its views on any pending bill relating to this chapter to *the proper legislative committee.*

The original 1931 statute *did not,* any more than Wisconsin's present Unemployment Compensation Act, prescribe that the Industrial Commission must appoint as members of the Advisory Committee individuals nominated by the leading employer organization and the leading labor organization.

In fact, however, that is what the Industrial Commission did originally and has done since, in order to assure that the Committee would be truly representative.

The employer representatives have all been nominated by the Wisconsin Manufacturers' Association, whose members employ a majority of the workers covered by the law.

The labor representatives have all been nominated by the Wisconsin State Federation of Labor, which was and is Wisconsin's leading labor organization. (For instance, when President Henry Ohl died last year, after serving more than 8 years as one of labor's three representatives on the Committee, the Federation's executive board really designated the new Federation president to be Henry Ohl's successor on the Advisory Committee,—though the actual appointment was of course made by the Industrial Commission.)

The fact that the employer members and labor members of the Advisory Committee are really representatives of their respective *groups* has had much to do with the Committee's influence and the weight its recommendations carry, not only with employer and labor groups, but also with the Industrial Commission, the Legislature and the Public generally.

In the actual functioning of the Committee, the emphasis is always on reaching eventual agreement between the two sides of the table.

Though I serve as presiding chairman, and do a good deal of talking both on technical and policy matters, I've never exercised any voting right I might possibly have. (For the chairman to help one side outvote the other side would be contrary to our conception of the Committee's functioning.) Note the following quotations from an Industrial Commission pamphlet on the law, published in January, 1936:—

> In March, 1932, shortly after the Wisconsin Unemployment Compensation Act was passed, the Industrial Commission created an Advisory Committee to assist the Commission in interpreting and administering the new statute. This Advisory Committee consisted of three labor representatives (J. F. Friedrick, Fred E. Gastrow, and Henry Ohl, Jr.) selected by the Wisconsin State Federation of Labor; and of three representatives chosen by the Wisconsin Manufacturers' Association (Fred H. Clausen, George F. Kull, and H. J. Mellum.) Arthur Altmeyer served as presiding chairman of the Advisory Committee, until he took a federal position in 1935. Since that time Paul Raushenbush (now director of the Commission's unemployment compensation division) has served as chairman of the Advisory Committee.

As you know, and as your letter suggests, the Industrial Commission has long used various other advisory committees in connection with its other functions and divisions. Though I am less familiar with the other committees, the following comment may help to remind you of a few facts as to their membership and scope.

In each case, the Commission secures nominations from labor and employer groups, and generally also from other interested groups which the Commission believes should be represented on the given committee. Usually the Commission secures several names, and selects from them in making any appointment. In all cases, unanimous recommendations are sought, so far as possible.

The Employment Service State Advisory Council, which has functioned for some years now, is set up consistently with the 1933 Federal Wagner-Peyser Act.

It is appointed by the Commission, from nominations made by the various organizations. Its present membership includes 5 employer representatives, 5 labor representatives, 2 members representing veterans, 1 representing women, 1 representing farmers, 1 from vocational rehabilitation, and 2 representing the public generally.

It meets, on the average, only once or twice a year—partly because its scope and usefulness have been considerably limited by the degree to which the policies and procedures of state employment services have been fully prescribed by federal regulations. (This has become increasingly true recently, in view of the tie-up with national defense.)

The Advisory Committee on Workman's Accident Compensation is assembled biennially to consider and recommend amendments to the Legislature. Its statutory basis is somewhat less clear and explicit than in the unemployment compensation field. However, the Industrial Commission secures nominations, from which it appoints several prominent labor leaders, several recognized representatives of employers, a few representatives of the leading insurance companies doing this type of business in Wisconsin, and a few lawyers practicing in the industrial field. This group usually meets for a day or two,—with the commissioners and the director· of the Workman's Compensation Department.

The Committee's recommendations, which have generally been accepted by the Legislature, carry weight not only because of the technical competence of the Committee's members but also because of their representative character.

In developing and revising its various *safety codes*, the Commission appoints a special committee to deal with each separate code. In creating such a committee, the Commission again secures— from labor and employer organizations—nominations of individuals who are both representative and technically qualified in the particular field in question (such as building, electrical, boilers, tunnels, dust, etc.). Nominations may also be secured from any technical or professional group having special knowledge but no direct financial stake in the nature of the code (e.g., doctors).

The various safety code committees, as you doubtless recall, function actively over an extended period in preparing a new code, or when comprehensively revising an old one. They remain subject to call thereafter, and are consulted on new developments or interpretations.

In short, the use of advisory committees by Wisconsin's Industrial Commission has been long continued, and markedly successful,—largely because of the technical knowledge and the truly representative character of the various committees down through the years.

The Commission's use of advisory committees seems to me a fine practical application and example of the democratic process,— and a good demonstration of how well that process can work.

> (Signed) Paul A. Raushenbush, Director
> Unemployment Compensation Dept.
> Industrial Commission of Wisconsin.

# Appendix iii

## JOHN R. COMMONS' POINT OF VIEW*

### By the Editor, KENNETH H. PARSONS

In America we think concretely according to the common-
law method of individual cases and precedents, conformable
to our judicial sovereignty; while the Europeans think
abstractedly in deductive terms handed down from Jus-
tinian, Napoleon, Adam Smith, or Ricardo. If we generalize,
as attempted in this book, we discuss only general principles, leaving their application to investigations of the particular cases. In this way has arisen the American common-
law method. This American system of custom, precedent,
and assumptions is with difficulty comprehended by European economists and jurists who operate under a system of
codes constructed originally by dictators on the model of
the perfected Roman law and changeable only by legislatures. It is even understood with difficulty by the British,
whose legislature is superior to the judiciary. Reliance on
codes ends in *revolutions,* whereas the common-law method
*gradually* eliminates the enforcement of contracts when
found, in particular cases, to work injustice.[1]

In these words John R. Commons has not only given us his
interpretation of what is distinctive about American social
thought, he has also characterized succinctly his own method, as
I understand it. This is as it should be. For few, if any other
economists have so directly and intimately experienced the great
structural changes that have occurred in the American economy
since the Civil War. As the rise of urban industry has converted
this country from an agrarian to an advanced industrial nation,

*From *The Journal of Land and Public Utility Economics,* August, 1942,
Vol. XVIII, No. 3, pp. 245–266. Reprinted by permission.

[1] J. R. Commons, *Institutional Economics,* New York, The Macmillan Co.,
1934. Quotation re-arranged from pp. 713, 223.

Commons has participated in the labor movement as a printer, research student, an inventor and administrator of industrial government, and as adviser to a host of public officials. As he has served the American people in countless ways in their struggle as citizens to achieve a tolerable degree of order and security, by experiment and trial and error, he has gradually worked out a comprehensive point of view. This essay is an attempt to give an exposition of the fundamentals of his position, and to suggest some of the issues that his theories present in relation to other approaches in social analysis.

## I.

Essentially, Commons has been attempting to work out a theory of economics which shall be adequate both for the analysis of economic problems and the guidance of social action in resolving the difficulties. It may very aptly be called a system of political economy. This may appear to be an odd description of an effort whose most comprehensive statement is entitled *Institutional Economics*. Yet the subtitle reads, "Its place in political economy." He somewhere suggests that he has carried this vision of a comprehensive political economy since his student days under Dr. Ely at Johns Hopkins. Whether he was studying labor unions, proportional representation, city finances, administrative commissions, the banking system, or institutional economics, it would seem there has been this wider frame of reference and the larger goal.

In this sense, he has been working in the great tradition. Yet his formulation centers in a distinctive way around the issues presented by social control, the acceptance of the process as of the nature of social things, collective action, the reality of economic power, conflicts of interest and social valuation. In addition, he has attempted to work out the problems of the relation of government to the economy, the functioning of the firm in its relation to the whole economy, and the significance of the legislatures and courts for economic life—which presumably any political economy must do.

To analyze such an array of problems obviously requires a

comprehensive, theoretical viewpoint. Here Commons has been courageously creative although in general he belongs to the American pragmatic school. The apt remark of Professor Morris appears to apply to Commons quite as well as to Mead, toward whose work it was directed: "Darwinism, the experimental method, and democracy are the headwaters of the pragmatic stream.[1] There is great similarity in fundamentals, it now seems to me, between the work of Commons on the one hand, and that of John Dewey and the late G. H. Mead on the other. Yet Commons has evidently worked through the basic methodological questions independently. He does not appear to have followed the work of Mead; he has some footnote references to Dewey in his recent works, but the most frequent and almost exclusive class reference, as I recall, was to Peirce. He returned time and again to the essay on "How to Make Our Ideas Clear." [2] Peirce also shares with Hume the title to Chapter IV of *Institutional Economics,* in line with the general policy in the book of crediting the "pioneers of insight."

Thus Commons shares in the deep faith of pragmatists (or instrumentalists) generally in the possibility of human intelligence for working out the problems of social conduct, for it is within such conduct that both mind and selves are developed. Commons' attention to the problems of social control and his definition of an institution as "collective action in control, liberation, and expansion of individual action " [3] may be taken as suggestions of his position on these issues.

## II.

If one word were to be taken as describing the nature of the economy, or society generally, in Commons' formulation, it would probably be "organization." This would serve merely to set off the grand conception from other general descriptions such as mech-

[1] Charles W. Morris, Introduction to G. H. Mead, *Mind, Self and Society,* University of Chicago Press, 1934, p. x.

[2] Reprinted in Charles S. Peirce, *Chance, Love, and Logic,* New York, Harcourt, Brace & Co., 1923, pp. 32–60. First published in *Popular Science Monthly,* January, 1878, New York, D. Appleton & Co., Vol. XII, pp. 286–302.

[3] J. R. Commons, *Institutional Economics,* New York, The Macmillan Co., 1934, p. 842.

anism or organism.[1] The essential point would be that, as organization, the social structure would be the resultant of and embodiment of the designs, purposes, and activities of human beings who had lived and worked in it. But this is merely a gross description of the nature of the universe of study.

We are nearer the foundation of the viewpoint when we consider the social process. Whatever else may or may not be said of Commons' attempt to formulate a general theory of economics, it seems to me that it is always struggling with problems of process analysis. And the process investigated is fundamentally social.

This brings the analysis to a focus upon social relationships—relations between persons. In the time sequence these relationships change; their changes are, of course, a matter for investigation. Economic relations, economic facts, are selected or particularized from the larger continuum of the social. This common ground of phenomena in the social serves as the foundation for the possible integration of the social sciences toward which Commons' analysis has been directed, at least implicitly. He has tried to formulate an analysis which would give a foundation for the coordination of the social sciences, especially law, ethics, economics, and political science. This coordination is made necessary by planning, by administrative and legislative direction of economic affairs—by social control generally.

By way of emphasis, and precaution, it should be noted that *social* as here used, is not something set off against the physical or natural as an exclusive category. Rather *social* is used as a category including the physical; for physical things—resources and production—are caught up into a system of social relations. This particular position has been presented forcefully and generally by Dewey,[2] but it is implied throughout, it seems to me, in Commons' analysis.

Commons' position, furthermore, accepts conflicts of interest as

[1] Commons frequently uses "concern" as equivalent to the here intended meaning of organization. Cf. *Institutional Economics*, pp. 619 ff.

[2] Cf., *The Social Intelligence in the Modern World*, The Modern Library, edited by Joseph Ratner, pp. 1059–69; originally published as *Social as a Category, Monist*, April, 1928, pp. 161–177.

natural and necessary ingredients of the social process.[1] There is individual action and collective action (perhaps individual action within collective action). In this action there are conflicts of interest. But there is more than conflict, there is mutual dependency and the achievement of order. Assuming that this is the nature of things social, the general question becomes one of how we go about building a stable society or a functioning economic system. For this much is clear, if social phenomena inherently contain the elements of conflict, dependence, and order, then they are not something analyzed and settled once for all in the past, but are continuously and eternally recurring as problems to be dealt with.

We may now recur to the statement at the beginning of this section, and ask the question of how an economy as an organization is related to the social process. The answer may be even more general, for not only is organization achieved within the social process, but also valuation and production, if social, is an inclusive form of interaction. The fundamental phenomena are social activities—individual action and collective action. By means of devised social procedures the relationships between individuals are stabilized or regularized; organizations are these stabilized relationships. Wherever alternatives are weighed and choices made within the achieved organization there is the phenomenon of valuation; Commons has devoted his thought especially to social valuations. Within organization, too, are achieved that coordination and integration of activity by which the raw materials of nature are converted, by production, into goods and services useful to mankind. It will be noted that these distinctions are a tentative marking off of different phases of behavior. Though provisional, they may be helpful in exploring the whole of the formulated point of view. Of the four—activity, organization, valuation, and operations—we turn first to the analysis of activity.

### III.

It is the activities of and relations between persons that constitute the core of social phenomena. Consequently, a truly social

[1] *Institutional Economics*, p. 3.

analysis would presumably center upon the analysis of social relationships. At any rate, this is what Commons has tried to do. Out of the great "seamless web" of society, he has fixed upon the transaction as the basic unit of investigation. Transactions are not only actions, they are social actions, joint actions. Consequently, transactions involve individual behavior, or actions.

Since economic actions, or behavior, are merely aspects of the more inclusive social actions, an analysis of economic behavior, which is central to Commons' purpose, requires some marking off of economic behavior as such. Yet it is not easy to point precisely to what Commons means by economic behavior or activity. This difficulty stems from the practice, which is basic to his viewpoint, of using definitions as tools for investigating the ongoing social process rather than as basic propositions whose contents are to be explored by deductive reasoning.

In general, economic behavior is the activity of citizens as they go about the business of making a living, producing, and acquiring wealth, in the actual world of affairs. He once wrote defining his conception of economics, " . . . we begin with man's relations to his fellow man in the process of exploiting nature and distributing the proceeds by inducements and sanctions." [1] Again: "Our subject matter is the transactions of human beings in producing, acquiring, and rationing wealth by cooperation, conflict, and the rules of the game." [2]

In its simplest form the principle of economy means proportioning the parts, or resources, to maximize their effectiveness. "The word 'economy' itself means the whole activity of proportioning the parts so as to get the largest result  or the minimum effort. Hence the term 'economy' has always meant a part-whole relationship." [3] Where the concept of economy is related only to the physical relationships of man to things, either of producing a maximum of goods from the available resources, or of maximizing the satisfaction of wants through the consumptive process, economizing may be a relatively simple and individual activity.

[1] "Anglo-American Law and Economics," 1926 (mimeo., p. 41.)
[2] J. R. Commons, *Institutional Economics*, New York, The Macmillan Co., 1934, p. 121.
[3] *Ibid.*, p. 621.

But where the individual is a citizen making his living through the give and take of a succession of transactions, proportioning or economizing becomes a complex of activity. This process of economizing breaks up into a repetition of transctions, where the complex economic behavior is guided by the will, which is analyzed by several different principles.

Professor Commons usually designates five distinct principles of economic action, although he has varied the number at different stages of his own formulation, and suggests that other persons may find a different number of principles more useful. The five principles of economic behavior are: efficiency, scarcity, futurity, the working rules of collective action, and sovereignty.

These principles, he seems to say, are inherent in the structure of social action, at least in that phase of social action which is economic behavior. It is most important to understand that Commons defines a principle as "a supposed similarity of actions" in which the flow of time is essential. "Because a principle involves the sequence of time it is a similarity of cause, effect or purpose." [1] The reference to cause, effect, or purpose refers to the conception of action in a social process. Action involves purpose through choice; and it involves cause and effect which are defined as relating to control through attention to the limiting factor.

The idea back of this formulation of principles is fundamentally an attempt to relate ideas to action, wherein both ideas, as principles, and the knowledge secured by their use, are relative to action. These principles have operational rather than existential status. They are essentially abstract ideas, defined for the purpose of investigating activity; or they are general conceptions arrived at by analysis and abstraction from the actual behavior of persons as they go about making a living in the actual world of affairs. As principles they represent the lines of actual choice and action, whether the actors know it or not, because they are implicit in the collective behavior of persons in the actual world.

The principle of efficiency relates to the similarities of activity in so far as it is directed to overcoming the resistance of nature. It relates to power over physical processes, and as an aspect of

[1] *Ibid.*, p. 94.

economic behavior it relates to the processing of materials into commodities. Ultimately, and in broadest social terms, it relates to the different forms of labor overcoming the "niggardliness of nature," converting materials into embodied uses or utilities for human purposes.

The principle of scarcity relates to the negotiations over prices and quantities. It is the similarity of actions in bargaining over the terms of transfer of ownership and delivery of physical goods.

The principle of futurity relates to expectations. Economic behavior rests upon the anticipation that the future will bring a similar, though variable, repetition of opportunities and hindrances as experienced in the past or moving present. Purposes, values, and expected consequences are the grounds for choices made in the present to be realized in the future.

The principle of working rules relates to the repetition of activities in which collective action creates order and stabilizes the wills of the participants by defining the rights and duties of each. It is the similarity of activity in custom, precedent, and statute law by which expectations are made secure. It is the ultimate principle which makes living in society possible by stabilizing the wills of those having superior bargaining power or authority.

The principle of sovereignty relates to the use of force toward legal inferiors by their superiors; the evolution of the state represents the extraction of the power of physical violence or force from private persons and its lodgment in the hands of authority. The principle of sovereignty relates to expected repetition in use of this force. It is the similarity of action in what the sheriff or other officials may do if the authoritative working rules are violated. "To the extent that the individual is clothed with this sovereign power of the state does he rise from the nakedness of slave, child, woman, alien, into the armament of a citizen, and his going concern rises from a conspiracy into a corporation." [1]

"These five part-principles constitute, in their interdependence, the whole of the principle of willingness . . . As principle, it is

[1] J. R. Commons, *Legal Foundations of Capitalism*, New York, The Macmillan Co., 1924, p. 121.

the expected repetition, with variability, of the total of all human acting and transacting within the limiting and complementary interdependence of the principles of scarcity, efficiency, working rules, sovereignty, and futurity. The functional relations are such because a change in one dimension changes all the others, and thus changes the whole transaction or concern. If efficiency increases, then scarcity diminishes; a variation of working rules occurs, as well as of expectations of the future, and perhaps of the use of sovereignty." [1]

Since the principles are intended to explain what the human will must contend against in economic behavior, they also serve to define the field of fact for economics. It is evident that the field of fact which Commons seeks to investigate is social. Yet as social, the phenomena are continuous with the physical. For economic behavior is concerned in part with the physical world; livelihood can be attained only by subjecting nature's forces to the human will. These physical events are endowed with value for purposes of human choices and action with reference to them. Through custom, organized collective action, and the power of sovereignty, working rules and the wills of persons are stabilized so that security of expectations is achieved. The integration of these diverse aspects is achieved in actual affairs by the human will.

Professor Commons' treatment of the will, or the principle of willingness, is one of the crucial aspects of his social theory. It is not a "free will"; rather he is concerned with the freedom of choice which sets the limits to a discretionary will. The limits of freedom to choice are partly natural, partly socially determined. But the social process with the "billions of valuations in billions of transactions" moves "forward on that energy which we call the will." [2]

In choosing, which includes acting, the will is purposeful—forward looking. "The will is always up against something. It is always performing, avoiding, forbearing, that is, always moving

[1] J. R. Commons, *Institutional Economics*, New York, The Macmillan Co., 1934, p. 738.
[2] J. R. Commons, *Legal Foundations of Capitalism*, New York, The Macmillan Co., 1924, p. 8.

along lines, not of least resistance like physical forces without purpose but of overcoming resistance, . . . with a purpose looking toward the future."[1] Yet in the acting, the will does not go to the limit of its power. It is the only force which can place a limit on its own performance. It forbears to exercise its full power except in times of great crisis.

The individual is, then, a purposeful, discretionary actor. Action has three discernible dimensions: performance, avoidance, forbearance. This is as true of action and reaction with nature as in the negotiation or dealing with other persons. Performance is the overt aspect of choice; yet the will forbears, placing a limit on the degree of power exercised. The limit of avoidance is set by society which defines, by collective action, what the actor as well as all other parties must not do under the circumstances.

It is by the process of choosing (selecting and acting) within associations that individuals become personalities. "Individuals . . . learn the custom of language, of cooperation with other individuals, of working toward common ends, of negotiations to eliminate conflicts of interest, of subordination to the working rules of the many concerns of which they are members. They meet each other, not as physiological bodies moved by glands, nor as 'globules of desire' moved by pain and pleasure, similar to the forces of physical and animal nature, but as prepared more or less by habit, induced by the pressure of custom, to engage in those highly artificial transactions created by the collective human will. . . . Instead of individuals the participants are citizens of a going concern. . . . Instead of mechanical uniformities . . . they are highly variable personalities."[2] Sometimes he speaks of individuals as institutionalized personalities.

Since each individual is to some degree a center of discretion and influence, agreements in transactions are achieved by negotiation. The consensus necessary for joint action may be reached by the power of persuasion between economic equals, or by the coercion of the stronger over the weaker. This field of activity is

[1] *Ibid.*, p. 79.
[2] J. R. Commons, *Institutional Economics*, New York, The Macmillan Co., 1934, pp. 73–74.

covered by Commons' term, *negotiational psychology*. It is by negotiation that parties which are involved in conflicts of interest, because of scarcity of opportunities, achieve that reciprocal alienation of what each wants but must secure from the other.

Whether the choosing is between natural opportunities or between the proprietary opportunities, through negotiation, "the human will has the strange but familiar ability to act upon a single factor, out of hundreds and thousands of complex factors, in such a way that other factors shall, of their own inherent forces, bring about the results intended." [1] This observation leads to the related doctrine of complementary and limiting factors which forms the core of his interpretation of economic behavior. In terms of social activity, the complementary and limiting factors are routine and strategic transactions. Since thought directs attention to the limiting factor, this doctrine is basic to Commons' conception of control. On the physical level control consists of manipulation of the limiting factors; in social affairs control finds its characteristic expression in the role of leadership influencing the collective will at the strategic time and place. His theory of causation stems from the same root; the cause is that which controls the limiting factor.

"Of course, if all the complementary factors become limiting factors at one point of time, then none of them is strategic, and the matter is hopeless." For a business the result would be bankruptcy; for society as a whole, revolution. Generally, "the limiting factors are *not cumulative* at a point of time—they are *successive* during a sequence of time. The most important of all investigations in the economic affairs of life, and the most difficult, as we shall find, is the investigation of strategic and contributory factors. It is none other than a universal principle of the human will in action." [2]

The argument so far may suggest why Commons considers the transaction as the minimum unit of investigation among economic and social relations. It is a social relationship of man to man; it is where the minds and wills of persons meet in the give

[1] *Ibid.*, p. 89.
[2] *Ibid.*, p. 90.

and take of the social process, with the ingredient conflict, mutuality, and achieved order. Behind these transactions are the actions of individuals. As a lone personality one may, and does weigh his alternatives and formulate his choices, yet action in society can follow only by coming to terms with other citizens and the officials of organized society. "Thus the ultimate unit of activity . . . must contain in itself the three principles of conflict, dependence, and order. This unit is the transaction. . . . Transactions intervene between the production of labor of the classical economists and the pleasures of consumption of the hedonic economists simply because it is society that, by its rules of order, controls ownership of and access to the forces of nature." [1]

Commons makes the transaction the unit of investigation because he is attempting to reduce collective action to the simplest form of social relationship. Yet the transactions are not all of one kind. They differ according to the issue of the transaction and the status of the participants. Commons distinguishes three types of transactions: bargaining, managerial, and rationing.

Bargaining transactions occur between persons who are legal equals; in case of dispute the adjudicator holds them equal before the law. If they are economic equals, the negotiators reach agreement by the mere persuasion of personality; if they are economically unequal, there may be coercion, as in case of the disparate withholding power of a workman bargaining with a corporation over a job. The subject matter of a bargaining transaction is the familiar price of the market, although more precisely it pertains to the terms of alienation of ownership.

The managerial transaction occurs between parties which stand in the legal relation of superior and inferior; it represents a command-and-obedience relationship. The typical situation includes a foreman and a workman. One orders; the other obeys. In terms of subject matter managerial transactions pertain to the processes of physical performance, as the construction of a machine, or the physical delivery of goods.

It is evident that bargaining and managerial transactions are

[1] *Ibid.*, p. 58.

interdependent and not clearly separate in fact. They are related as limiting and complementary factors. "As a bargainer, the modern wage earner is deemed to be the legal equal of his employer, induced to enter the transaction by persuasion or coercion; but once he is permitted to enter the place of employment he becomes legally inferior, induced by commands which he is required to obey." [1]

The third type of transaction, the rationing transaction, also pertains to persons in the legal relationship of superior-inferior. However, the rationing is done by means of negotiation and agreement among persons who have been authorized to apportion the benefits and burdens. The allocations of tax burdens has long been the typical rationing transaction between the concern and the general politico-economic organization. Recently the government has been rationing allotments and benefits to farmers, for example, through the agricultural adjustment programs. Currently, rationing transactions are supplanting, more and more, the usual bargaining transactions as the government assumes direct control of the economy under the war emergency. Within a going concern with the legal form of a corporation, a typical rationing transaction would be the directors formulating a budget or voting a dividend. [2]

Professor Commons distinguishes types of transactions from one another by means of both economic and legal relationships. For example, bargaining transactions occur between persons deemed equal by the law although there may be a world of difference in economic power. This combined analysis of legal and economic relationships is a dominant feature of his whole scheme of thought.

Throughout the formulation, individual action and transactions are recognized as derivative from, or ingredient to, social action. Indeed, the attempt to actually analyze collective action, in relation to the functioning of the economy, is one of Commons' major purposes. The twentieth century is the age of collective action. The problem is how can we understand and control, somewhat,

[1] *Ibid.*, p. 65.
[2] *Ibid.*, pp. 67–68, 876–903.

these great collective pressures and activities. The case is made urgent, in Commons' view, by the viewpoint of individualism which has dominated so strongly the economic thought of the past century.

Conformable with the general viewpoint and the facts to be investigated, Commons has taken as his definition of an institution *collective action in control, liberation, and expansion of individual action.* Within this formula may be seen the implicit recognition of the predominant significance of the social, of the achievement of individuality within the social nexus, of the operation of social controls upon social relationships—as well as the means by which social organization is achieved within social action.

## IV.

The acceptance of the evolutionary or process point of view requires that any system of economic or social thought shall conceptualize somehow the mode by which organized activity emerges from more rudimentary forms. This emergence in Commons' thought may be suggested by the relation between customs and going concerns.

As the unorganized form of collective action, "custom is the mere repetition, duplication, and variability of practices and transactions."[1] Customary behavior, then, is stabilized social behavior, affording to the individual the expectation that the usual ways of doing things may be continued. Yet customs vary; indeed from among the variable customs, selections are made, consciously or habitually, by the human will.

These elemental forms of collective action are the resources from which those practices and relationships are chosen which are extended, developed, and integrated into social organization. Landlords and tenants hit upon social arrangements which are mutually beneficial; travelers upon a common highway learn that if everyone drives to the right passage is facilitated and made more secure; business men discover practices and procedures that are helpful to them. Through wide acceptance such practices become customary. From among these countless ways

[1] *Ibid.,* pp. 44–45.

of social behavior, mankind has selected practices and made them more secure and of general application. The classic case of this function in the Anglo-American tradition is the common-law method of selecting good practices and making them into the law of the land.[1] These regularized social relationships are the forms of social organizations: their great function is to create security of expectations—for individuals, associations, concerns. But the problem is an eternal one, since the achievement of order and security of expectations occurs within the ongoing social process.

Social relations are stabilized by defining the limits within which individual behavior is allowed discretionary action. Essentially this consists in defining the limits of avoidance for action. Persons have duties to avoid specified acts. Speaking more generally, in terms of Commons' analysis already noted, all acting is performing, avoiding, or forbearing. Collective working rules define the dimensions of avoidance; within these limits persons perform or forbear. That is, working rules define the limits within which an individual is allowed to exercise his own will. Fundamentally, it is the exercise of wills which is canalized or controlled. And this occurs at both the customary and the organized levels of social action.

As the wills of the participants become stabilized in the processes of collective action, it then becomes possible to organize going concerns. In most general terms, a going concern is an organization of coordinated activity; it is collective behavior with a common purpose, and a collective will, governed by common working rules.[2] Going concerns, as units of organization, occur in all phases of social life.

The state, itself, is a going concern, developed out of the stream of collective action.[3] In our democratic constitutional form of government the discretionary powers of the officials running the concern are defined and limited by the general legislative and judicial procedures, culminating in the United States in the judi-

[1] Commons' *Legal Foundations of Capitalism* (Macmillan, 1924) deals with this problem extensively. See especially pp. 214–312; "The Rent Bargain"; "The Price Bargain"; and "The Wage Bargain."

[2] *Ibid.*, p. 145.          [3] *Ibid.*, pp. 149 ff.

cial supremacy of the Supreme Court. As a going concern the state has taken over the power of violence; the exercise of this power is the function of sovereignty. Since the state gives us the status of citizenship and the citizen must make his economic behavior conform to the rules of the state, Commons includes the principle of sovereignty as one of the principles of economic behavior.

The state, or states—including all branches—through its officials and employees, defines the working rules by which the individual's behavior is organized. By working rules, duties are imposed upon persons; this imposition of duties creates correlative rights in other persons. Both property and what Commons terms the status of individuals stem from these rights, which are quite literally the expectation that the state will impose duties on other persons.

This may be made more explicit by a brief sketch of Commons' formulation of the economic status of individuals or concerns. We are free to plan and direct our own lives and concerns to the extent that we have stable roles or zones of discretion within which we can exercise our own wills. This is the organizational aspect of security of expectations. These zones of discretion are created primarily through the operation of the (law) working rules of the state. These working rules define the status of individuals and concerns. To the extent that the state imposes duties on all other persons, we have rights. In terms of status, to the extent that other persons are under duties, I am in the status of security; their conformity gives me the status of security commensurate with my rights. However, beyond these relationships there is the status relationship of liberty-exposure. To the extent that other persons are under no obligation or duty to respect my person or property I am exposed to their liberty. In terms of a business concern, a business is exposed to the liberty of its customers to buy where they please. But a business in debt to a bank must conform to the rules for paying debts. The conformity of the concern to these rules gives the bank the status of security, with respect to the debt.

Similarly, property is related to the procedures of the state. Property is an object held for the owner's exclusive use, sale or disposal. But property rights are the social relations which the state vests in the owner of property. Again, these rights are created only by the imposition of duties upon other persons. Thus, property rights are literally social relationships stabilized according to law. When one buys property, he really buys rights to property; and when he buys the rights to property he is buying the expectation that the state will use its powers to support the purchaser's claims to the property.

Commons has traced out, especially in his *Legal Foundations of Capitalism,* the long, halting judicial procedure by which the meaning of property has been changed. In the original common-law conception, property meant a physical corporeal thing held for one's own use. Gradually, property came to mean the sale or exchange value of the thing rather than the physical object.[1] This shift from things for use to rights of sale changes the meaning of property from things to expected behavior regarding things. Thus Commons concludes, "The term 'property' cannot be defined except by defining all the activities which individuals and the community are at liberty or required to do or not to do, with reference to the object claimed as property." [2] This has the effect of recognizing that both liberty and economic power are aspects of private property.

These are some of the essential relationships in social organization within which business concerns are organized for the purpose of producing wealth and acquiring income. The head of a concern must get the concern going and keep it going. In most general terms, this directive function is the will in action. The head of the concern evaluates the alternatives and chooses from among them. But since the concern is organized in a social context or situation, the opportunities must be acquired before they can be used. And acquisition requires that the head of the firm

[1] *Ibid.,* pp. 11 ff.
[2] J. R. Commons, *Institutional Economics,* New York, The Macmillan Co., 1934, p. 74.

(or his representatives) must come to terms with the owners of the opportunities through negotiations and transactions.

The critical or strategic aspect of the opportunities, either for purchase or sale, is their position in social organization. When one buys or sells commodities, he both transfers title to them and actually moves the commodities. But, it is as property rights, titles—not things—that commodities are actually integrated into social organization. Thus unless a business man is living in a society where social relationships have been ordered and stabilized so that he may count on the state to enforce some necessary minimum of duties on other persons, he does not have sufficient security of expectations to build and operate a going concern. Labor differs from commodities fundamentally in that a worker is not allowed by law to sell himself into servitude; he can sell only his willingness to work.

Social organization, then, creates the roles within which the world, both as resources and as markets, is available as opportunities to the management of a concern. It is by transactions with other parties that these opportunities are actually brought into the going concerns. Since a going concern functions within the time sequence (social process), it is really the expectation that transactions will continue in the future that keeps a concern going.

Through bargaining transactions, the head of the concern acquires title, the rights to use or withhold, in the commodities and labor. Through managerial transaction the persons within a concern are directed in the transformation of the raw materials into processed goods—as, when, and where the management directs. Within a going concern, bargaining transactions are related to managerial transactions as complementary and limiting factors. The third type, rationing transactions, is similarly included in those concerns where authorized persons ration out the burdens and benefits, such as dividends. The expected repetition of all transactions is a going concern. "The whole is a going concern. It is a joint willingness of all participants: the willingness of employees and managers to maintain and operate the plant; the willingness of customers to buy, of investors and bankers to lend, of material men to sell, and of others to participate. The so-called 'right' of each to participate and to have compensation for participation is the intangible property of liberty and exposure. But the right of each individually to have compensation for his previous services is the incorporeal property of debt, wherein the concern is the debtor." [1]

Essentially, what Commons is seeking here, it may be assumed, is some way to analyze the operations of a concern so that the results of the analysis shall be relevant to social action and the time sequence. To do this, the analysis operationally reduces the concern to a number of different social relationships which have wider ties to the social structure. This approach treats a concern as a succession of decisions and transactions. The head actually builds up a concern, gets it going, and keeps it going by the transactions into which he enters on behalf of the concern. Commons implicitly classifies these transactions in terms of the control exercisable over them. Transactions in the moving present, or immediate future, are strategic; those which recur without attention are routine. Thus, first one transaction and then another becomes strategic only to pass over into routine for some period of time.

The implicit relationships of property to the going concern can now be made explicit. Through bargaining transactions workmen or suppliers agree to deliver materials or services. The laborer delivers his labor power through managerial transactions. Until payday he is creditor to the concern; similarly with all services and materials. The creditor-debtor relationship is legally one of right and duty. The security of the creditor is the conformity of the debtor to the duties of payment imposed by law.

The creditor-debtor relationship is an instance of incorporeal property. Incorporeal property rests on the duties of performance; it is the expected fulfillment of promises made. In one of its. fundamental aspects it rests upon the negotiability of debt. This great social invention actually permits the purchase or sale of mere promises to pay much as any tangible commodity.

[1] *Ibid.*, p. 422.

Except as negotiations lead to agreements which are enforceable, as the payment of debts, the relation between persons within a concern is that of liberty-exposure. The workman is exposed to the liberty of the foreman to fire; the employer is exposed to the liberty of the workman to quit. The bankers have the liberty to refuse to lend, the customers the liberty to refuse to buy. In the nature of the case there are no duties of performance. Here the duties are merely of avoidance. Either party may withhold what the other needs but does not own; the withholding is limited by the resources and alternative opportunities of the bargainers. The concern must depend on the "good will" of the parties for their continued participation. Broadly speaking, this expectation of continued beneficial transactions is intangible property.

The significance of Commons' property analysis could be made more clear, no doubt, by following the argument through other parts of his thought. He has traced out the processes by which debts have become negotiable; he then makes negotiable debts the foundation of his transactional theory of money. The capital value of the individual firm and property are shown to be essentially the same set of relationships from two different points of view. Property is a set of social relationships which ties the future to the present through expectations of stabilized behavior regarding other persons and things; the value of a concern consists in private title to them. But further pursuit of the argument regarding property could only make more emphatic one major inference which can already be drawn. The analysis so far reveals that the power of the state, the functioning of the state, is an integral part of every business at every moment simply because the very objects of purchase and sale—property rights—are themselves created only by the unseen pressure of the state which stabilizes the wills of the participants by imposing duties upon them.

In his review of "Institutional Economics," Max Lerner remarks: "This knitting of state authority into the texture of accepted economic material constitutes the real significance of Professor Commons' work. While his framework is large enough to include all forms of collective action in control of individual action, he actually concentrates on the legal sanctions."[1]

It is not an exaggeration to say that the analysis of property relations is an integral part of Commons' thought throughout his formulation. Methodologically this differs greatly from what is usually called economic analysis. But Commons, contrary to the prevailing practice of economic theorists, does not "assume" private property or ownership as a starting point and then work out the implications of economizing under static conditions. Rather, he sets out to make an analysis of economic processes, in which he finds property relations to be an important part. The fundamental difference between Commons' and the more usual approaches, therefore, appears to turn on the question relating to process analysis, more than on property as such.[2] At least this much can be said, Commons has found that the meaning of property has changed greatly and significantly as the Anglo-American politico-economic organization has gradually emerged into the modern money and credit economy, called capitalism. This is especially important in revealing the development of economic power, which looms so large in valuation processes in the current economy.

## V.

Commons' analysis of valuation is formulated in what he calls a theory of reasonable value. This is obviously a theory of social valuation—an integral part of the theory of the economics of collective action. It roots in his analysis of bargaining transactions. Since transactions are joint actions they require conjoint valuations or agreement upon valuations. He has described it as

---

[1] *Harvard Law Review,* 1935, p. 363.

[2] Commons makes an interesting comment on Veblen's position which bears rather directly on this point: "Veblen, when he changes from entities to processes, must change from corporeal property which contains no pecuniary process of buying and selling, to intangible property which is none other than the pecuniary process itself." J. R. Commons, *Institutional Economics,* New York, The Macmillan Co., 1934, p. 658.

"a theory of the joint activity and valuations of individuals in all transactions through which the participants mutually induce each other to a consensus of opinion and action." [1]

The issue of reasonableness in this theory of valuations arises in connection with the bargaining power of the participants to the transaction. Reasonableness relates essentially to the question of how much disparity of economy power is tolerable in agreements over prices. Bargaining transactions occur between parties equal before the law, but who may have greatly unequal economic power. This economic power roots, in turn, in the power of property—coincident with the court's expanded meaning of property from a corporeal thing held for one's use to the value of access to market—including the right to withhold from others. "Thus, with the legal power to withhold commodities and services finally recognized in law, reasonable restraint of trade, according to the court's ideas of reasonableness but contrary to the antitrust laws, comes to have a standing in law; and its equivalent bargaining power, or intangible property, comes to have a standing in economics. For restraint of trade *is* bargaining power, and reasonable restraint of trade is reasonable bargaining power." [2]

As a theory of valuation, this is a radical departure from the usual procedure in economic theory. Instead of individual valuation, we have social valuation. Instead of a theory of valuation at the limit of perfect competition, we have valuations in the zone of private power. Instead of valuations of resources in terms of the incremental values to one individual or concern, we have valuations between two individuals or concerns.

It is also evident that Commons' analysis recognizes that valuation is an aspect of social action and social organization. We may generalize this position and see that Commons has been interested in a different problem than that which orthodox price theory has analyzed. Seemingly, he makes a social analysis, upon the assumption that private enterprise means just that—the working of each private person or business in its own interest,

[1] *Ibid.*, p. 25.
[2] *Ibid.*, p. 344.

assuming the risks of business, driving bargains for himself, adjusting operations to the point of maximum profit for self, and so on. The point is that he has not been concerned to formulate an analysis pointing to the maximum return to the private firm; rather, if I understand him, he has been interested in analyzing the structure of opportunities, within which private liberty and economy operate. The opportunities available to an individual, or firm, are a function of social organization and action. In one place he speaks of "social opportunities owned, controlled, or withheld by other individuals, in a world where there is no equilibrium at the cost of reproduction simply because there is not perfect freedom, perfect equality, or perfect promptitude of competition." [1]

Commons does not mean that no evaluation of alternatives is made by the individual as a basis of choice. Nor would there be any necessary inconsistence between Commons' thought and the formulation of an ideal pattern of resource use for the individual firm, wherein one follows out the implications of efficiency of resource use to its logical limit under given conditions. One can even go farther. Presumably the individual can work out any ideal pattern of valuation as a vision for guiding his own course, combining efficiency, utility, security, play, and leisure (or anything else within the law)—provided he can make ends meet. But wherever an individual or head of a concern would act upon the basis of these individual valuations in a way that requires joint action, there is also social valuation.

However, it does follow necessarily, I infer, that prices are always the resultant of social valuations, rather than the outcome of some mechanical or physical process. Prices are the issue in bargaining transactions, wherein two individual wills meet and agree upon a joint performance of payment and delivery of goods. This is true, Commons would hold, even though the bargaining took place under any conceivable degree of competition—or the lack of it.

This follows from his conception of bargaining. It is a very broad concept and includes both the offering of goods (or serv-

[1] *Ibid.*, p. 331.

ices) and the power to withhold them. If all transactions were carried out near the conceptual limit of perfect competition, then the bargaining power would be just the mere offering of goods and services, and price would be equal to the cost of production. At the opposite conceptual limit (monopoly), potential partici-pants might have sufficient withholding power to fail indefinitely to reach an agreement. Commons' conception of bargaining power is so general as to include the ability of a participant at either extreme or at any intermediary position—in relation to the oppor-tunities of the particular time and place.

This is the common ground beneath all prices, and the basis upon which the issue of reasonableness is decided. In the com-mon-law tradition of the Anglo-American economy, these ques-tions have been settled by the courts. This is preeminently true in America where the Supreme Court is supreme over all other branches of government. Most of Commons' analysis of reason-able valuation, consequently, has been devoted to a study of court decisions. In order to decide the reasonableness of particular cases, the common-law courts developed the principle of a willing buyer and a willing seller; where both parties were willing, the sale was fair—and there was fair competition.[1]

The issues confronting the courts are increasingly difficult as conflicts of interest, collective action, corporations, and the great aggregations of power in private property become more charac-teristic of our economy. Yet, Commons' position implies that the question of the degree of private power that is tolerable is ulti-mately a judicial question. Though fairness is the issue, the de-cisions could not turn solely on justice, for there is always the more basic problem of order.

Although Commons' analysis of social valuation has been cen-tered on judicial decisions, the theory is of wider import. Infer-entially, at least, he suggests that any theory of social valuation must be based upon principles for deciding disputes and resolv-ing conflicts. This seems to follow necessarily from the conception of the social process as containing conflicts, dependence, and

---

[1] Cf. J. R. Commons, "Fair Return," *Encyclopedia of the Social Sciences,* New York, The Macmillan Co., 1932–35, Vol. 6, pp. 56–58.

order. The problem of social valuation is to achieve a common valuation so that order and mutuality can be achieved.

By drawing the inferences a bit further, it is suggested in Commons' thought that social valuations are of a different order than individual valuations. Social valuations are a part of the achieving of a stable and tolerable social organization. The values here appear to be order, justice, equality, security, etc., as well as economy. To the individual, either as a person or a concern, the consequences of the social status of these values are incorporated into the opportunities (or disopportunities) which are the individual's alternatives. And it is the structure of these opportunities which gives us the dimensions of freedom and liberty—in short, individual discretionary action. Of course if the social order collapses, or the economy of which we are participants stops functioning, then the stable opportunities disappear and everything dissolves in starvation, anarchy, or revolution.

In terms of social ethics, Commons holds that we do not settle disputes by reference to some broad philosophy of the social good. Instead, the conceptions of the social good must be derivative from the way we settle disputes. In short, social ethics is concerned with the settlement of disputes.[1]

In Commons' view, there are two theories of the origin of ethics. "One was the individualistic theory of the maximum of pleasure in a world of abundance, where the individual could not injure others by taking all he wanted. The other was the social theory of conflict of interests in a world of scarcity, where the individual may injure others if he takes all he wants. On the foundation of the latter theory ethics is an historical process developing out of the decisions of economic disputes and there is no dualism of ethics and economics."[2] Commons accepts the latter theory.

[1] I am indebted to Professor Charner M. Perry of the University of Chicago for assistance in understanding the fundamental issues in this phase of Professor Commons' thought. Cf. Charner Perry, "The Arbitrary as Basis for Rational Morality," *International Journal of Ethics,* Vol. 43, 1932–33, pp. 127–144, and "Principles of Value and the Problem of Ethics," *Revue Internationale de Philosophie,* July 15, 1939.

[2] J. R. Commons, *Institutional Economics,* New York, The Macmillan Co., 1934, p. 225.

In the preceding sections we have attempted to present a broad outline of Commons' thought relative to activity, organization, and valuation. We now turn to a brief consideration of some of the issues that arise in analyzing the operations of the economy in relation to these basic theoretical conceptions.

## VI.

The distinction in terms of activity between bargaining transactions and managerial transactions runs throughout Commons' analysis; it appears in the distinction between ownership and wealth, between withholding and producing, between scarcity and efficiency. It is indeed none other than the making, throughout the economy, of an analytical distinction between the proprietary aspect or ownership point of view in contrast with the production of things—goods, uses, and services. Where traditional analysis assumes that all scarce goods are owned, Commons analyzes the property, ownership, bargaining activities as variables coordinate with his analysis of production.

The essence of the distinction may be noted in terms of the problem of proportionality. The principle of proportionality is, of course, a universal principle; Commons uses it formulated as the principle of limiting and complementary factors. "The limiting factor is the one whose control, in the right form, at the right place and time, will set the complementary factors at work to bring about the results intended." [1] When the proportioning of the complementary and limiting factor is looked at from the volitional standpoint, we have routine and strategic transactions. These transactions are the actual process by which the human will in our modern economy actually controls the physical and social environment.

It is through the social relationship of managerial transactions that the management of a concern controls physical processes. The coordination and repetition of the transactions create the organization of a going plant—and keep it going. In such plants wealth is created by turning the raw materials of nature into forms which embody uses. By bargaining transactions, the busi-

[1] *Ibid.*, p. 628.

ness man purchases the raw materials and sells the finished product. The organization and repetition of these transactions (together with some rationing transactions) create the going business. The integration of the going plant with the going business is a going concern.

In this way, the processes of production are separated out, for the purpose of analysis. The productive processes include all the activities of mankind in overcoming the resistance of nature. As a process it is measured in terms of ratios of input to output. The input is labor and materials. The output is something which mankind deems useful at the current stage of civilization, else it will not be made. The way in which the productive processes are interrelated with the financial operations of concerns requires that production of things be limited in the interest of price and returns. But the restriction is withholding, not production. The production of use values exemplifies the principle of efficiency. It is the activity of mankind in subduing the forces of nature to their own purposes.

In general terms and from a broad social viewpoint efficiency is measured by man-hours in relation to output. Commons concedes that the attempt to measure efficiency in these terms has limitations when applied to individual concerns, since the labor of any one concern is only partially direct labor. Yet viewed in the large, socially and historically, all production is attributable to labor—mental, manual, and managerial. The logic of Commons' position in this particular, as well as his insistence that man-hours are the proper social measurement of efficiency, roots in the Ricardian doctrine of the niggardliness of nature. Nature is not productive; it merely offers differing degrees of resistance to man's efforts to turn natural forces to human purposes. A wheat field naturally produces weeds, grass, or brush, not wheat.

It should be noted, however, that the fundamental problem is independent of the proposed method of measurement. The problem is—how can, and does, mankind living in a society convert the forces of nature into uses and services? It is into this phase of economic activity that the stable physical relations are integrated. The physical combinations and proportions react in their own terms independent of their prices. Yet such combinations are more than mere physical motion. The basic physical and mechanical processes are combined and proportioned in accordance with human purposes, including the intent to economize on labor. It is the human purposes which have converted the mechanical or physical actions and reactions into machines and going plants.

Thus Commons restricts production to the process of turning out use values. The qualities of objects, as objects, which make them useful do not change with the quantities produced, although the significance of these uses to the individual changes with the quantities, their relative scarcity. At different stages of civilization, different things are wanted, as carriages have given way to automobiles. To supply these wants is a task of physical organization. Natural forces or materials are converted into uses or services by collective effort through managerial transactions which are integrated into going plants and going concerns.

Bargaining transactions occur over transfers of ownership. It is through these transactions that the production process is supplied with materials and the output disposed of. This is the income-outgo relationship. It is through the bargaining transactions that the going concern is actually related to other firms—to resources and markets. Commons generalizes this relationship from a social point of view under the name of scarcity, the relation between quantities wanted and quantities available. This is the familiar relationship of supply and demand, whose effects upon transactions are measured in terms of money.[1]

It may be noted that Commons has herein distinguished two pairs of relationships, input-output, income-outgo. Input-output are a part of the physical processes of production; income-outgo are a part of the proprietary or business processes. For example, output is not income for the wage worker, because his output is a physical transformation of his employer's materials. "It depends on who owns the output. The output of the slave is the income of the owner. The output of the laborer is the income of the employer. The input of the laborer is man power. His output

[1] *Ibid.*, pp. 261–262.

is use value. The money outgo of the employer and equivalent income of the laborer is the money wage. There is no necessary or natural connection between use value and money. They are measured by two different systems of measurement, which are inconvertible." [1]

This distinction between input-output and money income-outgo follows from Commons' separation of efficiency (production) from scarcity (transference of ownership). It has not been uncommon in discussion of proportionality for economists to use dollar inputs as the ground for arriving at the point of maximum efficiency, the "least cost combination." In discussing Black's analysis in *Production Economics* [2] Commons remarks that this latter method of calculating efficiency is "important and useful in the private management of . . . concerns," but that it leads to social fallacies.[3] He has traced out what appear to him to be the many fallacies in economic thought which have been involved in the failure to distinguish things from ownership, producing from withholding, in short, what Commons calls efficiency from scarcity.[4] "Thus the classical economists did not distinguish output from income, or outgo from input. The distinction was concealed in the double meanings of cost and value. They assumed that, of course, a man's output was his income." [5]

The order of problems which he has been intent upon studying may be seen by reminding ourselves, for example, of the problems of reasonableness arising in the field of scarcity. Also, in the realm of efficiency Commons has been interested in such social issues as who get the benefits of technological improvements. Without distinguishing scarcity from efficiency, i.e., if money is taken as the measure of efficiency, he observes that a business man who makes a high net income by beating down wages may be held to

---

[1] *Ibid.*, p. 287.

[2] John D. Black, *Introduction to Production Economics*, New York, Henry Holt and Company, 1926.

[3] J. R. Commons, *Institutional Economics*, New York, The Macmillan Co., 1934, pp. 276–277.

[4] This is essentially Veblen's distinction between industry and business.

[5] J. R. Commons, *Institutional Economics*, New York, The Macmillan Co., 1934, p. 286.

be just as efficient as one who pays high wages but has a superior organization.

Without attempting here to appraise Commons' criticisms of the tradition on these issues, I would point out some of the premises implicit in his analysis. Commons is attempting in this phase of his thought to analyze the actual operations of concerns; not to formulate an ideal pattern of resource utilization as a policy guide for the concern. It is "logically" true that cost equals value at the limit of perfect competition: Commons' analysis is always pointed toward actual events, i.e., somewhere in the field of what is now called imperfect competition. Thirdly, Commons' reference point is social, not private. He has defined efficiency and scarcity with reference to investigations into two differentiated aspects of social action. Too, the going concern, the firm, in Commons' thought, is always, so far as I am aware, a concern with employees. His analysis is not aimed at analyzing the economizing of the self-employed entrepreneur. The reference point is social, fundamentally social action.

The measurement, for Commons, of input-output and income-outgo is the measurement of performance; and basically the performance is social. This follows from his attention to the two-sided collective action that relates persons to firms, or firms to each other, rather than to the "net income" economic position of the firm.[1] This directs attention to the gross income and gross outgo of the concern. Commons insists that to do otherwise conceals the conflict of interests. The courts can deal only with the gross income and gross outgo aspects of the concerns, for it is here that the conflicts arise which call for adjudication.

This taking of the social viewpoint, with reference to performance, income and outgo, has some rather startling implications. Commons concludes that it is the courts who have been responsible for the adoption of weights and measures. It was the social necessity for devising measures of performance that led to the adoption of standard units of measurements, dollars, pounds, tons, yards. When conflicts come before courts, there must be some way of

[1] Cf. especially his paper, "Institutional Economics," *Proceedings of American Economic Association, Supplement,* March, 1936, pp. 237–249.

determining whether the agreements have been carried out. Since all contracts or legal agreements are potential cases for adjudication, then all must be enforceable at law. If one party agrees to pay $100 for 100 bushels of No. 3 red winter wheat and the other agrees to deliver 100 bushels of wheat of specified grade for $100, it is objectively ascertainable whether or not each performed his part of the contract.

Thus we are led again to the point Commons makes so often: it is the stabilization of the duty relationships which gives security of expectations, and it is the necessity of this security that leads to the making of duties precise. "Units of measurement are, indeed, defined historically and not logically, for they are historical institutions developed from custom or law in order to make precise the administration of justice. All units of measurement are 'nominal' just as language is nominal. Yet they have reality. Their reality is collective action, for they give precision to the working rules that determine how much or how little shall be paid or performed by individuals or corporations." [1]

With this insight, Commons' theory seems to me to come "full-circle." By this argument he shows how a social process acquires the forms which are the basis of modern business concerns. He has analyzed the way general organization, valuation, and now specific and measurable forms have been achieved. If this be true we are justified in pointing to some of the possible issues that may be related to this genetic explanation of the appearance of measureable forms in the social process. The general question is: When and why does mathematics apply to social existence? Although Commons has made no comment on this issue, so far as I know, his analysis suggests that mathematics applies as far as social activities have been regularized and made precise by units of measurements imposed in the interest of order and justice.

At least this much can be said, given such a genetic explanation: one does not need to assume a Newtonian, mechanical universe in order to generalize from the fields of research and inquiry in economics where mathematical analyses have proven fruitful.

[1] J. R. Commons, *Institutional Economics,* New York, The Macmillan Co., 1934, p. 468.

Here, I merely throw out suggestions, but this position does offer promise of giving a basis for a genuine general theory based upon social categories, yet incorporating mathematical analyses to the full where the social relations to be analyzed have actually been quantified and regularized in the course of social action. Furthermore, this may suggest why statistical and mathematical procedures are not sufficient for the study of policy—as Professor Knight once observed in lecture. Policy and social control require analysis of social organization, valuation, and action. To concentrate upon statistical methods may lead one not only to lose reference to the distinctly social, but also to concentrate upon the outcomes and residues of social action rather than its basic structure.

## VII.

The argument so far has attempted an exposition of what we consider to be the essential features—the broad structure—of Commons' thought. Yet, a few further observations may be in order, regarding issues implicit in it.

The interest in social control, for example, runs deep in Commons' thought. This, I take it, is one of the basic reasons for the combined legal and economic analysis. When he was called upon to assist in the drafting of bills for the legislature he found that they not only had to meet the requirements of soundness in economic analysis, but that they must also be held reasonable by the courts. And he noted that either action by a legislature in regulating the terms of contracts or collective action by a trade union regarding the conditions of employment might be considered an infraction upon the liberty or the property of the employer. In the American political economy such infringement must be done within the "due process of law" which is judicially determined.

The relating of the analysis to both legal and economic premises, then, is essentially a method of tying ends and means, form and content together. It makes possible practical judgments on what to do in actual affairs. Evidently Commons' mind could find no rest by merely pointing out ends or goals that might be achieved.

Whatever visions of the ideal he may have projected, there is the persistent attempt to deal correlatively with the means of realization.

Correlative with this is Commons' conception of causation. The strategic or limiting factor once controlled is the cause of the new state of affairs.[1] "In nature, things merely 'happen.' But out of the complex happenings, man selects the limiting factors for his purposes. If he can control these, then other factors work out the effects intended. The 'cause' is volitional control of the limiting or strategic factors through managerial or bargaining transactions. The 'effects' are the operations of the complementary factors and the repetition of routine transactions."[2] This is the causal relation in purposive human behavior—which purpose is, in part, to modify, to control the social processes. Strategic becomes literally strategy.

These elements combine to give an interpretation and emphasis which are unusual. The "economy of the mind" which Commons practices requires attention to the strategic or limiting factors. It seems a reasonable inference that these conceptions of causation and control are basic to the selection of the transaction as the basic unit of investigation. It is just where the wills of men meet that controls can be exercised. The transaction is the strategic nexus of social actions. Also, since physical possession follows legal control, then attention can be centered on the latter.[3]

If these be reasonable interpretations of Commons' approach, they raise basic questions regarding the treatment of property by

[1] Mead has expressed a similar view. "Generally, it [cause] is some condition which can be changed in order to bring out a different result." G. H. Mead, *Movements of Thought in the Nineteenth Century,* Chicago, University of Chicago Press, 1936, p. 277.

[2] J. R. Commons, *Institutional Economics,* New York, The Macmillan Co., 1934, p. 632.

[3] The conception of cause appears to explain the method of analyzing the history of economic thought, which so puzzled Lerner in his review of *Institutional Economics*: first one issue and then another has become strategic in the development of economic thought. The man who resolved the difficulty was accepted by Commons as a "pioneer of insight." In this way, for example, MacLeod is placed on a par with the great masters because of his insight into the significance of property as the subject matter of economics. Lerner, *op. cit.,* *Harvard Law Review,* Vol. 49, p. 632.

economists. Commons' long attention to property relations appears to me to be rooted in two deeper issues. He appears to accept the process approach as necessary in social analysis. In short, social facts are social only if taken in the sequential setting.[1] Secondly, he is attempting to make an analysis relevant to democratic social control. The question which his analysis presents here is precisely this: If economists are to make their analyses relevant to the problems of social control, do they not have to include the study of property?

Commons' pioneer work on administrative commissions may also serve to illustrate his attention to planning and control. One can almost sense on every issue that Commons is attempting a formulation that will be relevant to the decisions which some strategically placed person must make—such as judge, legislator, governor, or especially the head of an administrative commission. It is natural, then, that Commons' theoretical writing should be at its best in his discussion of these commissions. Here one can see how his insight into the history of social thought, the decisions of the courts, due process of law, social conflicts, social efficiency, and the psychology of laborers and business executives all blend into what might appear superficially to be simple suggestions regarding what to do next.[2] Administrative commissions are held to represent the emergence of a fourth branch of government—a fact-finding branch empowered to make investigations into the conflicting claims of the various interests, to gather facts according to a procedure conformable with the due process requirements of the law, all for the purpose of determining a reasonable course of action between wide possible extremes, in the use of governmental powers within the economy.

This system of theory Commons has worked out by means of his participation in social affairs. He has referred to it as a compass which has enabled him to find his way through the maze of conflicting situations which he has experienced. It is, then, a gen-

[1] Cf. John Dewey, *Logic*, New York, Henry Holt and Co., 1938, Chapter XXIV, esp. pp. 501–502 for critical comments on this point.

[2] Cf., *Institutional Economics*, pp. 840–873; *Legal Foundations*, especially pp. 354–356; also "Legislative and Administrative Reasoning in Economics," *Journal of Farm Economics*, May, 1942, pp. 369–392.

eral theory, and he has wrestled with the fundamental problems of definition which make possible the movement of thought from one aspect of experience to another. This problem cannot be discussed here; but it may be noted that Commons' basic categories are inclusive. All acting is performance, avoidance, or forbearance. All institutions are collective action in control of individual action. All transactions are bargaining, managerial, or rationing. This persistent effort to find the similarities beneath the differences appears to be implicit in his attempt to build a theory out of analyses of actual social relationships. For society is no truncated affair. Stern necessity requires that the inherent conflicts shall not tear it apart; it is continuous through achieved cooperation, conjoint action, communication, and institutions. Thought can deal with this range of problems only by a theory which embraces the basic issues involved.

Commons nowhere suggests, so far as I know, that all economic analysis should follow the pattern of his own thought. It is fundamentally a question of purpose. There are many problems where detailed analyses of the structure of social action are not necessitated; studies of velocity of turnover, in Commons' thought, or the calculations of the influence of quantity on price, may stand as examples. The significance of Commons' thought in this context appears to me to be in showing a possible way of moving from the problems where a mechanical, marginal analysis approach is fruitful to the broader questions of social organization, valuation, conflicts, and control. Furthermore, these are the problems which now threaten civilization and present the great challenge to social thought. For those who seek insight and inspiration in dealing with them, Commons' work may be a treasury of suggestions. His thought is complex and difficult. His writings report the reflections of an exploring mind in search of the fundamental relations in social life, not a mind expounding the implications of assumed basic propositions.[1]

[1] Comment by Professor Commons to the editor of the *Journal of Land and Public Utility Economics* upon reading the essay: "It is a magnificent analysis and summary . . . I feel Parsons has done very much indeed to clarify my arguments with which I have struggled back and forth these twenty years."

# Index

[ 377 ]